CONGO SQUARE

AFRICAN ROOTS IN NEW ORLEANS

CONGO SQUARE

AFRICAN ROOTS IN NEW ORLEANS

FREDDI WILLIAMS EVANS

FOREWORD BY
J. H. KWABENA 'NKETIA, PH.D.

UNIV. OF LA. AT LAFAYETTE PRESS
2011

ISBN (paper): 978-1-935754-03-9

University of Louisiana at Lafayette Press
P.O. Box 40831
Lafayette, LA 70504-0831
http://www.ulpress.org

This book is printed on acid-free paper.

Library of Congress Cataloging-in-Publication Data:

Evans, Freddi Williams.
Congo Square, New Orleans / by Freddi Williams Evans;
foreword by J.H. Kwabena `Nketia.
p. cm.
Includes bibliographical references and index.
ISBN 978-1-935754-03-9 (pbk. : alk. paper)
1. Congo Square (New Orleans, La.)--History. 2. New Orleans (La.)--History.
3. African Americans--Louisiana--New Orleans--Social life and customs. 4.
Meetings--Louisiana--New Orleans--History. 5. Sunday--Louisiana--New Or-
leans--History. 6. African Americans--Louisiana--New Orleans--Music--History
and criticism. 7. African American dance--Louisiana--New Orleans--History.
8. New Orleans (La.)--Social life and customs. 9. African Americans--Com-
merce--Louisiana--New Orleans--History. 10. Community life--Louisiana--New
Orleans--History. I. Title.
F379.N57C663 2010
976.3'35--dc22
2010037423

Editorial assistance by Dr. Paulette Richards, Georgia Institute of Technology.

Front cover: *Danis 1* by Elizabeth Calett; cover art © Elizabeth Catlett/Licensed by VAGA, New York, NY.

Rear cover: seated chief-musician playing a sanza (kaponya), Chokwe people (Angola) School of Muzambe, wood; courtesy of the New Orleans Museum of Art, bequest of Victor K. Kiama 77.135.

To each and every person of African heritage
who worshipped, danced, sang, played music,
or sold wares in Congo Square.

CONTENTS

Foreword by J. H. Kwabena `Nketia, Ph.D.................................ix

Acknowledgements xiii

Chapter 1   Introduction..1

Chapter 2   The Legacy of the Gathering Place...................9

Chapter 3   The Significance of the Gatherings 23

Chapter 4   The Gatherers..47

Chapter 5   The Musical Instruments..............................63

Chapter 6   The Songs 75

Chapter 7   The Dances..89

Chapter 8   The Economic Exchange 109

Chapter 9   Conclusion 115

Chapter 10   Epilogue 119

Timeline of Events Relevant to Congo Square...........................135

Notes 165

Selected Bibliography..187

Image Credits..196

Index..197

Seated chief-musician playing a sanza (kaponya), Chokwe people (Angola) School of Muzambe, wood.

FOREWORD

J. H. Kwabena `Nketia, Ph.D.
Director, International Center for African Music and Dance
University of Ghana, Legon-Accra

It is a pleasure to write a foreword to this book on Congo Square, for it is the work of someone who combines her knowledge and experience of the historical and cultural experience of an eventful location with relevant data garnered from documentary sources and uses her personal knowledge of Africa as a frame of reference.

As Langston tells us in *The Big Sea*, the first volume of his autobiography, at age twenty-one when he worked on the S.S. *Malone* as a sailor, his first sight of Africa was a sea of boundless joy. He writes:

> All those days I was waiting anxiously to see Africa. And finally, when I saw the dust green hills in the sunlight, something took hold of me inside. My Africa, Motherland of the Negro people! And me a Negro! Africa! The real thing, to be touched and seen, not merely read about in a book.[1]

He knew of course that many of his own people may never have this kind of first-hand experience, and that he could use the print medium to bring Mother Africa to their consciousness. He was also aware that healthy international relations are built on knowledge, understanding, and mutual respect and that he could contribute to these by sharing his experience with Americans. Accordingly, he wrote and published *My First Book of Africa*, an introduction to Africa, and followed this in 1960 with the *African Treasury*, a collection of short stories and poems by African writers in order to bring home the reality of our common legacy.

When I read Freddi Williams Evans' book on Congo Square, I had the feeling that she felt the same way when she visited Africa. It was a return to Mother Africa for knowledge and insights that cannot be gained from merely reading about Africa. Aspects of African American culture that she had taken for granted in her own environment, but which confirmed the presence of Mother Africa in New Orleans, now assumed a new meaning.

This reality struck me quite forcibly when I first came to the United States in 1958 as a Fellow of the Rockefeller Foundation. A few days after my arrival in New York, I moved from downtown Manhattan to a temporary apartment on

Amsterdam Avenue close to Columbia University. From time to time, I thought I heard the sound of drums but could not believe my ears because the idiom was very African. I traced it to a park in Harlem where some African American boys were playing games. Some played basketball while others just ran around or danced now and then to the sound of the drums. The body movements fascinated me. Indeed every ripple convinced me that the boys must be African boys playing in Harlem and not African Americans. So after this experience, every time my mind wandered back to Africa, I found myself taking a walk in the direction of the sound of the drum, to Africa in Harlem. It struck me also that comparative studies of African American idioms of African drumming would reinforce our knowledge of the dominant characteristics of this art, a topic which has begun to attract the attention of scholars.[2]

When I moved from New York to Evanston, Illinois, I learned a great deal more about this culture and the forms of behavior it manifests in certain activities. I lived with a black family, and Melville Herskovits now and then took me to the store front churches in Chicago—I suppose to watch my reaction—for he knew that I could not fail to recognize the African qualities in the mode of worship, the movement and handclapping that accompanied some songs, the verbal responses and shouts, the incidence of spirit possession, and so on and thus confirm his own observations documented in *The Myth of the Negro Past*.[3] The songs I heard were, of course, not traditional African songs, yet there was something in the singing style, handclapping, and modes of expression that seemed familiar and which I felt would repay detailed comparative study.

As I reflected on all these, it occurred to me—as I also tried to make sense of the stylistic differences I noticed—that the relationship between African and African American cultures is on a deeper level than their surface manifestations, and that what needs to be identified are the deep structures or the roots that generate the surface features as well as the specific roles, functions, and meanings assigned to them.

In this connection it might similarly be profitable to look closely at the enculturative processes that lead to continuity or what early anthropologists described as "survivals" and "retentions" in both African and Afro-American cultures, processes that facilitate music cognition or lead to certain types of rhythmic behavior and modes of rhythmic expression—the habit of externalizing perceived beats, the habit of integrating sound and movement, or communicating through sounds, and the tendency to elaborate on the concept of play in performance.

Another important point that occurred to me is the relationship between tradition and creativity. It seems that the structures that maintain a tradition are not easily discarded, because on a deep level, it is these that give a culture its identity. The details of these structures can be changed by successive generations, for what seems important in African American culture is not just reproducing tradition but making something fresh or new out of it.

The experience of teaching African Americans African drumming and dancing at the Institute of African Studies at the University of Ghana later confirmed this orientation, for as I watched the response of many of our African American visitors or talked to them, it seemed that the mastery of the traditional forms was always a means to an end. It was the subsequent creative use, including possible transformations and extensions they could apply in the context of their own art, that was foremost in their mind. This seemed to be true also of great artists who tend to approach the African experience in a more subtle and sophisticated manner.

When Max Roach spent three months in Ghana studying African drumming and xylophone music, his intention was not to go back to America and reproduce what he learned. On the contrary, his interest lay in acquiring a better sense of the organization and generative processes of this music which he could use creatively in his own way.

I believe that these observations are also true to some extent of the African response to the African American experience. What attracts the attention of Africans in African American cultural expressions and modes of behavior are not just the elements that are identical but the creativity evident in the changes applied to familiar forms and the innovations that have taken place. Some creative musicians learn African American music in order to derive from it models they can use in their own way. That is why some African musicians who thought they could establish themselves as creative and performing musicians in the African American tradition have turned back in order to develop their own varieties based on their own indigenous cultural resources and the challenge of their environment.

This attraction is also why African musicians hold African American musicians in such esteem and are so excited whenever an African American musician or important person visits Ghana. New Orleans jazz musician Louis Armstrong's coming to Ghana in 1956, the year before independence, was like a big dream. Musicians from Ghana rallied around him and went to meet him with their own realization of new music because we had highlife and were creating new African popular music. The idea that perhaps we could even have some dialogue with him was very inspiring. The following year, jazz musician Wilbur De Paris performed for Ghana's Independence celebration, for which I served on the Arts Committee. He represented the kind of thing that we thought we needed to know because, like Louis Armstrong, he was an example of someone who reminded us of the strength of African culture that has survived on the other side of the Atlantic.

It is always good for us, as Africans, to see what we call "survivals," for lack of a better word, because they are indications of African culture as it was—its distinct characteristics. When you have that reinforced after many years of exodus, it means that there is something in the culture that *can* survive in spite of the changes taking place—and it brings into our consciousness the importance of making sure that what we have continues and forms the basis of the new culture. Congo Square is evidence of what happened. A culture that is able to survive is not any kind of culture—it is resilient. It is able to transform itself and yet keep its vitality.

What has struck me is the fact that Congo Square has attracted so much attention because it is really a reminder of something very important for the culture. Interest in it has not subsided; yet, it is still like a big puzzle—but a puzzle that is not something trying to find a solution. It is a puzzle trying to find confirmation of the historical fact. The historical fact is not something one can erase. But every time you look at it, it gives you as if a renewal of the fact and, therefore, gives you a basis for looking forward.

ACKNOWLEDGEMENTS

This book is the result of a collective effort. I owe special thanks to Kalamu ya Salaam for his mentorship, the use of his private library, and his leadership of NOMMO Literary Society along with the Amistad Research Center's Congo Square Research Initiative; to Dr. Paulette Richards for her editorial direction, travels with me to out-of-town archives, and translations of French documents; to Professor J. H. Kwabena `Nketia for providing the book's Foreword; to Dr. Gwendolyn Midlo Hall for her assistance and encouragement; to Elizabeth Catlett for use of *Danis I* as the cover, and to Brenda Square (Amistad Research Center) and Dr. Stella Jones (Stella Jones Gallery) for their assistance; to Dr. Zada Johnson, Warren Jones III, and Dr. Michael White for their collegiology; and to the project's photographer, J. R. Thomason, for his expertise and dedication.

My appreciation extends to the following people for their valuable contributions: Ausettua Amor Amenkum (Kumbuka African Dance and Drum Collective), Carol Bebelle (Ashe Cultural Arts Center), Marie Brown (Marie Brown Literary Agency), Dr. Raphael Cassimere, Karen Celestan, Dr. Teri Chalmers, Carol Haynes, Lolis Eric Elie, Dr. Ina Fandrich, Luther Gray (Congo Square Foundation), Dr. Anita Harris, Dr. Joyce Marie Jackson, Ulrick Jean-Pierre, the late Dr. Morris F. X. Jeff, Dr. Tom Klinger, Keith Weldon Medley, Dr. Kazadi wa Mukuna, Dr. Cassandra Murphy, Dr. Jerah Johnson, Royce Osborne, Everrett G. Parker, Dr. Clyde Robertson, Kysha Brown Robinson (Runagate Multimedia), Kwame Ross, Ned Sublette, Bill Summers and the Summers Multi-Ethnic Institute of Arts, Barbara Trevigne, Jennifer Turner (Community Book Center), Dr. Jerry Ward, Jr., Dr. Dwight Webster (Christian Unity Baptist Church), and Vera Warren Williams (Community Book Center).

I wish to thank the archivists, librarians, and staff who have assisted me over the years at the following institutions. Some of the people listed may no longer work at the institution associated with their names, however they were there when they provided assistance with this book: the Amistad Research Center (Rebecca Hankins and Brenda Square); The New Orleans Public Library (Wayne Everard, Greg Osborn, and Irene Wainwright of the Louisiana Division, as well as Valencia Hawkins in the African-American Center); Tulane University (Dr. Wilbur Meneray and Leon Miller from Special Collections, as well as Alma Freeman and Bruce Raeburn from the Hogan Jazz Archives); Dillard University Library (Dr. Annie Malessia Payton); The New Orleans Jazz and Heritage Foundation Archives (Rachel Lyons); The Historic New Orleans Collection (Sally Stassi,

Mary Lou Eichhorn, and John Magill); The Louisiana State Museum (Charles E. Siler, Shannon Glasheen, Carolyn Bercier, and Dr. Charles Chamberlain); The Southern University at New Orleans Library (Shatiqua Mosby-Wilson) and Archives (Linda Hill); Xavier University Archives and Special Collections (Lester Sullivan); The University of New Orleans Library, Special Collections (Florence Jumonville and Marie Windell); Cammie G. Henry Research Center, Northwestern State University of Louisiana (Mary L. Wernet and Madeline Meziere); The Louisiana State Library (Mark Wellman); Houghton Library, Harvard University (Betty Falsey); The John Hay Library, Brown University (Alison Undy); and The Library of Congress (Jose Walters Johnson). My thanks also extends to everyone associated with the University of Louisiana at Lafayette Press for their hard work and dedication to this project.

Along the way, the Louisiana Endowment for the Humanities and the New Orleans Jazz and Heritage Foundation provided funds to support aspects of this project for which I am grateful.

Finally, I thank the following family and friends for their inspiration and support: Dr. Akita C. Evans, Melvin and Shenell Evans, Ray and Dianne Williams, Shadric and Sara Williams, David and Beverly Miller, Peter and Joyce Evans Henderson, Dr. Melvin and Dora Evans, Carlton and Gwen Charles, and Dr. Peter and Tina Frempong. I acknowledge the teachings and values that my parents, the late Rev. R. L. and Carrie Cotten Williams, imparted in me. Above all, I thank God.

Chapter 1

INTRODUCTION

It is the Sabbath! A Sabbath in New Orleans! here the noisiest day of the week—so full of strange contrasts, of lights and shadows, crossing and recrossing each other; of the grave and gray, saints and sinners, each engaged in his vocation—that he may well tremble for his art who attempts to fix it, living, upon canvass.[1]

In 1724, under French rule, the *Code Noir* of Louisiana established Sundays as non-work days for all inhabitants of the colony, thereby extending the privilege of a weekly holiday to enslaved Africans. The opportunity for those enslaved to engage in recreation and revelry on Sundays continued under Spanish as well as American rule. Popularly recognized as their "free day," African descendants gathered in the ways of their traditions on Sunday afternoons at various locations in New Orleans until 1817 when a city ordinance confined them to one gathering place. The designated location was a public space in the back of town commonly known as Congo Square.

Henry Knight, who visited the city two years later, in 1819, reported that the Africans met in the Square on the Sabbath evening and "rocked the city with their Congo dances."[2] The incredible noise that emanated from the dancing, drumming, clapping, and singing of over five hundred gatherers on February 19 of that same year drew civil engineer Benjamin Latrobe to the gathering place. That Sunday, Latrobe entered circles in the Square and observed that, "the allowed amusements of Sunday, have, it seems, perpetuated here, those of Africa among its inhabitants."[3] Although Latrobe considered what he heard and saw to be highly distasteful, he captured the essence and most significant aspect of the affair—the perpetuation of African cultural traditions. The performance styles and practices that characterized those gatherings reflected the ones found in the regions of Africa from which the gatherers originated. They also mirrored those found in other parts of the New World where slaveholders had taken enslaved Africans who originated in the same regions.

In Congo Square on Sunday afternoons, to different degrees over time, African descendants spoke and sang in their native languages, practiced their religious beliefs, danced according to their traditions, and played African-derived rhythmic patterns on instruments modeled after African prototypes. This Af-

1

rican population also bought and sold goods that they made, gathered, hunted, and cultivated much in the style of West African marketplaces. Even when those who gathered at Congo Square performed European music and dance forms, accounts confirm that traditional African practices persisted. Such conscious and willful continuation of African culture in Congo Square conveys the agency of the gatherers in celebrating and preserving their heritage.

This book presents accounts and descriptions of the songs, dances, musical instruments, and marketing practices that typified the gatherings in Congo Square as well as examples of similar practices that existed in Haiti, Cuba, and other parts of the West Indies. The parallel performance styles and practices witnessed in those locations provide a picture of the persistence and consistency of African cultures in the Americas. They also demonstrate New Orleans' previous relationship with Caribbean countries and Congo Square's influence on the perpetuation of African cultural traditions in North America. Congo Square was the venue, the place and space, for Africans to engage in African-derived cultural practice, particularly the performance aspect. While not every African-derived cultural practice that occurred in New Orleans took place in Congo Square, the repeated gatherings and long-term perpetuation of African culture that existed there established the location as ground zero for African culture in New Orleans. Congo Square in New Orleans was central to the survival, preservation, and dissemination of African-derived performance practices which influenced local as well as national popular culture.

Several scholars have discussed the influence of African cultural practices on cultural practices in the Americas. Among the earliest and most well-known of these was cultural anthropologist Melville Herskovits, whose work challenged long-standing myths that discounted the cultural connection between Africa and black people in the Americas. Herskovits' work documented the existence of this connection as well as the impact that it has on the cultures and everyday lives of African descendants. His research also established that certain cultural traits had been transmitted to people of European descent.

This study focuses on one location in North America and explores the influence of the long-term African cultural practices that occurred there. While it contributes to the larger discussion of African cultural influences, the questions that remain and difficulties faced deserve discussion and establish the need for continued research.

A major challenge encountered lay in the reliability of sources. Writers perpetuated myths and mystique by repeating information without seeking primary sources or disregarding eyewitness accounts. Narratives and newspaper articles seldom provided specific time periods, informing sources, or bylines; and, when either of these elements did accompany such information, other ones often remained in question. As the Sunday gatherings existed during French, Spanish, and American rule, a reference to the time period and circumstances under which events are said to have occurred is important. The timeline provided in this book will prove helpful, and dates or time periods frequently appear within the text.

The most pervasive images of dances in Congo Square derived from Edward W. Kemble's (1861–1933) sketches, originally published as illustrations for George Washington Cable's (1844–1925) article, "The Dance in Place Congo." Kemble's and Cable's mid-nineteenth century birth dates preclude them from having witnessed or remembered the antebellum Sunday gatherings in Congo Square—although they may have witnessed dances at other times or locations. During his career, Kemble authored "Kemble's Coons," a series of cartoons that derived their humor at the expense of African descendants and Irish and Chinese immigrants. Kemble also illustrated Mark Twain's *Adventures of Huckleberry Finn* and the 1892 edition of *Uncle Tom's Cabin*. Perhaps his most memorable creation is the "Gold Dust Twins," a branding logo for Lever Brother's washing powders which illustrated the conceit that the product could bleach even the darkest stains as the dark-skinned twins turn white in the bath.[4]

Kemble's depictions provided the stylized imagery of dances in Congo Square for an article of questionable reliability. Published in *Century Magazine* in 1886, Cable's article refers to early nineteenth century gatherings but does not cite or indicate originating sources. Some scholars, including Gilbert Chase, accuse Cable of lifting some of his material verbatim from Médéric-Louis-Elie Moreau de Saint-Méry's writings about St. Domingue and paraphrasing much of it for sensational effect.[5] Yet, facts do exist in Cable's writing, as cross-checking less questionable sources—particularly travelers' accounts—indicates. His writing contributes to our understanding of the Sunday gatherings; and his collection and publication of Creole songs are noteworthy. Still, for this as for many other sources, it was necessary to cross-reference in order to clarify contradicting information, present novel concepts, and connect concepts and events—thus the extensive endnotes for each chapter.

For example, cross-referencing revealed that the often quoted Hélène d'Aquin Allain never witnessed the dances in Congo Square nor knew anyone who had. Her 1883 publication, *Souvenirs D'Amérique Et De France, Par une Créole*, comments on an excerpt from Moreau with the statement that she "imagined" the dances in Congo Square were identical to those dances Moreau described in his book on St. Domingue. Allain included descriptions of Moreau's dances along with his description of a Voudou service for a serpent deity in her narrative. As Carolyn Morrow Long has stated, since the 1880s, writers have disregarded or forgotten Allain's source and have consequently accepted and repeated her description as the "classic New Orleans Voodoo ceremony, complete with queen, snake, gris-gris, bloody animal sacrifice, and sexual debauchery."[6] Similarly, some writers—including the one who wrote the 1932 *Times Picayune* article "Voodoo

E. W. Kemble's depiction of a dance in Congo Square, based on descriptions by George Washington Cable.

and Orgies Held Sway Here"—named Congo Square as the location of that ceremony. Allain, Cable, and others drew heavily, if not completely, from Moreau. While the dances at Congo Square resembled performances in the West Indies and descriptions from those countries are included for reference sake, this text relies primarily on firsthand accounts witnessed in Congo Square.

Another example of repeated material without a byline or originating source is the 1879 *Daily Picayune* article entitled "The Congo Dance." It refers to gatherings in Congo Square that took place sixty years before the publication date. A portion of this article reappeared in the back of the 1976 republication of Cable's *The Dance in Place Congo & Creole Slave Songs*. Additional cross-referencing indicated that William Wells Brown included an excerpt of this article in his book *My Southern Journey or The South and Its People* published in 1880. As in the previous case, Brown did not indicate where he obtained the information for his narrative. His book, published after he traveled to several Southern states during the winter of 1879–80, includes accounts of that journey along with accounts of slavery as he had experienced it, heard it described, and read about it. Brown reportedly traveled as far south as Huntsville, Alabama, but did not reach New Orleans. He did make several trips to the city in 1832 while hired-out by his owner as a handy man for a slave trader. At seventeen or eighteen years of age, Brown's job included preparing fellow enslaved men, women, and children for the auction block.[7]

Brown's use of the newspaper article was not unlike his inclusion of news articles in *Clotelle*, often cited as the first American novel written by a person of African descent. In the end, Brown's report does not represent a voice from within the circle which is important for achieving authenticity and accuracy. As accounts from those who actually danced in the Square during the antebellum years have not surfaced, questions regarding the content and interpretation of activities remain. Also missing are interpretations from people of African descent who, as members of the same culture, could have provided reliable information, even if they only observed from the sidelines.

Eyewitness accounts of the gatherings in Congo Square during the post-Civil War era have come from interviews conducted by the Federal Writers' Project during the 1930s and 40s. These interviews relative to Congo Square centered on the legend of Marie Laveau and on the practice of Voudou. By the mid 1880s, the mythology of Voudou had become institutionalized—with contributions from writers such as Allain, Cable, and Lafcadio Hearn. Some writers on the subject sensationalized this belief system and way of life and failed to distinguish between Voudou as an organized religion with formal initiation rituals and voudou as a belief system influencing customary behaviors. As the belief and practice of Voudou grew in adherents and transcended economic, social, and racial lines, at the same time, the ritual practice itself was becoming commercialized. A national firm manufactured, advertised, and sold charms along with powders, and some ceremonies themselves had become a spectacle with announcements published in local papers. In addition to not distinguishing between the public spectacle and the meaning of Voudou religion, writers increasingly associated the words "Voudou" and "orgy" as seen in the newspaper article that referred to Congo Square, "Voodoo and Orgies Held Sway Here."

Valuable observations about Congo Square have come from travelers who, often amazed by what they witnessed in New Orleans on Sundays during the pre-Civil War era, recorded events in journals. While their observations are reliable and valuable, their interpretations, when given, remain questionable. For example, the word "Congo" carried a specific and a general meaning. It referred to a particular dance as well as any African-derived dance performed by black people. When travelers wrote that African descendants performed "congo dances," "their congo dances," "a congo dance," "congo," or "the congo dance," semantically, the meaning may appear clear. However, many writers used these terms interchangeably, thus generating questions about their interpretations. On the other hand, when the dancers themselves stated that their dance was "the Congo dance," a specific dance and ethnic group can be associated with the interpretation.

Since past experiences and prejudices can color interpretations, participant observation fosters the deepest understanding. However, none of the print sources fell into this category. Indeed, most observers who wrote about Congo Square's activities during the period of enslavement documented a group of people whom they did not understand linguistically, spiritually, or culturally and whom they considered inferior. This belief that Africans were inferior and subhuman often revealed itself in the language and terminology used to describe Congo Square gatherers and activities. Since the barrage of these terms may negatively impact the self-image of high school students and other young readers, appropriate words placed in brackets replace offensive terms that originally appeared in quoted passages. In some antebellum documents, including city ordinances and letters from the mayors, writers used the word "Negro" to refer to enslaved persons and the word "colored" referred to free people of color. Historically, writers of the Harlem Renaissance campaigned to have "Negro" recognized as a proper noun spelled with a capital *N*. In this text, quoted passages that include "Negro" written with a lowercase *n* will show it written as "negro" with [*sic*] to indicate the spelling found in the original document. Although flawed in some ways, such reports of the Sunday gatherings as well as those of related activities provide essential documentation.

The varying usage and meaning of key terms presented another challenge for this study. Generally, the term "Congo" referred to the people and cultural practices that originated from the Kongo and Angola regions of West Central Africa.[8] However, writers also used it generically to refer to something black or of African origin—as noted in some newspaper articles and travelers accounts. Such usage of the word suggests that the name "Congo Square" may have referred to the location or place for "blacks." Along these lines, John Kendall wrote that the name "Congo" derived from the custom of enslaved Africans meeting and dancing there on Sundays. The earliest identified use of the term "Congo" to refer to the location known as Congo Square occurred in 1786 when Bishop Cyrillo (Cirilo Sieni) issued a pastoral letter that denounced "Negroes who at the vespers hour, assembled in a green expanse called 'Place Congo' to dance the bamboula and perform the rites imported from Africa by the Yolofs, Foulahs, Bambarras Mandigoes, and other races."[9]

Interestingly, the Bishop did not list the Kongos among those African ethnicities, although by 1786, their numbers had increased in the colony, and the Bamboula dance originated with them. In the text above, the term "bamboula" appears to refer to a specific dance—"the Bamboula dance." In other examples, it referred to a dance rhythm and a drum—"the Bamboula rhythm" and "a Bamboula drum." At the same time, a general use of the term "bamboula" appeared in newspaper articles and eyewitness accounts—for example, "the Bamboula songs," "a Bamboula dance," and "their bamboula dances."

Gov. Estaban Miró responded to the Bishop's complaint about the Bamboula dance by forbidding *los tangos, o bailes de negros* (the dance of the blacks) before the end of vespers. His ordinance indicates that the Africans also danced on the main plaza of the city. Like "bamboula," the word "tango" carried a generic meaning, seen in this passage, as well as other meanings. It denoted a rhythmic cell and a specific dance as well as a drum and a place of dance. Sharing another commonality with the word "bamboula," the word "tango" and the tango dance originated with the Kongo nation. The governor's use of the Kongo-derived term "tango" indicates the early Kongo-Angola influence in the New World.

Questions that remain about word usage, the gaps in the timeline of the Congo Square gatherings, and the history of particular dances in New Orleans are among the many indications for further study. The continued quest to find additional primary source documents about the gatherings—particularly accounts from the African descendants who gathered there, as well as documents from the French and Spanish periods, remains important for further illumination and understanding of Congo Square's history and its influence on the culture of New Orleans and North America.

Chapter 2

The Legacy of the Gathering Place

Before European explorers arrived, the location of Congo Square and its vicinity lay in the proximity of an Indian portage, a transportation route that Native Americans traveled between the Mississippi River and Bayou Choupic. Jean Baptiste Le Moyne, Sieur de Bienville, who founded New Orleans, renamed the bayou Grand Bayou de St. Jean, or Bayou St. John in English. The elevated land along the bayou and the portage attracted several of the thirty-plus Native American nations that populated Louisiana; and, historian Daniel Usner pointed out that members of some of those nations used the portage as a fishing/hunting/gathering station as well as a transportation route.[1] In a history of New Orleans, John Kendall specified a type of gathering that occurred near this portage stating that before the foundation of the city, Native Americans celebrated their corn feasts in the vicinity of Congo Square. Although Kendall did not identify the nation or nations that hosted those festivals, the Quinipissa, Acolapissa, Ouma (Houma), Chitimachas, Tunicas, and Bayogoulas among others are known to have, at some point, resided or camped in the area that became New Orleans.[2]

Regarding the corn feasts, the first play written in Louisiana, in 1809, "La Fête du Petit Blé ou l'Héroisme de Poucha-Houmma," translated "The Festival of the Young Corn or The Heroism of Poucha-Houmma," commemorated those kind of events—though not specifically the ones held at what is now Congo Square. Native Americans reportedly celebrated those festivals with religious fervor;[3] and according to local lore, they considered the area of Congo Square to be holy ground.

The high and dry land ridges along the bayou provided habitable sites for Native Americans and later French settlers as some of the first land grants in the colony developed along Bayou St. John, the Indian portage, and Bayou Road. Archaeological excavations have unearthed evidence of prehistoric Native American settlements near Bayou St. John as well as in the French Quarter, the latter of which dated between A.D. 1200 and 1600. The Native American guide who led Bienville and his crew into the area on March 9, 1699, took them along that Indian portage. They accessed the Mississippi River and the site where New Orleans would eventually rise via the Gulf of Mexico to Lake Pontchartrain to Bayou St. John and then along the portage.[4]

A plaque that commemorates the occasion stands on Decatur Street, across from Jackson Square, near Café Du Monde between St. Ann and St. Peter streets.

It reads:

> New Orleans - First sighted as Indian Portage to Lake Pontchartrain and Gulf in 1699 by Bienville and Iberville. Founded by Bienville in 1718: Named by him in honor of Duke of Orleans, Regent of France. Called the Crescent City because of location in bend of the Missisissippi.

A 1728 map of New Orleans shows the portage running through the French Quarter on St. Ann Street. Near what is now Dumaine Street, the portage branched off and continued on both St. Ann and Dumaine. Those branches merged around what is now Burgundy Street and ran to the northeast of what became known as Congo Square (see top map at right).

Although the French explored the area in 1699, Bienville's brother, Pierre Le Moyne, Sieur d'Iberville initially established a settlement at what is now the Gulf Coast area of Mississippi and years later at Mobile Bay. As a royal colony, King Louis XIV, after whom Sieur de la Salle named the Louisiana territory, governed all affairs from France. Regarding the colony's development and growth, historian Gwendolyn Midlo Hall reported that by 1706, only eighty-five subjects of the French king inhabited the colony, over half of whom were soldiers in his army. By 1708 soldiers, along with enslaved Native Americans, still constituted the majority of the 278 inhabitants. Those Frenchmen who did settle in the colony received scant provisions from the king and suffered from famines, fevers, and other illnesses. They traded with Native Americans for food, adopted some of their agricultural and survival techniques, and at times some of them resided with the Native Americans for sustenance and security.[5]

In 1712, the king granted the colony to Antoine Crozat, who, as proprietor, managed the political, demographic, and economic growth of the territory. However, after five years and minimal progress in these areas, Crozat returned Louisiana to the King. In 1717, the regent, Philip, Duke of Orleans, granted the colony to John Law's Company of the West, which, after merging with other companies, became the Company of the Indies. With approximately four hundred French settlers in the territory, including men, women, and children, Law's main goal was to provide Louisiana with new colonists.[6]

Bienville founded New Orleans in 1718 just in time for the large number of anticipated settlers and relocated to the area that year. Law, however, did not easily reach his goal to populate the territory as few Frenchmen willingly migrated to the distant unknown and undeveloped land. Therefore, to assist in populating the colony and to rid French towns—particularly Paris—of undesirable citizens, a royal edict authorized the transportation of criminals to Louisiana. This arrangement included those in jails and hospitals as well as those still at large. In 1719, smugglers, vagabonds, prostitutes, thieves, the "incorrigible," and

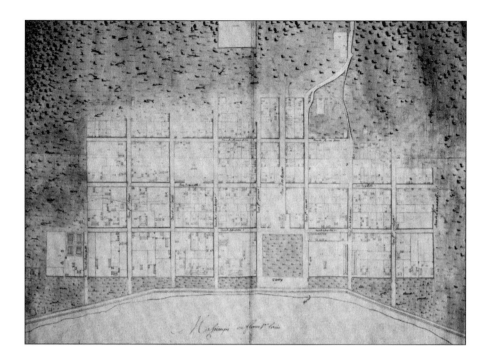

New Orleans as it was in 1728 (above) and 1731 (below). Note the Indian portage that connected the rear of the city to Lake Pontchartrain.

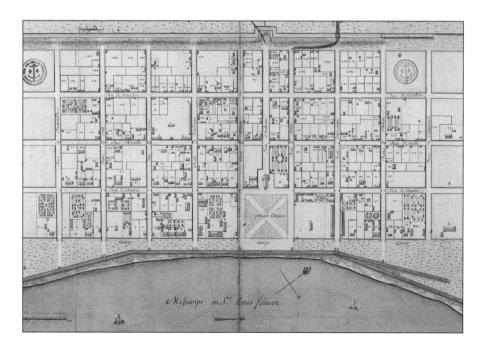

those with other social ills populated the Louisiana colony. In Paris, the Company
of the West employed a brigade of guards derisively called the "Bandouliers de
Mississippi" (Mississippi Bandits) to clean the city of its rabble. These guards
operated under the authority of police officers and received a bonus from the
Company of the West for every person secured.[7] However, not only did the deportees who survived the voyage and conditions in the Mississippi Valley prove
to be undesirable citizens, they lacked the labor capabilities required to build the
colony as well as the skills required to survive in it. Glenn Conrad stated that the
1,000 to 1,200 forced immigrants were "unequipped by nature and profession to
be colonists" and "remained for the most part non-functional dependents within
the colony."[8]

With a change in recruitment methods, Law offered Frenchmen and other
Europeans large tracts of land called "concessions" or "grants" and smaller tracts
called "habitations." His offer sometimes included the forced and indentured
labor of some of the deportees who had been sent to the colony, paid travel
expenses for entire families, horses and oxen for cultivation of fields, pigs, sheep,
chickens, furniture, kitchen utensils, and food supplies until the first harvest, and
enslaved Africans on credit. In addition, Law advertised the wonderful land of
Louisiana as having friendly and cooperative Indians, plenty of wild game, gold,
silver, copper, and lead mines.[9]

His incentives worked. Between 1717 and 1721, the extent of John Law's
era in Louisiana, more than seven thousand French colonists, voluntarily and in-
voluntarily, populated the territory. Yet, despite the large number of newcomers,
among those who survived illnesses, hunger, and attacks by Native Americans, few
possessed the skills necessary to provide their own sustenance.[10] The labor of enslaved Native Americans had also proven to be problematic as well as insufficient
for the laborious tasks at hand. Their familiarity with the surroundings made it
easier for them to escape, and fellow enslaved Africans could conveniently escape
along with them. Enslaved Native Americans also posed a threat to the security
of French settlements, and their enslavement impeded French/Indian diplomatic
relationships. The thriving economy of St. Domingue and other French colonies
in the West Indies modeled the notion that the labor of enslaved Africans could
ensure the development and ultimate survival of Louisiana. Interest in enslaved
African labor existed from almost the very beginning of the colony. Bienville
proposed to French colonists in the islands an exchange of two enslaved Native Americans for one enslaved African. They rejected his proposal, but shortly
thereafter John Law's Company, upon its takeover of the colony, moved swiftly to
fulfill its contract with the Crown to provide a certain quota of enslaved Africans
to serve the Louisiana colonists.[11] By that time, African presence already existed
in the colony although relatively limited.

Approximately twenty blacks resided in the colony prior to 1719 when the first two ships that brought enslaved Africans to Louisiana, *L'Aurore* and *le Duc du Maine*, landed 450 bondsmen. Hall found that the first documented evidence of enslaved Africans in the territory appeared in 1709 when Bienville managed to acquire them for himself. Having arranged a ship to St. Domingue at the King's expense, Bienville and another colonial official, D'Artaguette, had the ship stop in Havana under the pretext of acquiring powder and there secured several enslaved blacks.[12]

Ship captains and traders initially landed and marketed enslaved Africans on the present-day coast of Mississippi, particularly before 1721 when New Orleans became the capital of Louisiana. Shortly after, at least by 1724, newly arrived enslaved Africans and those who had not been sold to colonists resided at the Company's Plantation, also known as the King's Plantation, located across the river in Algiers away from the New Orleans settlement. This distant location aimed to alleviate the security and safety fears of local rulers and residents. In 1726, Louisiana colonist Le Page du Pratz accepted the position as manager of this plantation. He had arrived in the colony in 1718, resided on Bayou St. John for a short time, and moved to Natchez where he operated a plantation for eight years before returning to New Orleans. In his book, *The History of Louisiana*, Le Page described the King's Plantation as being only partially cleared and totally disorganized when he arrived there. He stated that the blacks stayed in cabins that were scattered everywhere and possessed pirogues that they used to steal from plantations across the river. Under his management, the bondsmen finished clearing the land, set up a camp with huts organized around a central space, enclosed the camp with a palisade that only had one entrance, built an overseer's cabin outside the palisade, and built an infirmary for the enslaved who had ailments. Le Page destroyed the pirogues that belonged to the blacks, put an end to their Sunday assemblies, and encouraged neighboring plantation owners to do the same.[13]

By the time Le Page took over the King's Plantation, the number of enslaved Africans brought to the colony had increased to more than two thousand. These Africans provided the labor needed for private plantations, and those bound to the Company's plantation developed the colony's infrastructure and produced large crops of tobacco. African labor generated products for local sale as well as export, and the Africans brought agricultural and technological skills that helped to provide the sustenance for everyday survival. Thomas Marc Fiehrer stated that they "themselves constituted the specialists who brought the crops along."[14] An example that supported this statement developed with the arrival of the first cargo of enslaved Africans to Louisiana in 1719. The Company of the Indies instructed the captains to purchase three to four barrels of rice for seeding from Africa along with Africans who knew how to cultivate the crops. Rice soon became a chief grain crop in the area as well as the staple for Louisiana Creole and later Cajun cuisine. Some of the other food items that originated in Africa

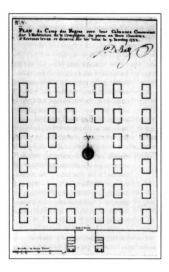

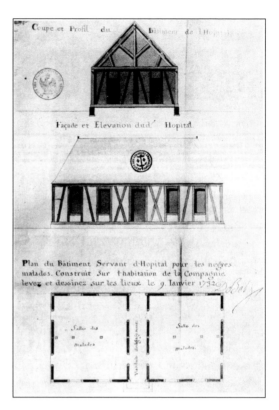

Camp for Africans on Company Plantation (above); hospital for Africans on Company Plantation (at right); and enslaved Africans on the King's Plantation, 1732 (below).

include watermelons, guinea fowls, okra, and pigeon peas.[15]

As with rice, slave traders purchased and brought Africans to the Louisiana colony who knew how to process indigo. Those Africans had routinely developed dye from indigo plants that grew uncultivated along the rivers in the Senegambian area. Indigo plants also grew wild in Louisiana, but processing experiments did not begin in the colony until 1721. Indigo also became an export product of the early Louisiana colony.[16]

Along the same lines, attempts with sugar cane production began in the early years of the colony at the Mississippi fort with cane seed brought from Santo Domingo. The Jesuits fortified efforts in 1751 by bringing additional cane seed from Santo Domingo along with forty enslaved Africans who knew how to cultivate the crop. It was a series of events, however, that eventually led to the growth of the Louisiana sugar industry. The independence of St. Domingue (Haiti), the expulsion of Frenchmen from Cuba and the subsequent flight of sugar planters to Louisiana, the advancement in sugar processing techniques, and the labor of enslaved Africans made sugar the mainstay of Louisiana's economy.[17]

Africans brought many other skills as well. Some of them were cooks, merchants, metal workers, language interpreters, lumberjacks, healers, navigators, sail makers, ship builders, silver and goldsmiths, jewelry makers, engravers of metal and stone, caulkers, sounders, potters, wet nurses, basket weavers, leather workers, wood carvers, cloth weavers, and horse trainers.[18] While it may be semantically incorrect to refer to them as blacksmiths, cowboys, construction workers, seamstresses, tailors, etc., some of the Africans worked with metals, herded cattle, built dwellings, and made garments having acquired the skills that those titles represented when they were in Africa. Labor categories and skills that some of the Africans possessed—having acquired some of these in the colony—appeared on the 1721 census list of residents in the Louisiana colony where the commandant of blacks included "a house outfitter, a turner, a barge maker, a carpenter, two joiners, two armourers, an edge-tool maker, a black-smith, a harness-maker, a tobacco-curer, a carter, sixteen ship's captains, some sailors, etc."[19]

In addition to physical labor, technological skills, food items, and food ways, the Africans brought their cultural memory, their religions, music, and dances to colonial New Orleans; and, at every opportunity, they strived to observe the cultural dictates that remained central to who they were. Early on, as it was a work-free day for all inhabitants of the colony, Sunday became the day that they honored their traditions. The *Code Noir* or Black Code of 1724 outlined policies for governing and living among the enslaved. One of the fifty-plus articles mandated that the colonial subjects observe all Catholic holidays and refrain from working on those days and Sundays. As a customary day for leisure and diversion, this article impacted the opportunity afforded the enslaved Africans to commemorate their cultural practices and mirrored customs in other French colonies like Haiti

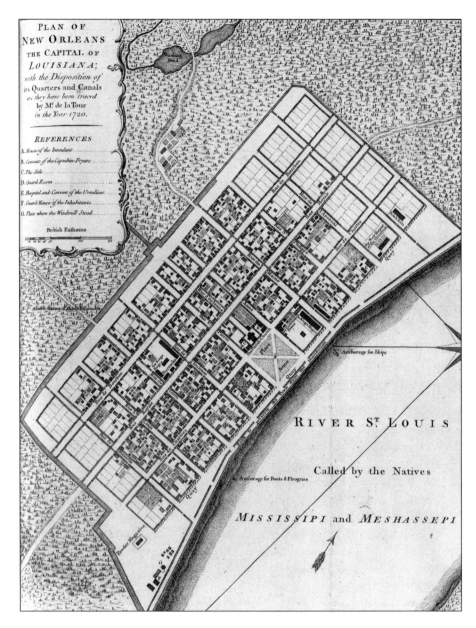

PLAN OF
NEW ORLEANS
THE CAPITAL OF
LOUISIANA;
with the Disposition of
its Quarters and Canals
as they have been traced
by Mr. de la Tour
in the Year 1720.

REFERENCES

A. House of the Intendant
B. Convent of the Capuchin Fryars
C. The Jail
D. Guard-Room
E. Hospital and Convent of the Ursulines
F. Guard House of the Inhabitants
G. Place where the Windmill Stood

British Fathoms

RIVER St. LOUIS

Called by the Natives

MISSISSIPI and MESHASSEPI

New Orleans as it was under the French.

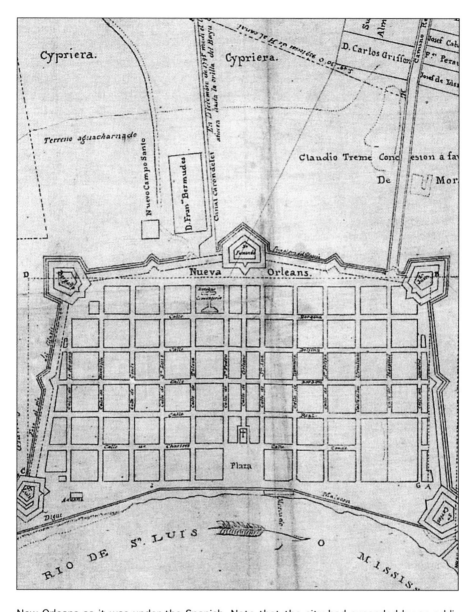

New Orleans as it was under the Spanish. Note that the city had expanded by an additional two blocks away from the river and that fortifications had been added; Fort Ferdinand (near the center of the map) was located in the immediate vicinity of Congo Square, which was part of the land identified here as the "Claudio Treme Concession."

where the same laws existed.

By 1726, when Le Page du Pratz returned to New Orleans, the *Code Noir* had been in effect for roughly two years and enslaved Africans customarily assembled for dancing and recreation on Sundays throughout the area. In the original French text of his book, he wrote that every Sunday there would be at least four hundred blacks on the Company's Plantation including two hundred and fifty who lived there. With over two thousand enslaved Africans in the colony at that time, the type of Sunday gatherings that Le Page witnessed also occurred on other plantations on both sides of the river. Le Page appealed to plantation owners and those in authority to abolish such assemblies on their plantations because of the danger they posed to the colony. Although he claimed success in bringing an end to such gatherings, the extent and long-term effect of his influence is not known. In 1734, with a change of governors, from Etienne Perier to Le Moyne de Bienville, all of the enslaved Africans on the plantation were sold to colonists, and the elimination of Le Page's position prompted his return to France.[20]

Early on, the vicinity of present-day Congo Square became another location that African descendants used to celebrate their cultural practices. Plantations and other operations in the area that utilized the labor of enslaved Africans included the Company of the Indies' brickyard, which manufactured red brick for the colony. Charles Chevalier de Morand, an employee of the Company of the Indies, who arrived in the colony before 1720, established the city's first brickyard on what was at that time an arm of Bayou Road and is now Governor Nicholls Street. When the Company of the Indies failed in 1731, Morand purchased the brickyard and surrounding land. With Bayou St. John allowing access to the young settlement, officials built a fortification line in 1730 to protect the city. They placed the line along Dauphine Street, two blocks toward the river from the present location of Congo Square, consequently leaving the Square outside of the city limits.[21] An 1881 newspaper article stated that this location functioned as a gathering place for enslaved Africans from the earliest days of the city. Bienville reportedly laid it out as a meeting place for them since it lay back of the city, a favorable location for such a purpose.[22] With the establishment of colonial New Orleans, the vicinity of present-day Congo Square's significance as a location of festivities for local inhabitants was restored and the legacy of the vicinity as a gathering place was renewed. During its span of history through the antebellum years, it was not only the location of African-derived performances and practices, but also of recreational, social, spiritual, cultural, and political events for all inhabitants of New Orleans.

Colonial authorities brought Congo Square into the city limits in 1760 when they redesigned and relocated the rear fortification line—moving it outward, away from the river. Archaeological excavations in the square revealed this second fortification line, as well as the third one, which the Spanish built in 1794 and named Fort San Fernando (Fort Ferdinand). With the demolition of this fort in 1804 at the onset of American rule, city officials moved to incorporate the area into the city commons.[23] The surrounding area, which Morand once owned, belonged to Pablo Moro (Moreau) during Spanish rule. Within years of his acquisition, a large portion of the property fell into the hands of Moro's grandson-in-law Claude Tremé. The neighborhood adjacent to Congo Square took the name Tremé from its owner, who in 1810 subdivided a large portion of his property and sold it as house plots. The new land owners included colonial settlers and white immigrants from Saint Domingue; however, the majority of them were free people of color—and mostly women. Many of the people of color were also immigrants from Saint Domingue.[24]

Sections of the Square served as a burial ground and later a loading dock for the Carondelet Canal, a man-made waterway that stretched into the vicinity. In 1795 when digging the canal, workers unearthed coffins at what was then Fort Ferdinand, which were believed to have belonged to members of the military. Completed in 1796, the canal served to extend Bayou St. John inward and essentially connect Lake Pontchartrain to the walls of the city. Residents played games including raquette on the grounds—thus at times turning parts of the Square into a sports field. This ball game originated with Native Americans and gained popularity among enslaved Africans, free people of color, and Europeans.[25]

In 1816, Cayetano's Circus opened in Congo Square as it had in previous years. The city granted permits for circuses at other locations in the city along with Congo Square, which continued to host circuses in the 1860s.[26] This public space played host to carriage shows, horse shows, foot races, bullfights, cockfights, and kite flying by the Chinese who lived in the vicinity. For many decades, beginning as early as 1813 and likely earlier, residents came to the location to view firework exhibitions and in later years to watch hot air balloon ascensions. Policemen held drills on the grounds, and Mardi Gras parades ended there.[27]

Designated as the new Place d'Armes in 1851, Congo Square became the location of military drills on Sundays; and the Globe Ball Room opened doors within its boundaries during the same year. Congo Square housed the cannon that signaled the nine o'clock curfew for the enslaved. This curfew and signal continued until 1862 when Union forces took control of the city during the Civil War. An old fire alarm bell that gave nine strokes at the hour replaced the cannon and remained for many years.[28]

Congo Square was the location of political gatherings, union meetings, and campaign rallies. In 1864, over twenty thousand Louisianans gathered there to celebrate the Emancipation Proclamation. The following year, residents came to commemorate President Lincoln after his assassination. In the late 1800s, city planners added a fountain to the public park; and in the early 1900s, they installed playground equipment, a swimming pool over time, and eventually a large sculptured eagle at its center. It was the location of open-air concerts, the first Jazz Festival in 1949, the first New Orleans Jazz & Heritage Festival in 1970, and numerous other festivals and community events over the years.[29]

Place Publique, Place des Nègres, Place du Cirque, Circus Park, Circus Place, Circus Square, Congo Park, Place Congo, Congo Plains, Place d'Armes, and Beauregard Square were among the official as well as unofficial names of this location. Some of those who provided interviews for Federal Writers' Project staff referred to the location as the "Negro's" and "Negro Square." Some travelers and observers called the location "the commons," "Congo ground," "Congo green," "the green," and "the green expanse." Traveler Timothy Flint, who mentioned the brilliant green carpet of clover that covered the ground in the winter, called the location the "parade ground."[30]

Yet, even when official names existed, a popular name was Congo Square, and it is the name that remains today. From the city's earliest days until the mid 1800s, people of African heritage—enslaved and free—gathered, discontinuously, on Sunday afternoons and conducted the activities that have brought worldwide notoriety to the location. The celebration, acculturation, and transformation of African performance styles and cultural expressions at that location influenced local and national popular culture and set Congo Square apart as a historically significant location.

The phenomenon of Congo Square, nevertheless, should not serve to romanticize the location nor the urban system of slavery that existed in New Orleans. In fact, a bitter side contrasted the more pleasant side of Congo Square's history and thus established it as a location of both happiness and sorrow. Longstanding oral history has held that enslaved Africans were sold in Congo Square, and a city ordinance of 1829 supports this assertion. In March of that year, a city council resolution forbade traders or owners to display enslaved persons in public squares for the purpose of selling them or hiring their labor. The ordinance identified several squares by their street locations and Rampart Street, referring to Congo Square, was among them. While this ordinance prohibited such activity from ordinary traders and owners, subject to fines, it excluded sales of enslaved people conducted by public officials of the state, meaning that sanctioned transactions continued in the city's public squares.

Congo Square was also the location of all executions, save one, that officials carried out in New Orleans between 1803 and 1834, and sources indicate that some of those executed were of African heritage. In addition, officials located a pillory, a device used to publicly punish offenders, as well as a whipping post in the Square. Other consequences for charges against the enslaved included branding with the fleur-de-lis, addition to a chain gang, a prescribed number of lashings administered by the jailer, and confinement in jail.[31] Particularly after 1803, the beginning of American rule, New Orleans' reputation regarding slavery and the slave trade gained prominence. One of the fears of enslaved Africans throughout the South was to be "sold down the Mississippi" to New Orleans, which became the largest slave market distribution center in North America during the decades preceding the Civil War.[32]

Such harsh conditions for the enslaved in New Orleans did not begin with American rule. Throughout the city's antebellum history, enslaved Africans endured arduous physical labor—clearing swamps, draining ditches, digging canals, building levees, driving piles, stripping and splitting trees to prepare lumber for vessels and houses, and yielding plantation crops. Their "half-day of half freedom" on Sunday afternoons in Congo Square ended at sunset when police dispersed the crowd. Punishment ensued if by the nine o'clock curfew, signaled by cannon fire, the enslaved were not back in their places ready to resume their servitude.[33]

"Bon soir dansé. Soleil couché." "Good night dance. The sun has set," some sighed as they returned to their regulated existences. Yet, a degree of consolation abided. Come Sunday of another week, they could reunite and revive their cultural heritage in Congo Square.

Congo Square in the snow, February 15, 1895.

Chapter 3

THE SIGNIFICANCE OF THE GATHERINGS

The Sunday culture in New Orleans impacted the existence and continuation of the gatherings at Congo Square, and the African cultural practices that persisted at those events impacted the popular culture of New Orleans and the nation. This exchange of influences, along with a combination of other factors, contributed to the historical significance of the gatherings in Congo Square. Those factors include:

- the Square's longevity as a gathering place
- Congo Square's international influences
- the documentation of the gatherings
- the openness of the gatherings
- the magnitude of gatherers
- the economic exchange
- New Orleans' Sunday atmosphere
- the diverse backgrounds and transcultural exchange
- the perpetuation of African-derived rhythmic cells
- the influence of the African cultural practices

CONGO SQUARE'S LONGEVITY AS A GATHERING PLACE

From the time of their arrival in the Louisiana Colony, enslaved Africans sang and danced in traditional styles. Le Page du Pratz, who lived in the colony at several locations from 1718 to 1734, observed gatherings of hundreds of Africans on Sundays dancing the Calinda and indicated that these dances took place on the King's Plantation, as well as at private plantations. The writer of a *New Orleans Democrat* article along with historian Jerah Johnson pinpointed the rear of the city, Congo Plains, as the location for such events from the earliest days of the city.[1] Consequently Congo Square's legacy as a gathering place, which began with Native Americans, resumed during the eighteenth century with African descendants and eventually citizens of all backgrounds. It was a cultural continuum that existed during all three periods of rule—French, Spanish, and American. Travelers' accounts, city ordinances, police codes, newspaper articles, and other documents trace the Square's history and show that people of African heritage gathered there off and on under various conditions until at least the 1850s.

While the legacy of the Sunday gatherings at Congo Square in New Orleans is significant, it is not unique: 1) Sundays were generally days of rest and recreation for those enslaved throughout the Americas; 2) enslaved Africans gathered and danced in urban as well as rural settings in other states although laws and conditions may have varied—among these were the Pinkster dances in New York and the Jubilees in Philadelphia; 3) many urban areas designated public squares (typically remote and less desirable locations) for the recreation of enslaved Africans—for example, in Philadelphia, Pennsylvania, the public square utilized by enslaved Africans during the early colonial period also held the name Congo Square, as indicated on the historical plaque at the location now called Washington Square. Located in the historic district of the city, over time this square served as a pasture, a burial ground, and a place of recreation for enslaved Africans. Reportedly, some of the enslaved came there to pray, dance, cook traditional African foods, and converse in various languages with free Africans before being sold on the auction block. The word "Congo" in the square's name referred to the part of Africa now called the Democratic Republic of the Congo.[2]

Referring to a period before the American Revolution, the *Annals of Philadelphia*, published in 1830, stated that on the last days of their jubilee enslaved Africans engaged:

> in dancing the whole afternoon in the present Washington Square, then a general burying ground—the blacks [*sic*] joyful above, while the sleeping dead reposed below! In that field could be seen at once more than one thousand of both sexes, divided into numerous little squads, dancing and singing, "each in their own tongue," after the customs of their several nations in Africa.[3]

While other public gathering places that hosted large numbers of enslaved Africans did exist in North America, such as this one in Philadelphia, New Orleans' Congo Square existed for a longer period and until a later date. This no doubt led Dena Epstein to conclude, after her extensive documentation of African music in the New World, that regarding the mainland of North America: "Only in Place Congo in New Orleans was the African tradition able to continue in the open."[4]

Congo Square's International Influences

Although located on the mainland of North America, the French-ruled Louisiana colony shared connections with St. Domingue (which became Haiti) and other colonies in the French West Indies. Under Spanish rule, the colony held similar relations with Cuba, which was the seat of the Spanish colonial administration. Such commonalities often led to the receipt of enslaved Africans from the same region or country in Africa and sometimes from the same cargo. It also led to mutual laws (e.g. the *Code Noir* under the French) for governing the enslaved across several territories, exchanges in commerce and population, and similarities in culture. The chapters in this book on the songs, dances, and musical instruments illuminate some of those shared cultural practices.

New Orleans' connection to the French and Spanish West Indies, particularly Haiti and Cuba, expanded with the success of the Haitian Revolution and impacted the Sunday gatherings at Congo Square. While some Haitians fled to New Orleans between the years 1791 and 1804 as a result of the insurrection, a vast number of them sought asylum in Cuba because of its geographical proximity to St. Domingue. In 1809, however, with the outbreak of war in Europe between France and Spain, officials expelled French refugees from Cuba and other Spanish colonies who did not pledge allegiance to the Spanish crown from those colonies. Among the thousands who fled to Louisiana from Cuba, 3,226 were enslaved Africans, 3,102 were free people of color, and 2,731 were white. The majority of these immigrants remained in New Orleans increasing the city's population from 17,001 in 1806 to 24,552 in 1810.[5] Such interchange between New Orleans and parts of the West Indies did not end in 1810 as Flugel, a traveler to the city, noted in his April 1817 journal entry. One Sunday afternoon around four o'clock, Flugel stood among spectators in Faubourg Ste. Marie observing enslaved Africans dancing. He wrote:

> As I was looking on a sailor told me that a few months ago, he had come from Havana where he had sailed with some slaves from the coast of Guinea. Among them was a son of Pepin, a King of the Congo, who had been recommended to a merchant-house, Fernandez of Havana, who were to expedite him to Port au Prince, St. Domingo, where he now lives.[6]

The increase in the city's black population also increased attendance at the Congo Square gatherings as well as at social and religious assemblies throughout the city. The ever-present threat of slave uprisings and anxiety over the influence that such meetings would have on them became a reality with the slave revolt of January 1811. Within a week following the revolt, city officials passed an ordinance that restricted social gatherings for enslaved persons to Sundays at places that the mayor designated. Two years later, in his letter to the council dated January 16, 1813, Mayor Nicolas Girod requested permits for Negroes to gather and dance at three different locations: Faubourg Ste. Marie, Fort St. Ferdinand, and Faubourg Marigny. An 1815 map of New Orleans and suburbs shows all three areas with Fort Ferdinand being the only designated location with set boundaries as well as the one located at the center of the city. Although the mayor did not

specify locations within the Ste. Marie (later St. Mary) and Marigny neighborhoods, public squares did exist in both parts of the city. In 1815, Jacques Tanesse
designed a map of the city which identified the square in Ste. Marie as Place Publique (presently Lafayette Square) and the square in Faubourg Marigny as Place
Washington (see map at right). In 1817, six years after the 1811 ordinance, the
city council reissued and revised that order restricting the Sunday assemblies of
enslaved people to only one location, which the mayor would appoint. Although
Congo Square became the sole venue for Sunday gatherings, neither the letters of
Mayor Augustin de Macarty, extending several years following the ordinance, nor
the notes of the city council have surfaced that reveal the official designation.

Congo Square had served as a gathering place for dancing since the earliest
days of the colony; however, it was only one of several locations frequented on
Sunday afternoons until 1817. African descendants gathered and danced along
the levee, in backyards, in vacant lots, on private plantations including the King's
Plantation, and at other locations in the city including, for a period of time, Plaza
de Armes, the main square of the city located in the front of St. Louis Cathedral.
Numerous other gathering places in the city have been identified that were not
necessarily associated with or identified as locations for dancing including the
public square where Fort St. Louis previously stood. The Haitian Revolution and
subsequent events including the expulsion of French citizens from Cuba, the
large influx of Haitian immigrants, the 1811 Slave Revolt, the constant threat
of additional uprisings, and the city's growth in population as well as physical
expansion all impacted the efforts of city officials to control Sunday activities.
This control resulted in the use of Congo Square as the sole location for African
descendants to assemble.

THE DOCUMENTATION OF THE GATHERINGS

The timeline at the end of this book provides chronological documentation of the gatherings and other events pertinent to the history of the Square.
It notes primary and secondary sources including travelers' accounts, city ordinances, police codes, newspaper articles, letters from mayors, an autobiography,
and local eyewitness reports. Gaps exist in this record because neither ongoing
reporting nor ongoing gatherings occurred. Over the years, several writers referred to the periods of prohibition for the gatherings including James Creecy
who made several trips to New Orleans beginning in 1834. He wrote that the
Congo Square dances had been terminated more than once, "but the Creole propensity for those amusements is so strong that their friends are soon placed in
power again, and the wild frolics are hailed by acclamation. . . ."[7]

Several factors may have influenced such interruptions after 1817 when
an ordinance confined all assemblies to one location. These include: the growth
and development of the neighborhoods in the city, including Tremé; the politi-

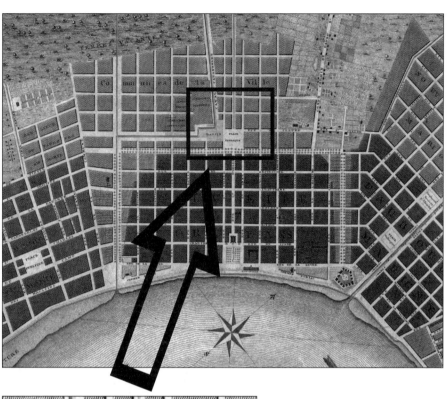

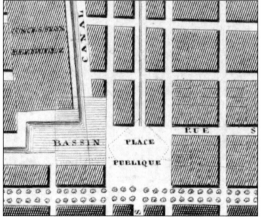

Plan of the City and Suburbs of New Orleans in 1815 by J. Tanesse. Congo Square is identified as "Place Publique."

Note also the square labeled "Place Publique" in Faubourg Ste. Marie and the square labeled "Place Washington" in Faubourg Marigny.

cal as well as demographic Americanization of the city; the division of the city government into three municipalities in 1836; the appropriation of Congo Square for other functions on Sundays; the anxiety over abolition activities and slave insurrections; and the increased restrictions on people of African descent, both enslaved and free.

Possibly identifying a period of prohibition, Henry Kmen stated that the Sunday gatherings in Congo Square appeared to have ceased shortly after 1835. While no new ordinance appears to have suspended the dancing privileges around that time, the division of the city government in 1836 and the finding of Joseph Tregle, Jr., present a probable explanation for Kmen's observation. Although the Nat Turner insurrection and other national events in the early 1830s plunged the South into fear, Tregle indicates that the hysteria did not peak in Louisiana until late 1835. Reports from all parts of the state described threats of insurrections encouraged by abolitionists and the distribution of abolitionist literature.[8]

Newspapers published such reports particularly in August of that year, and authorities in various parishes passed new resolutions regarding the enslaved. Officials in East Feliciana Parish restricted enslaved Africans to their residences or plantations, especially on Sundays—unless in possession of a pass in writing, stating their business, their place of destination, and the period that they would be absent. In Ascension Parish, new laws also banned Sunday gatherings for enslaved people. The governor's address to the Legislature in January of 1836 demonstrates the depth of the concerns regarding the abolition movement referring to the northerners as traitors to humanity, their country, and its constitution.[9]

Slaveholders in New Orleans as well as those in other areas of the state held meetings and called for tighter controls of those enslaved. Authorities in New Orleans maintained that if the state's laws pertaining to the enslaved— called the "Black Codes"—were efficiently enforced, they would provide adequate protection in every emergency. The forty articles of that code, adopted by the Americans in 1806, regulated the activities of enslaved people and included a provision for free people of color. One of the articles established that those enslaved should be free to enjoy Sundays or paid fifty cents for Sunday work, excluding certain positions like house servants and carriage drivers. However, another article forbade them to assemble. With promises to reinforce the Black Code in hand, slaveholders in New Orleans then sought to deter abolitionists, to prevent the dissemination of their pamphlets, and to control free people of color.[10] Consequently, while authorities in New Orleans may not have instituted a new ordinance during this period, they may have enforced an existing one. The city council resolution to allow enslaved Africans and free people of color to gather in Congo Square under police surveillance in 1837, the year following the city's reorganization, suggests that there had been an interruption in the Sunday gatherings.[11]

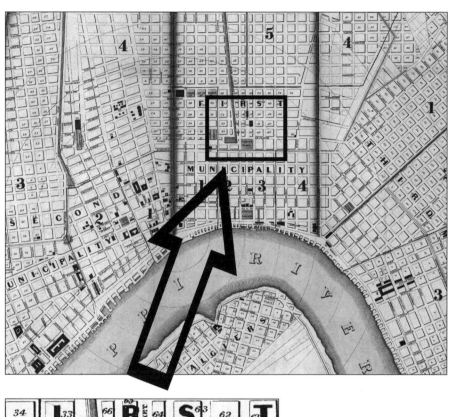

Norman's Plan of New Orleans & Environs, 1845 by Henry Moell-hausen. Congo Square is identi-fied here as "Circus Place."

In the early 1840s, newspaper articles indicated that private and "unlaw-ful" balls for the enslaved took place in homes and backyards. An 1841 *Picayune* article reported that an unlawful "Negro ball," at "half past two o'clock on Sun-day morning . . . was in full tide of successful operation." Authorities arrested thirty-four enslaved people, and their owners had to pay the prescribed fines. An 1843 *Daily Picayune* article told of a black, public ball involving traditional African dance that authorities detected in the yard of a house in the Third Municipality one Sunday afternoon. That same year, the *Daily Picayune* shed light on the plight of Congo Square and the apparent effort to keep visitors out. "We yesterday no-ticed that this common, so long let free to loafers and cattle, is being put in chains. Do the authorities fear that it would go away?"[12]

In 1845, citizens petitioned the First Municipal Council on behalf of the Sunday dances. The resulting ordinance granted permission for the enslaved to gather and dance as long as such merriment took place before sunset and was not offensive to public decency. The ordinance restricted gatherings to four months, May 1 to August 21, from four to six p.m., with written consent from owners and under police supervision. An 1845 news article stated that the ordinance restored the ancient privilege of resorting to Congo Square and referred to the dances ob-served during those gatherings as "Regular Ethiopian Break-Downs."[13] The term "Ethiopian" referred to the African-derived culture that permeated the event, and the word "regular" implied that the events were standard.

An 1846 *Daily Picayune* article and A. Oakey Hall's account of New Or-leans, written in 1846 and 1847, reveal that enslaved Africans danced in Congo Square after 1845. Contrary to the 1845 Ordinance, which limited dancing to the months of May through August, the 1846 gathering took place in March. The ar-ticle further indicated that the gatherings were ongoing: "No stranger . . . should fail to visit, of a Sunday afternoon, the square in Rampart Street, commonly called Congo Square. . . . Every fair Sunday afternoon he [master of ceremonies] may be found at his post."[14] Both accounts lend evidence to the performance of African-derived dance and musical instruments.

In December of 1848, the *Daily Picayune* published a review of the city's public squares. Regarding Congo Square, which was in grave neglect, the article stated, "The negroes [*sic*] are the only ones who patronize it."[15] The article also mentioned that circuses continued to exhibit there. In January 1851, city offi-cials designated the Square as the new Place d'Armes where the military would conduct drills on Sundays. In February of that year, the Globe Ball Room, later known as Globe Hall, opened on the corner of St. Peter and St. Claude within Congo Square. Newspaper articles announcing the opening of the splendid room and the upcoming Masquerade Ball stated that a "selected Band of Music under the direction of a good leader will execute the most modern Waltzes, Polkas, and Contre dances." Dancing continued at this site through the season of amusement

336. *(a)* Attendu qu'un grand nombre de citoyens de la Première Municipalité s'est adressé à ce conseil, afin que des danses d'esclaves soient permises le dimanche, sur la place du Cirque;

Attendu qu'un divertissement de ce genre, lorsqu'il a lieu en plein jour et qu'il n'offense en rien la morale publique, peut être toléré en le plaçant toutefois sous la surveillance de la police ;

Résolu que, du 1er Mai au 31 Août de chaque année, les esclaves qui auront une permission écrite de leur maître, pourront se réunir le dimanche sur la place du Cirque et y danser depuis quatre heures de l'après-midi jusqu'à 6 1[2 du soir.

Résolu que les commissaires de police des 3me et 5me districts, l'officier commandant le poste du faubourg Trémé, et cinq hommes de la police de jour devront veiller à ce qu'aucune infraction aux ordonnances de police n'ait lieu, pendant qu'il sera permis aux esclaves de danser sur la place du Cirque.

[*a*] Ord. 28 Avril 1845, Jour.

1845 ordinance from the First Municipal Council, which sanctioned gatherings in Congo Square.

as well as beyond with references to outdoor dancing over the years. Author and musician Maude Cuney Hare interviewed a woman who told of the dances at Congo Square during that time. While the interviewee did not mention the Globe Ball Room, the venue or situation to which she referred was similar to the ball room in that it excluded enslaved persons. Hare wrote, "I am told by an elderly Creole neighbor who remembers those early days, that as late as 1855 Place Congo was open only to free persons of color and members of the white race and that the dance which lasted from two until nine on Sunday afternoons was a noticeable event in the life of the old city."[16]

In 1856, a city ordinance made it unlawful to beat a drum, blow a horn, or sound a trumpet in the city. A week after this ordinance passed, the city council passed an additional one that prohibited all public balls, dances, and entertainment without permission from the mayor. Although officials restated the latter ordinance in 1857, a clause provided an opportunity for enslaved Africans to again assemble and dance or play ball or cricket with permission from the mayor for a particular day and ending at sunset.[17] While no newspaper article or city document has been located to indicate whether requests were made and honored, the fact that officials established the law suggests that there was a need for it and that the opportunity to assemble existed.

Newspapers do show that as the Civil War approached, tension mounted and restrictions on the gatherings and movement of enslaved as well as free people of color increased. Authorities discouraged people of color (enslaved and free) from assembling in public and in private to the point of arrests, beatings, and fines; and an 1858 ordinance made it unlawful for them to assemble.[18] The police, however, arrested those whom they caught assembled in private settings long before this ordinance passed and overwhelmingly linked the gatherings to the practice of Voudou. An 1850 *New Orleans Daily Picayune* article expressed concern over the rapid increase of these secret meetings, which were reportedly of injury to the enslaved because they brought them in contact with disorderly free people of color and mischievous whites. It was therefore of utmost importance for the police to disband them.[19]

Newspaper articles from the early 1850s reveal police efforts to comply with this mandate. In 1851, they arrested a free man of color and several enslaved people along with him charging the free man of color with keeping a disorderly house. The *Daily True Delta* reported, "This African superstition still obtains among the colored population in the lower part of the city (First Municipality)." Five days later, the same newspaper, the *Daily True Delta*, reported another gathering in the First Municipality and stated, "Nothing tends more to demoralize the servile population than gatherings for such purposes, and the police are doing well to break them up wherever they find them." The following day, the *Daily True Delta* reported the arrest of a dozen people in a house on Burgundy for "practicing the Voudou rites. . . . There was but one slave among them, all the rest were free." The police fined each person ten dollars. An 1854 article entitled *Voodoo Dance* stated, "This dance is a sort of African . . . rite or mystery, which has been introduced into this country . . . and handed down from sire to son for ages. . . . A few white persons of the city have become proselytes to the African faith, and occasionally join with them in these rites." Police arrested the people of color involved and charged them with disturbing the peace.[20]

In February 1857, prior to the passage of the 1858 Ordinance, police arrested nearly thirty people of color, enslaved and free, who gathered at the Orleans Ballroom for a masonic meeting. Police beat the enslaved, charged the free people of color with unlawful gathering, and fined them. Upon its enactment, the 1858 ordinance forbade people of color, whether enslaved or free, to assemble for religious services or any other purposes without white supervision. As a result of this ordinance, authorities closed St. James African Methodist Episcopal Church,[21] founded in 1844, and seized its property. Before this action took place, authorities had placed the church under surveillance, harassed some of its members, and stationed patrols at the church doors to prevent enslaved persons from attending services. The church remained closed for four years, reopening in 1862 after Union forces occupied New Orleans under General Benjamin Butler.[22]

When addressing such arrests, restraints, and charges of Voudouism, Marcus Christian noted that they grew in volume as the Civil War approached and noted that authorities made no reports of Voudou dances or arrests near Congo

Square, which many had considered the traditional meeting place of the followers of Voudou during antebellum years.[23] Regarding Congo Square at around
that time, an 1864 *Daily Picayune* article stated that "his [the formerly enslaved]
dancing days in Congo Square are over; the banjo and the violin are heard there
no more." Despite the relentless efforts of authorities to end the assemblies and
dances of the enslaved people, reports indicate that gatherings of various levels
continued at some locations.   Federal Writers' Project staff interviewed black
New Orleansians in 1940 who observed dances and musical performances during
their lifetime, which included the period of slavery. One interviewee, Miss White,
who was born in 1855 and was eighty-five years old at the time of the interview,
remembered a dance hall in close proximity to Congo Square and stated that:

> when she was a girl at school, she resided on Barracks street
> [*sic*] between Rampart and St. Claude. . . . Directly opposite her
> home on the down town side of the street was a hall for colored
> people. Every Saturday night, the slaves were permitted to at-
> tend a dance at that place.
>
> As they were well-behaved, the neighborhood did not object to
> the location and the dances that were given there.[24]

As indicated in these accounts, African descendants, enslaved and free,
continued to gather and dance after the prohibition of the Sunday gatherings in
Congo Square. The locations for their gatherings varied, but dance halls located
in the vicinity of Congo Square were popular and free people of color owned
many of them. Those businesses as well as the culture that they represented
continually faced attacks by the authorities. One dance hall located in the vicinity
of Congo Square (then Beauregard Park) where African descendants held dances
on Saturday nights remained in operation as late as 1906. Early that year, Beauregard Park commissioners requested, in writing, assistance from Mayor Martin
Behrman in shutting down the hall. The commissioners' report to the mayor in
August indicated that their efforts had been successful.[25] Such loss of venues
continually threatened the survival of African cultural performance practices.

THE OPENNESS OF THE GATHERINGS

Varying conditions and restraints governed the Sunday gatherings in Congo Square over the years. However, when they did take place, the gatherings remained open to African descendants regardless of legal status, labor category,
and location in the city or surrounding area. The ordinances of 1817 and 1845
required police supervision. The latter of these ordinances required the enslaved
to have written permission from slaveholders and limited the gatherings to two

A "slave pass."

hours, for four months, with eight supervising policemen. The conditions set by the latter ordinance, however, were apparently amended or short-lived as a news article indicated that a gathering occurred the following year during a time that contradicted the order. Regarding the required passes, Frederick Olmsted, who visited the city in the early 1850s quoted a newspaper article that called for a regulation of the manner in which passes were issued stating: "Forging passes . . . has now become a regular business in New Orleans . . . any Negro can obtain a pass for four bits or a dollar."[26] Such transactions affirm the openness and inclusiveness of the events during authorized periods.

THE MAGNITUDE OF THE GATHERINGS

Not only did the gatherers come from diverse backgrounds, they came in masses. As travelers estimated the numbers that they reported and ongoing records do not exist, the pinnacle of attendance at Congo Square remains in question. However, the attendance no doubt increased after the 1817 ordinance restricted all gatherers to a sole location.

Travelers and local eyewitnesses left varying accounts regarding the Sunday afternoon crowd; yet, all reports provide a picture of the vastness of the gatherings. In 1819, Latrobe observed five to six hundred persons in the Square. However, he documented the gathering in February of that year, one of the coldest months in New Orleans.[27] The time of year compounded by the fact that many of the enslaved did not have shoes and were poorly clad—some nearly naked—suggests that Latrobe's number does not represent the largest assembly of African descendants in Congo Square.

Captain Canot recorded in his journal, later published as *The African Slave Trade*, that "we have heard the tom-tom, and witnessed the mystic dance of thousands of native Africans and their lineal descendants in Congo-square, New Orleans."[28] John Lay, a Buffalo merchant, who traveled to the New Orleans in 1822, recorded in his journal that, on a Sunday, he witnessed a Congo dance attended by five thousand people.[29] He did not indicate whether that number referred only to the dancers, the spectators, or to both. Henry Castellanos (1828–1896), who stated that he described Congo Square as he knew and saw it in his book, *New Orleans as It Was*, reported that African descendants came to the gatherings by the thousands.

An 1845 *Daily Picayune* article published shortly after the ordinance that restored dancing stated, "thousands of Negroes congregated in and about Congo Square on Sunday afternoon. . . . Some two or three weeks since an ordinance was passed restoring to them their ancient privilege of resorting thither, and thither they now repair in countless throngs."[30] While some articles may have included spectators in the account, Latrobe's numbers did not. The inclusion of spectators in his description would possibly have increased his estimation to a thousand as well. Regarding the conduct of this magnitude of gatherers, Latrobe reported that "there was not the least disorder among the crowd," nor did he learn upon enquiry, that there had ever been any mischief.[31]

The size of Congo Square during the time of these observations differed from its current dimension of approximately 2.35 acres. James Creecy, who visited in the early 1830s, wrote that the Square contained five, six, or perhaps more acres. In 1930, city officials completed construction of the Municipal Auditorium, presently Morris F. X. Jeff Auditorium, which they located at what is now the rear of the Square. Until that point, Congo Square was a little over twice the size it is today, as it included the area on which the auditorium now stands. Jazz musician Harrison Barnes, born in 1889 and interviewed in 1959, recalled the size of Congo Square before the auditorium's construction. Globe Hall, to which he refers, opened in 1851 and stood on a corner of Congo Square at St. Peter and St. Claude. *Soards City Directory* listed the hall's address as 1210 St. Peter Street. Barnes stated:

> They used to have the Square right where the auditorium is now, that Square there, used to go straight across there, used to be named Congo Square. They changed it to Beauregard Square, and they had a hall used to call it the Globe Hall right there, where you could set down out in the square when they're going to have a dance there and they'll come outside and play two,

three numbers. That's where I heard Bolden [Buddy Bolden]
and Manuel Perez, all different Bands come around there, they
get out and play a coupla numbers.[32]

The number of African descendants who gathered at this location on Sunday afternoons and the long span of the gatherings indicate the significance of
the experience to those who assembled. Also indicated is the lure that these events
held for onlookers, many of whom were tourists of European ancestry. Not only
did the gatherings evolve as a tourist attraction, they were equally as popular
among locals. Traveler James Creecy, who recommended the Sunday event to
tourists, also noted that Creoles (locals) had a strong propensity for the amusements. Grace King stated that whites promenaded by to look at the scene, and
young men from the College of Orleans, in route to the theatre, always stopped
by to see the blacks dance "Congo."[33]

The Economic Exchange

Enslaved Africans came in masses, and many of them came with money
that they had earned from their slaveholders and/or outside endeavors during
their free time. In New Orleans, the buying power of the enslaved had long
existed and authorities acknowledged it early on. In 1772, the attorney general
petitioned the Cabildo "requesting that merchants of this city be allowed to sell
to negroes [*sic*] on Sundays and holidays before and after the divine services."[34]

This buying power of the enslaved extended to the gatherings at Congo
Square where the opportunity for enslaved persons to earn money during their
off-time produced wages to spend with black marketers on Sunday afternoons.
While free people of color and white spectators contributed to the success of the
marketers, it is significant that at the base of the economy at Congo Square were
merchants and customers who were enslaved. The exchange was an integral part
of the Sunday afternoon experience, which was true from the earliest assemblies.
Le Page du Pratz, who lived in the colony from 1718 to 1734, noted that when
the Africans gathered to dance on the King's Plantation and other neighboring
ones, there was also buying and selling. As an 1864 *Picayune* article stated, one of
the reasons that enslaved blacks came to Congo Square was to spend their surplus
money.[35]

The Sunday Atmosphere

There was no better time to have money than on Sundays in New Orleans.
In the Catholic-based, French-founded city, residents reportedly observed Sundays quite differently from their counterparts in Protestant locations where many
customarily regarded Sundays as solemn and subdued. James Creecy wrote that

New Orleanians did not neglect Holy Mass in the mornings, but the afternoons of the Lord's day were devoted to "amusements, fun and frolic of every description—always with an eye to much sport for a little expense."[36] Locals typically attended a cockfight, ball game, the circus, or a similar event in the afternoon, and a ball, opera, or theater, etc. in the evening. Businessmen opened taverns, cabarets, and various shops, while market women peddled their wares in parks, market places, and up and down streets. Locals as well as those visiting the city for the day, strolled through the markets, cruised the river, and frequented public parks. But, "back-a-town," people of African descent held high carnival in Congo Square. As stated in an 1864 *Picayune* article, "Congo Square was devoted on Sunday afternoons especially to the unrestricted pleasures of the negroes [*sic*]."[37] The Sunday afternoon atmosphere in New Orleans as well as certain laws and ordinances enabled such an accommodation for African descendants in the place known as Congo Square.

THE DIVERSE BACKGROUNDS AND TRANSCULTURAL EXCHANGE

The black population of New Orleans included a mixture of cultural backgrounds and influences, and the gatherings at Congo Square mirrored that diversity. The people who gathered there had come by way of the French West Indies, Cuba, other slave-holding states, and some had come directly from Africa. They had been born in different parts of the African continent, different parts of the French and Spanish West Indies, and different parts of North America—including Louisiana. To varying degrees, some of them not only encountered African, French, Spanish, Caribbean, and American cultures, but also Native American, German, and Italian as well as other influences that may have resulted from New Orleans' status as a port city. The transcultural exchange that developed at Congo Square on Sunday afternoons blended, intensified, and transformed performance styles. Nonetheless, elements of African cultural practices lay at the core of those New World styles, and traditional African performance styles and practices persisted alongside them.

THE PERPETUATION OF AFRICAN-DERIVED RHYTHMIC CELLS

The New Orleans rhythm known as the street beat, bamboula beat, second line, and even New Orleans beat, is an example of the influence that African-derived rhythmic patterns had on new performance forms throughout the African Diaspora. Now an integral part of New Orleans culture, this rhythm and its derivatives entered the city with enslaved Africans who had been brought to Louisiana directly from Africa and from the Caribbean—primarily Haiti and Cuba. Many of those who arrived in New Orleans from Cuba had fled there from Haiti.

As a result of the uprising, a large number of Haitians, both African descendants and French colonists, fled Saint Domingue and settled in Cuba. Many of the musicians of African heritage among them played for the quadrilles, minuets, and cotillions of the French elites who had also absconded to Cuba. As author Ned Sublette has pointed out, those musicians added their interpretation to the simple melodies that appeared in written form. They imposed African-derived rhythmic cells or patterns, one of which initially came to be known as "tango," a word of Kongo origin.[38] This rhythmic cell gained such prominence in Cuban music that it became identified with Cuba and received the name "habanera" meaning "of Havana."

habanera

Although African descendants, enslaved and free, already performed this rhythmic pattern in New Orleans, it received reinforcement—sometimes under the name "habanera"—from those Haitian immigrants of African descent who arrived from Cuba. They performed this rhythm on drums to accompany dances, and it appeared in the melody line of several Creole songs, both of which African descendants performed in Congo Square. Perhaps the most popular of these songs was *Quan Patate-Latchuite* which Louis Gottschalk's nurse Salley from Haiti taught him and on which he based his composition "La Bamboula – Danse des Nègres, Op. 2." Addressing this song's role in New Orleans culture, three-fourths of a century after the Congo Square gatherings ceased, Alice Nelson Dunbar wrote that every child could sing its melody. It is reasonable to suggest every child could also clap the habanera rhythm for the melody followed it.

Sublette noted that an important variant of the habanera cell developed when musicians tied the second note of the cell to the third.[39] In Cuba, the three-beat pattern that resulted is called the "tresillo," Spanish for "triplet." It is a distinctive feature of Afro-Cuban popular dance music including that of the Rumba Guaguancó. This three-beat rhythmic pattern also provides the foundation for several indigenous street songs in New Orleans including the popular Mardi Gras Indian chant *Hey Pockey Way*.

tresillo

The cinquillo is another identifying feature of Cuban music; and at the same time, it is the central rhythm of the Haitian meringue as well as the Puerto

Rican Bomba with a common influence being Haitian musicians of African ancestry.

cinquillo

Samuel Floyd, former director of the Center for Black Music Research
at Columbia College in Chicago, wrote that the tresillo often appears alongside
the cinquillo and may have derived from it. Both are widely used throughout the
Circum-Caribbean. New Orleans-based Afro-Cuban/Latin jazz percussionist Bill
Summers affirmed that in every Latin American and Caribbean country where
he has been and where there were black people, they play these rhythms. "It's the
basic groove for Black music period," he stated, quickly adding that, however "in
no form or fashion would these [rhythms] be all that was going on." The relationship between the two rhythmic cells led Floyd to recognize the entire complex of
genres in which they appear as a cinquillo-tresillo rhythmic complex.[40]

These rhythmic cells have origins in an African timeline pattern that permeated Cuban music and that received the name "clave." The research of profes-
sors J. H. Kwabena `Nketia and Gerhard Kubik identify African timelines as well
as their variations and derivatives. The clave rhythmic pattern forms the basis of
Afro-Latin and Caribbean musical styles and the tresillo rhythmic cell is found
within it.

clave

The tresillo and cinquillo cells were and continue to be a characteristic
feature of New Orleans music as well. They provide the foundation for the New
Orleans street beat. When studying the relationship among African descendant
musical forms that manifest in these cells, New Orleans-based percussionist and
researcher Michael Skinkus used the cinquillo and tresillo as templates to com-
pare the New Orleans street beat to the rhythms of the Haitian Petwo, Cuban
Rumba Guaguancó, and Northeastern Brazilian Baião. Skinkus found that the
difference in how the rhythmic cells are manifested in these various locations lies
in the part of the tresillo that receives the accent.[41]

Research studies also tie the cinquillo, tresillo, and clave rhythmic cells to
early jazz based on the frequency of their use during the developmental stages of
the musical form.[42] These were the rhythms and the influence on jazz that Jelly
Roll Morton referred to as the Spanish tinge. Preceding the rise of jazz, Creole

slave songs—songs that accompanied Ring Shouts on the Carolina and Georgia Sea Coast as well as in Louisiana—and Ragtime compositions embodied these rhythmic patterns.

These cells were not only performed in Congo Square nor were they only performed for and among people of African heritage as musicians of African descent frequently included them in European-based dance music. The published and unpublished compositions of enslaved African descendant Basile Jean Barès (1845–1902) present perfect examples. Barès, perhaps the most popular entertainer in New Orleans from the Union occupation in 1862 until the end of Reconstruction, performed along with his string band for Rex and other Carnival balls. His still unpublished piece, *Los Campanillas*, dating probably from the late 1880s, and the only music in Barès's own hand to have survived, embodies the habanera rhythmic cell. Barès wrote all of his music for piano, which includes either marches or European-style dances such as polkas, quadrilles, gallops, and waltzes.[43]

Although the habanera cell and its derivatives existed in some of those arrangements, the music performed for those types of events was not the predecessor or main influence on what is known as the New Orleans street beat. The impact of the gatherings in Congo Square on the perpetuation of those rhythms in New Orleans culture is significant. The long term repeated performances and practices by the masses passed from and through descendants contributed to the viability of the New Orleans street beat. Congo Square's role as a long-term, public venue for repeated performances by massive numbers of African descendants from diverse origins and musical orientations established it as a location that publicly preserved as well as disseminated cultural practices including these rhythmic cells. Such dissemination was also in part at the hands of spectators including white minstrels and circus performers who took these rhythmic cells and African-derived performance practices to other locations in North America and Europe. The memoirs of E. P. (Edwin Pearce) Christy, who appropriated songs, dances, musical instruments, and orchestration that he found at Congo Square, noted that in 1841, he organized the first band of Ethiopian minstrels. The members were proficient on several instruments and reportedly possessed the science and skill to play and sing African-derived songs with true precision and effect.[44]

As African descendants from various locations in Africa and the Americas joined the gatherings in Congo Square, they reinforced these familiar rhythmic patterns and joined the process of using them to create new musical forms. Likewise, African descendants who entered New Orleans bringing their musical heritage from rural areas and other states after the gatherings ceased and slavery ended readily perpetuated these often familiar cells and also participated in creating new musical forms.

Just as these African-derived rhythmic cells were not restricted to Congo

Compositions by African American pianist and composer Basile Jean Barès (1845–1902): *Los Companillas* (above) written in Barès own hand and *Grande Polka Des Chasseurs* (below), which was published in 1860 while he was enslaved.

Square, neither were they exclusive to secular music. The Bata rhythms of the Santeria religion as well as the music of Haitian Voudou contain them. The tresillo rhythmic cell persists in black Protestant churches in South Carolina through what outsiders refer to as the Gullah or low-country clap. Church members there don't usually refer to it by any name; it's just the way they clap.[45] As in this example, African American religious institutions, which for the most part remained segregated and isolated from European influences after emancipation, retained many African cultural practices such as these rhythmic patterns.

Floyd concluded that the cinquillo and tresillo motifs are more than basic rhythms:

> They stand as central symbols of African-diasporal musical unity transcending the boundaries of geocultural units and linking these units to each other and also to West Africa, the land from which a large part of this music derived. . . . Through it all, the rhythms of the cinquillo-tresillo complex infuse the carnival and festival bands, the second-liners, and the percussive beats and street singing of the standing and walking basers of the music.[46]

These are the rhythmic patterns of the New Orleans street beat, bamboula beat, second-line beat, and New Orleans beat. A study of these rhythms demonstrates New Orleans' past relationship with Caribbean countries and shows the influence of the African cultural performances and practices on New Orleans' culture.

THE INFLUENCE OF THE AFRICAN CULTURAL PRACTICES

The traditional African culture that existed at Congo Square unified gatherers, drew them in large numbers, and sustained the regular attendees. African descendants did not abandon traditional dance and music when European forms entered the scene nor did they limit these traditional performance forms to Congo Square or their backyards. Timothy Flint observed the Congo-dance in the streets in 1822.[47]

An 1843 *Daily Picayune* article reported a public "Black ball" at which the instruments, music, and dance were African. An 1846 *Daily Picayune* article referred to the dances performed that year in Congo Square as "African." Travelers also described seeing African dances and hearing African music in Congo Square during the 1840s, while Charles Dudley Warner, who visited the city in the 1880s, observed African songs and dances during a Voudou ceremony.[48] An 1887 *Times Democrat* article reported the performance of African songs and dances with African-modeled musical instruments in that year. New Orleanians who provided interviews for W.P.A. staff in 1940 specified African-influenced dancing and musical instruments.[49]

In many parts of the country, public performances of traditional African music and dance had long ceased. However, conditions in New Orleans enabled residents of African heritage to perpetuate and preserve these forms openly and with significant numbers of people. The African cultural practices in and around Congo Square influenced the evolution of indigenous performance forms. These New Orleans-based music and dance styles are integral to the local culture and serve to make New Orleans distinct. Those African practices that permeated the gatherings also influenced popular culture on the national level as evident through the minstrelsy career of E. P. Christy, a frequent spectator at the Sunday gatherings.

Born in Philadelphia, Pennsylvania, in 1815, Christy moved to New Orleans at the age of ten to live with family friends and eventually worked as a clerk in a mercantile house. His involvement with the entertainment world began as a youth when his infatuation with the circus led him on tour through the southern states with the Menagerie of Messrs. Purdy & Welch. Upon his return to New Orleans, Christy became the superintendent of a ropewalk with his previous employer, which required him to supervise a number of enslaved Africans. Christy's memoir states, "It was in this capacity that he acquired his superior knowledge of the negro [sic] characteristics, traits, humor, and melody which his observant genius has since turned to such golden account."[50]

Christy's daily exposure to this African culture found reinforcement at Congo Square on Sunday afternoons, which the unidentified writer of his "authentic biographic sketch" credited with having the ultimate influence on his minstrelsy:

> At this time it was the custom of the "[Africans]" to hold their holiday meetings at a spot known as "Congo Green," where, amid their mirth, music, dance and festivity, he [Christy], with the soul of an artist, and the tact of a student of nature's eccentricities, amassed those rich stores of entertainment which have long stamped him as the most truthful and pleasing delineator of Ethiopian humor and melody.[51]

Chisty's memoir, printed in another source, indicates the frequency of his visits to Congo Square:

> few of the meetings took place without Mr. Christy being a silent but close observer of their manners, and a willing student of the queer words and simple but expressive melodies—the singing of which formed the staple of their amusement in those welcome hours of festivity and relaxation.[52]

In 1832, at the age of seventeen, Christy joined the extensive Circus Caravan of Messrs. Purdy, Welch & Delavan where he performed for years in black-face as a Negro [*sic*] melodist, punster, and singer. In 1846, four years after form-ing his first minstrelsy troupe in Buffalo, Christy's Minstrels began a ten-year stint on Broadway making the troupe a New York institution. The troupe's tours through the U. S., Canada, and England established it as the world's preeminent minstrelsy act.[53]

Christy performed some songs just as he learned them from enslaved Af-ricans, but he also reinterpreted songs by harmonizing and scoring them. The resulting products were examples of cultural syncretism in which combined Af-rican and European elements created new performance styles. In collaboration with songwriter Stephen Foster, Christy's minstrel show songs, an ancestor of American popular music, proved to be lucrative. For example, the song *Old Folks at Home* (also *Way Down upon the Swanee River*), written by Foster but performed by Christy and originally published under Christy's name, reportedly sold 130,000 copies in three years.[53] Christy's memoir published in *The Age* stated, "Many of the 'colored gentlemen' whose old original 'Notes' have never failed, when issued by Christy, to demand cash returns."[55]

Likewise, Christy performed some dances just as he learned them, even retaining some of the names like "Juba." However, his choreographed jigs and caricaturized and racially stereotyped movements altered dances resulting in new forms—minstrel show styles. While Christy was not the first blackface minstrel, he was considered the most influential. His memoir stated that he organized the first Ethiopian minstrel band, and historians associate him with the devel-opment of the traditional three-part format of minstrel shows as well as the "walk-around," which became a traditional ending for the final act. During the "walk-around," each member of the ensemble, arranged on stage in a semi-circle, stepped into the center to dance his specialty in a competitive manner—as if to out do the other. This practice is prevalent in traditional African dancing except that the circle is closed and the spectators are also participants.

As with other minstrels, the standard instruments that Christy's band played included the banjo, bones, triangle, fiddle, and tambourine (which had a larger drumhead and fewer rattles than contemporary versions). African descendants used these same instruments to accompany African-derived dancing in Congo Square and at other locations in the country. Ken Emerson, author of *Doo-dah!: Stephen Foster and the Rise of American Popular Culture*, stated that this grouping of musical instruments, which he referred to as the minstrel band, was the forerun-ner of the jazz band, the bluegrass band, and the rock band.

No doubt other blackface minstrels stood among the spectators and bor-rowed from the public performances at Congo Square, which became a noted tourist attraction. Minstrel acts were popular features in circuses, and New Or-leans was once a principal point in the circus industry. The prevalence of circuses in the city once led the national historian of the Circus Fans Association to cite New Orleans as the circus capital of the United States. While not every circus held in the city pitched tent at Congo Square—also called Circus Square and Circus Park—Cayetano's Circus, the first recorded circus to perform in the city, did so with shows beginning in the early 1800s. Newspaper articles reveal that shows were typically held at mid-day as well as in the evenings and often included processions through the streets. An 1864 circus procession that began and ended at Congo Square featured ladies and men on horseback, three chariots, and a large African lion led by his keeper. The parade route of another circus held in 1864 revealed that the procession began at ten o'clock in the morning from the site of the circus in Congo Square and moved up Rampart Street to Canal Street then to Camp Street. It continued to Coliseum Place, to Race Street, to Annunciation Street, to Tchoupitoulas Street, to Julia Street, to St. Charles Avenue, to Esplanade Avenue, to Rampart Street, and back to Congo Square—the place of exhibition.[56]

As with Christy, some minstrels began their careers under the big top, in some cases performing as clowns. While Christy may have borrowed from other sources and locations—as did his counterparts—his memoirs, published during his lifetime, specified only "Congo Green" in New Orleans as having an influence on his art. At the time of his death by suicide in 1862, the estimated value of Christy's property alone ranged from $100,000 to $150,000. By all accounts, his appropriation of the African cultural practices that he found in New Orleans at Congo Square impacted the nation and made him wealthy.[57]

Christy's position at what he assumed was the top of a social hierarchy prevented him from recognizing that all points on a circle are equal creating no top or bottom. The philosophical concept of the hermeneutic circle addresses the problem of how and whether an observer can acknowledge the subjectivity of another. Although heavily influenced by the circles he witnessed at Congo Square, Christy regarded the participants as insignificant and inferior human beings. He responded to their contributions as a commodity rather than as a conversation. Failing to acknowledge Africa as the origin of those songs, Christy suggested that he was the first to use them to establish a national American music. He considered the melodies to have come from nature implying that he was the "first to catch the native airs as they floated wildly, or hummed in the balmy breezes of the sunny south, turn them to shape, and give them a local habitation, and a name."[58]

On the other hand, many performers who succeeded Christy did respect the subjectivity of the Africans and African descendants who formed their circles in the Square. The willingness to embrace the culture in spite of the distance in time and space from the original Congo Square gatherers has enabled musicians of all ethnicities to transcend many of the negative stereotypes left by Christy and other "Ethiopian delineators" and to continue the conversation.

New Orleans-based performers have indeed continued the conversation and embraced the cultural legacy as well as the African-based performance styles and practices handed down through generations. Neither acculturation nor syncretization can overshadow the influence inherently found in New Orleans' music, songs, rhythms, and dances including: the second line or parade beat, jazz funeral music, Mardi Gras Indian rhythms and chants, and early New Orleans jazz. That influence is attributed to the African descendants who perpetuated traditional performance styles in Congo Square and to those who continued those performances styles and practices after the gatherings ended.

The African influence on national performance styles via Congo Square is equally profound. Christy and other minstrels carried the songs, dances, musical instruments, and syncopated rhythmic patterns from Congo Square to the Broadway stage, and even to Europe. While they performed some songs and dances as they learned them, they also modified African-derived performance styles creating new styles in American dance, music, and theater with minstrelsy becoming the first American-born theatrical form.

Chapter 4

THE GATHERERS

Those who gathered in Congo Square on Sunday afternoons during the antebellum period reflected the city's ever increasing black populace. Expanding in number as well as diversity, this population included people from a multitude of African nations, some who had been brought directly to Louisiana, some who had come via French and Spanish territories in the Caribbean, and some who had come from other states. Included also were groups of offspring who had been born in the "New World." Enslaved and free African descendants in each of these categories brought cultural, social, and religious practices and influences to New Orleans and then to Congo Square on Sunday afternoons.

Gwendolyn Midlo Hall's research shows the geographical as well as ethnic origin of these Africans. Under French rule, traders brought Bambara, Mandinga, Wolof, Fulbe, Nard, Mina, Fon, Yoruba (Nago), Chamba, Adó, and Kongo-Angola people to Louisiana. These ethnic groups landed directly from Africa within the twelve-year span between 1719 and 1731. Two-thirds of them originated from the Senegambia region from a limited number of nations with relatively homogenous cultural practices; and others originated from the Bight of Benin and the Kongo-Angola region. As the founding contingent in the colony, these Africans adapted and blended languages, food ways, and cultural materials and practices to develop the Creole slave culture and language to which those who arrived later had to largely adjust.[1]

During the Spanish period, the Africans who traders brought to the colony originated in four main areas of the continent including the three locations involved under French rule along with the Bight of Biafra. These additional nations included the Caraba, Ibo, and Moko people. Among them were also Africans from Sierra Leone (the Kissy), the Windard Coast (the Canga), the Gold Coast, and Mozambique. Hall's research shows that during this period, Africans were primarily transshipped to Louisiana from the Caribbean and came less often directly from Africa. Voyages were initiated and carried out, for the most part, by independent planters and included ports in Jamaica, Martinique, St. Domingue, and, after 1790, Cuba. Records show, however, that the Africans on those voyages were not likely to have been born or socialized in these Caribbean countries. The clustering of African nations during this transshipment period of 1770 to 1803 shows that the Kongo represented the largest single African ethnic group in New Orleans.[2]

Such heavy presence of Kongo descendants in New Orleans remained true after American rule in 1803; and by 1820, the overwhelming majority of enslaved Africans in Louisiana were of Kongo-Angola origin. Not only did they comprise the largest single ethnic group brought to Louisiana, they were the largest nation that remained in New Orleans.[3] Without indicating the time period, Cable also referred to the Africans of the Kongo coast as the most numerous in the state. He further stated, "These are they [the Kongos] for whom the dance [Congo dance] and the place [Congo Square] are named."[4] One Sunday afternoon, fellow travelers who stood in the public square at Faubourg Ste. Marie with J. G. Flugel identified former Kongolese kings or chiefs among the dancers. Descriptive comments from other eyewitnesses note that some of the gatherers in Congo Square wore gris-gris (charms believed to have special powers) around their necks, some bore scarifications on their cheeks, and some had teeth filed to sharp points.[5]

Political circumstances and historical events such as the Louisiana Purchase impacted who could have attended the gatherings. With American rule, settlers from other states increasingly migrated to Louisiana, and many of the enslaved people who accompanied them were American-born. With the 1808 constitutional ban on the importation of Africans, the domestic slave trade introduced enslaved people from other slave holding states, particularly Virginia, Maryland, and South Carolina.[6] Africans from these locations brought their creolized languages, cultures, and musical influences to the city and to Congo Square. At the same time, traders continued to introduce Africans directly from the continent by smuggling them through the Louisiana swamps and bayous. This activity continued practically throughout the period of the Congo Square gatherings. The 1879 *Daily Picayune* stated:

> The slave trade, which had been abolished in 1807, was still kept up until as late as 1845, by cruisers which ran up the bayous and lagoons abounding on our coast, as [*sic*] safely deposited their cargoes at appointed places. Bayou Barataria was a regular thoroughfare for this trade.[7]

The article stated that many of the Africans who had been smuggled into the territory attended the Sunday gatherings in Congo Square. Their participation in the festivities contributed to the strength of the African traditions and cultural practices that persisted there.

Adding to the diverse Sunday population were Haitian refugees who entered the city by the thousands during the first decade of the nineteenth century, resulting from the revolution that led to Haiti's independence. The majority of the over nine thousand Haitian immigrants who entered New Orleans via Cuba, from 1809 to 1810, remained in New Orleans, tremendously increasing the city's population. Immigrants of African descent, enslaved and free, brought with them dances, songs, religious practices, and food ways that reinforced the existing African-derived practices.

According to eyewitnesses, African descendants gathered at Congo Square by the hundreds to the thousands. Among them were free people of color, enslaved laborers who were hired out, and those enslaved in rural areas, urban areas, domestic settings, the fields, etc. Maroons, previously enslaved Africans who escaped from slavery to live in organized communities in swamps near the city, reportedly attended the gatherings despite the risk of capture. While representatives from the various social and labor classes came to Congo Square, research indicates that some groups frequented the gatherings more than others. Findings also show that native-born Africans were more likely to have attended the gatherings than those born in America, particularly those who had gained some sense of status (i.e. skilled labor category). Researcher Gary A. Donaldson concluded that Congo Square was the focal point of a subculture of New Orleans' black population throughout the first half of the nineteenth century.[8]

Helping to define that subculture, James Creecy, who traveled to the city in 1834, reported that "the lower order of colored people and Negroes [sic], bond and free, assemble in great numbers in Congo Square, on every Sunday afternoon in good weather, to enjoy themselves in their own peculiar manner."[9] Along the same lines, George Washington Cable reported that house servants did not come to Congo Square as much as the field hands. These trends reflected the earlier observations made by Médéric-Louis-Elie Moreau de Saint-Méry in the French West Indies. He noted that many of those enslaved who worked in the house considered themselves to be socially above those who worked in the fields. They preferred the dances of their owners who allowed them to meet among themselves to dance.[10]

This preference for European-style music and recreation was also common among the enslaved in New Orleans whose owners rented or hired-out their labor. Some of them openly disregarded the Ordinance of 1817, which confined those enslaved to only one gathering place. Many of the hired-out also lived away from their owners and frequently resided among free people of color. On Sundays, some of them dressed in "princely style"—wearing the best broadcloth and the finest hats, headed for the balls and "carousals." Such balls or dances often began in the evenings and featured European instruments, songs, and dances. Sometimes, they hired-out rented carriages for themselves on Sunday afternoons and on special occasions like the opening of the Pontchartrain Railroad in 1831.[11]

Some of the hired-out provided their own living arrangements as though they were free and periodically reported to their slave-holders to whom they gave a portion of their earnings. "On the practice in our community of renting premises to slaves," an 1863 newspaper article stated, "such a course as that which has lately been tolerated should cease, and punishment be awarded to offenders."[12]

This practice, however, was far from new. A city ordinance as early as 1811 forbade all persons to rent any house, apartment, room, or closet by the month or day to any enslaved person in the Faubourgs and adjacent places in New Orleans, even with the authorization of his slave holder or a representative. Nonetheless, the practice was ongoing and widespread. James Stuart, who visited the city in 1830, wrote that all of the waiters in his hotel had been hired from their slave holders, and the hotel furnished their board. Along the same lines, James Thomas, who traveled to the city two dozen times between 1831 and 1861, wrote that not only did some of the bondsmen live outside the purview of their slaveholders, some hired their own time, operated their own businesses, purchased real estate, and managed to buy themselves as well as family members.[13]

Among the hired-out were harness makers, blacksmiths, furriers, hostlers, barbers, draymen, press hands, engineers, cobblers, printers, riverboat hands, midwives, bricklayers, carpenters, painters, druggists, and market women. Werner Wegener reported that large companies including the New Orleans Gas Company, the Pontchartrain and New Orleans Railroad Company, and the Red Brick and Tile Company owned large numbers of the enslaved who lived to themselves and carried passes with them.[14]

As Creecy noted, free people of color gathered at Congo Square as well, although many of them held dance and recreational preferences similar to the hired-out. Creecy added, "the 'haut ton' [high society] attended operas, theaters, masquerades, etc. The quadroons had their dashing, fancy balls, and dances, & etc."[15]

Regarding the dancers whom he observed at Congo Square in the 1840s, African descendant James Thomas wrote that most of them appeared to have been imported from Africa. During his observation in 1819, Latrobe, who entered four of the circles in the Square, noted that he "did not observe a dozen yellow faces." By this, he referred to people of mixed African and European ancestry called mulattoes. Although mulattoes represented a large number of free people, neither mixed ancestry nor skin hue determined the status of freedom. Some people of pure African ancestry acquired their freedom, as some mulattoes remained enslaved.

In addition to diverse backgrounds, gatherers also came from diverse locales in town. As reported by the *Picayune*, "They collected here [Congo Square] from all parts of the city." Along the same lines, the *Item Tribune* stated that "Negro field-hands from surrounding plantations and some from the city made it [Congo Square] their weekly gathering place." Some of these visitors came to the city to sell their wares in the marketplace and stayed afterwards to dance. Eleanor Early stated, "Country blacks came to town on Sundays with their masters' and their own produce for the French Market. They began selling at dawn and in the afternoon, when they were through, they went to Congo Square to meet their friends and celebrate." Historian Joe Gray Taylor wrote, "One of the favorite means of amusement for the Negro [*sic*] men during the holidays and on free Sundays was to go to the nearest town."[16]

The Sunday gatherings at Congo Square became a tourist attraction—no doubt one of the first in the city. Newspaper articles and travelers, like Creecy, often encouraged spectators to come. He wrote, "Hundreds of nurses, with children of all ages, attend, and many fathers and mothers, beaux and belles, are there to be found. . . . Every stranger should visit Congo Square . . . once at least, no one will ever regret or forget it."[17]

Tourists reportedly came by the hundreds, even thousands. However, they did not all come for mere entertainment as E. P. Christy indicated in his memoir. He and other performers came to acquire material for circus acts and minstrel shows. Their appropriation of the African cultural practices at Congo Square entertained the world and garnered substantial profits while simultaneously setting in stone stereotypical images of black behavior, speech, songs, and dances.

Louis Moreau Gottschalk (1829–1869), New Orleans native and world-renowned pianist and composer, also heard the music and observed the dances of Congo Square, whether as an observer at the Sunday gatherings or at other locations in the city. While no primary source provides evidence that Gottschalk actually witnessed the Sunday gatherings, the rhythmic patterns and song that accompanied the Bamboula dance, customarily performed there, influenced his piano fantasie, *La Bamboula—Dance des Nègres.* As a child the piano prodigy lived on Rampart Street and his musical development was heavily influenced by his black nursemaid Sally.

As Creecy noted, nurses of African heritage like Sally stood among the onlookers on Sundays and frequently brought the young children in their care. Other African descendants, including James Thomas, also joined the spectators. He wrote, "In the forties I used to go on Sunday to see the blacks [*sic*] dance. They were given a (what is now a park) large Square called Congo green."[18] When Thomas first visited New Orleans in 1839, he was only twelve years old and still enslaved. He reported in his autobiography that he acquired a counterfeit certificate of freedom prior to securing passage on a steamer to New Orleans.

While enslaved Africans and Native Americans may have forged some alliances during the early years of the Louisiana colony, reliable accounts that specify Native Americans dancing at Congo Square on Sunday afternoons have not surfaced. It is important to note that while accounts that have surfaced provide valuable information, they do not reveal everything about the gatherings. Along these lines, in 1831, traveler P. Forest observed Native Americans joining an African dance at a different location. He noted that on Sundays, African descendants from the city and the surrounding areas along with several Native American families that lived nearby met in a place called "The Camp"—a large green field on the bank of a lake about three leagues from the city—to share ludicrous pleasures. Forest's description included a popular French song that expressed the sorrow of a person lamenting the departure of Lisette, who abandoned "The Camp" for the pleasures of the city. Historian Jerah Johnson noted that "The Camp" was located on the edge of Bayou St. John.[19] Forest's account is significant in that it identified another Sunday gathering site for African descendants.

As indicated, those whom slave traders brought to Louisiana and who gathered in Congo Square originated from numerous African nations and diverse New World backgrounds. With them came not only their songs and dances but also their belief systems and practices. African philosopher and historian John Mbiti affirmed that "wherever the African is, there is his religion" for, he carries it to the fields, the beer party, a funeral ceremony, and even the house of parliament if he is a politician.[20]

So it was, the Africans brought their religions with them to the Louisiana colony, but the *Code Noir* required slaveholders to baptize and instruct them in the Catholic faith.[21] Some Africans of Kongo heritage had likely already been exposed to, if not converted to, Catholicism prior to their arrival in the colony, as missionary efforts in the Kongo began during the fifteenth century. These efforts initially targeted families of the nobility and extended to local villages during later centuries. Although many of the Africans accepted Catholicism in Louisiana, aspects of their traditional beliefs remained internalized, invisible, and immune to the law resulting in a dual existence of religious properties. That is, many Africans descendants essentially practiced Catholicism in public and traditional African belief systems in private.

What developed in general, however, was a New World religion that blended Catholicism with beliefs and practices from several African nations. In Louisiana, the name of the New World religion was Voudou, which derived from the Fon word "Vodun" meaning "spirit" or "Gods." In Haiti where the same laws for enslaved Africans existed, the name of the New World religion was Vodou (also Vaudaux, Vodun). In Voudou, as well as in other New World belief systems—including Santeria and Palo in Cuba and Candomblé in Brazil—dancing, drumming, and singing are unified and are central components of the ritual ceremony. This unified performance practice was also true of social dance styles. When addressing the dances in Congo Square, the distinction between what was religious and what was social became even more challenging for spectators considering that participants often performed both kinds of dances in circles. Such an overlap or commonality in performance practices reveals the thin line of distinction between the sacred and the secular and raises questions regarding the validity of the interpretations from onlookers about the activities that they witnessed at Congo Square.

Ethnic groups credited with the initial "emergence and resilience" of Voudou in Louisiana are the Yoruba and Fon, and the Kongo. Reportedly, the first two groups contributed their complex system of gods, while the Kongo contributed the complex system of sacred medicines. Consequently, many ritual experts from the Kongo surfaced as conjurors or root-persons in Louisiana and throughout the South. Hall's research revealed the connection between the Kongolese and the use of the term *wanga* in Louisiana, which meant a magical charm or ritual object. African descendants also used this term in Kimbundu, West Central Africa, South Carolina, and Haiti indicating not only common vocabulary but common belief systems in the African Diaspora.[22] Eyewitnesses observed enslaved Africans at the Sunday gatherings with charms (also gris-gris) around their necks. The use of such ritual objects was sometimes itself referred to as Voudou, which establishes the need to address the differences between Voudou as an organized spiritual system and "voodou" as customs or traditional behaviors. Many of those who wrote about what they observed and thought may have happened in Congo Square often used these terms and concepts interchangeably.

In Louisiana the practice of Voudou received strong reinforcement, as well as degrees of alteration from enslaved and free people of color who emigrated from St. Domingue. David Geggus, quoted in Hall, calculated that the Kongos were the largest African nation in St. Domingue during the years before the Haitian Revolution. The influence that these and other Africans from Haiti had on the spread of Voudou and their potential to inspire revolts revealed itself in the actions of Gov. Baron Hector de Carondelet, who in 1792 banned slave traders from importing them from the West Indies.[23] The minutes of the Spanish Supreme Councils of State read, "Consequently it would be well to prohibit very sternly the introduction [into these districts] of creole negroes [*sic*] and particularly those who might come from the French colonies. The [Negros] from the coast of Africa would be the only ones who might be admitted."[24] Louisiana planters also preferred enslaved Africans directly from the continent as opposed to the French West Indies, because the Voudou practices of Africans who lived in those colonies made them more difficult to control.[25]

With the success of the Haitian Revolution, however, the Louisiana colonists eventually faced enslaved Africans whom they least preferred—those from the French West Indies who embraced Voudou. As the majority of Haiti's white citizens fled or faced death, most of them carried with them the Africans whom they held in bondage. Initially, many of the white refugees fled to Cuba; however, the war between France and Spain forced these French settlers to flee again in 1809—this time to New Orleans. Although the French refugees readily received admittance to Louisiana, their African bondsmen did not. A federal law that prohibited the entry of foreign slaves into the United States had gone into effect in 1808. After much debate, the House of Representatives passed a bill that allowed them to enter the state based on the fact that the enslaved Africans were the main resources of their holders.[26]

With the majority of the Haitian refugees remaining in New Orleans, the increase in the city's population translated to an increase in the practice of Voudou. This practice manifested itself among the enslaved, free people of color, and whites, which resulted in an increase in secret meetings, open gatherings, and dancing. City officials acted quickly to control these assemblies after the Slave Revolt of 1811, which sent shock waves through the South and across the country.

Beginning on the evening of January 8, 1811, Charles, the enslaved African of Deslondes, and others, led over five hundred enslaved Africans in a revolt during which they marched toward New Orleans from nearby St. Charles Parish. Thomas Thompson's research on the revolt, published in *Louisiana History*, revealed that 120 newspapers across the country reported the news of the uprising. He wrote that, "the appearance of articles in newspapers in every state and territory where newspapers were published betrayed a national anxiety over the huge, and still largely foreign, slave population in newly acquired Louisiana."[27] Albert Thrasher, author of *On to New Orleans!: Louisiana's Historic 1811 Slave Revolt*, cites this uprising, which lasted approximately three days, as the largest slave revolt in United States' history.

On January 16, 1811, within a week after the revolt ended, the New Orleans City Council passed the Ordinances of 1811. The restrictions set forth by these ordinances regarding the bondsmen virtually restated the New Orleans Police Code of 1808, which itself reflected a 1795 city ordinance. The orders absolutely forbade the enslaved to assemble except at pre-approved funerals, or dances and sports. Meetings for the purpose of dancing or enjoying themselves were to take place only on Sundays, until sundown, at places designated by the mayor.[28]

In response to the 1811 ordinance, the mayor appointed three places for gathering and dancing in 1813 including Faubourg Ste. Marie, Fort St. Ferdinand, and Faubourg Marigny. With a majority population of African descendants, most of whom were enslaved, the flourishing of Voudou, and the ever-present fear of uprising, these regulations appeared for the third time in the Ordinances of 1817. The orders only permitted enslaved Africans to assemble for worship inside a church or temple during designated hours. Again, assemblies for purposes of dancing or other merriment were to take place only on Sundays, under police supervision, ending at sunset, and in open. However, this time, all gatherings were confined to one location, and the public Square back of town became the gathering ground.[29]

As Mbiti implied, the Africans brought their religions with them to Congo Square, but what were those religions and how did they worship? Early travelers reported witnessing religious and spiritual activities on Sunday afternoons; however, whether those writers, as spectators, witnessed traditional African rituals, syncretized New World religious practices, or customs and behaviors associated with either of these remains in question. In 1786, Bishop Cyrillo de Barcelona wrote that the Africans gathered in "Place Congo" to dance the "bamboula" and perform the rites imported from Africa. Christian Schultz, in 1808, observed them in the rear of New Orleans—presumedly Congo Square—performing their worship in the "manner of their country." He recorded that, the principal dancers or leaders adorned themselves with "wild and savage fashions, always ornamented with a number of tails of the smaller wild beasts, and those who appeared the most horrible always attracted the largest circle of company."[30]

Schultz's documentation of those leaders provides an example of continued African spiritual practices in Congo Square. Robert Farris Thompson's research shows that the Kongo tradition of wearing tails represented sacred medicine. In the Kongo, as well as in the South and other locations in the New World, the skins of small animals often served as the containment for medicines and objects that aimed to provide healing and good fortune.[31] This account provides an example of the system of medicines that the Kongo nation contributed to the Voudou belief system, as well as an example of the transference and continuation of African religious practices in Congo Square and the Americas.

After the Civil War, it appeared to city officials that the practice of Voudou grew. In actuality, emancipation nullified previous ordinances that prohibited assemblies and ended the control that slaveholders may have once exerted. An 1869 newspaper reported that the horror of African superstition was appearing with unusual frequency in the South, especially in Louisiana. Congo Square resumed its prominence as a gathering place for African descendants after emancipation. Eyewitnesses who spoke with Federal Writers' Project researchers in 1940 reported that followers of Voudou danced at night, weekdays and Sundays, and their accounts refer to the legend of Marie Laveau.

Joseph Morris, interviewed in 1940 while living at 803 North Claiborne Avenue, recalled seeing her in Congo Square:[32]

> They would be right in the middle of the square—some sitting down and some would dance and some would sing. They was dressed in the usual ordinary clothes. Most of the time old Da-pa Laba would dance (He was a healer, too, who worked with Marie Leveau). While they was dancing they had trained snakes that followed them and kept time with the singing. Then there was a big hollow tree in the square where everybody that believed in Marie Leveau would come and put money—fifteen cents, and liquor and cow peas—jumbalai. We used to sneak there and take the money and drink the liquor; we left the jumbalai. They wouldn't let us kids light around there too long, and later on when I was a young man I didn't know anything about her practices. But, I did go to her house on St. Ann Street. It was a double house with three brick steps and was one story.[33]

Newspaper articles including "A Voudoo Tree: Haunted Sycamore of Congo Square," published in 1891, provided stories on the hollow tree in the Square to which Morris and other interviewees referred.[34] Raymond Rivaros, who was sixty-four years old when interviewed by federal writers, witnessed Marie Laveau walk straight into Congo Square many a day, carrying her serpent in a box and not speaking to anybody. He recalled that "She would put the serpent by the fountain, dance around it a while, then pick it up, put it back in the box and leave without saying a word to anyone . . . two policemen were at each of the four gates at the square."[35] City officials completed the fountain in Congo Square to which Rivaros referred in 1885. Prior grooming of the location had taken place in 1884 for the Cotton Exposition, World's Fair.

Oscar Felix, seventy-two years old when interviewed in 1940, lived at 1220 South Prieur Street. As a follower of Marie Laveau, he shared insight into Voudou ceremonies, as well as the dances at Congo Square. Felix stated that participants conducted the ceremonies similar to the regular Mass of a Catholic church—only the leader would begin with a prayer to St. John in the name of the Father, of the son, and of the Holy Ghost:

> I must tell you about the dances in Congo Square. These weren't the regular ceremonies, because they were never held in public. But every Sunday in the evening they all would dance in the square from two until five or six o'clock, never later than six. Here we would sing and the men and the women would dance.
>
> That's right. They would do the Creole Dance. There's something else, too, I meant to tell you. O yes, in the square there was a big hollow tree. Two men could stand in it at the same time. Every Monday all the workers and the people who believed in and followed Marie Leveau would come to this tree. They would bring money—never less nor more than fifteen cents—either three nickels or a dime and a nickel. Everything they did was in three's; One–two–three; Faith–Hope–Charity; the Father–the Son–the Holy Ghost. These were just the beliefs and practices of her teachings. Whenever there was food placed in the tree somebody would always take it. You see, these things were put there for other people who needed them to take them and they always did. Nobody ever put anything in there that would harm anyone. Of course, the children would always look for candy and nickels and it was all right for them to take it. It was their way of paying for the use of the square and a way to help somebody who needed help.[36]

Zora Neale Hurston, who studied Voudou while visiting New Orleans in 1928, agreed with Felix stating that the dances of Congo Square were pleasure dances and their sole purpose was entertainment. She added that Voudou (hoo-doo) dances, on the other hand, were ceremonial and had religious purposes; and those ceremonies took place in New Orleans on Bayou St. John and the shores of Lake Pontchartrain. Non-initiates did not participate in those ceremonies and could not witness them.[37] Felix provided the following song, *Song of the Voudous on Congo Square*, during his interview with the Federal Writer's Project:

Chaute par les Voudou sur la place Congo	*Song of the Voudous on Congo Square*
Conduit moin la reine.	Lead me to the Queen.
Conduit moin dans château le roi.	Lead me to the King's Castle.
Conduit moin dans château le roi.	Lead me to the King's Castle.
Conduit moin dans palais mo roi.	Lead me to my King's Palace.
Si mo mourri jordi comme demain,	Should I die to-day as to-morrow,
Voyé dit yé vini voir moin.	Send tell them come see me.
Conduit moin la reine.	Lead me to the Queen.
Conduit moin dans château le roi.	Lead me to the King's Castle.
Conduit moin dans château le roi.	Lead me to the King's Castle.
Conduit moin dans palais mo roi.	Lead me to my King's Palace.
Si mo mourri jordi comme demain,	Should I die to-day as to-morrow,
Mouchoir madras méné moin couri.	Bandana kerchief led me to it.
Conduit moin la reine.	Lead me to the Queen.
Conduit moin dans château le roi.	Lead me to the King's Castle.
Conduit moin dans château le roi.	Lead me to the King's Castle.
Conduit moin dans palais mo roi.	Lead me to my King's Palace.
Tout péche oui, que mo fait -	All sins yes, that I committed –
Mo volé femme qui té pas pou moin.	Me stole woman that wasn't for me.
Conduit moin la reine.	Lead me to the Queen.
Conduit moin dans château le roi.	Lead me to the King's Castle.
Conduit moin dans château le roi.	Lead me to the King's Castle.
Conduit moin dans palais mo ro.	Lead me to my King's Palace.
Si vous voir nainaine zabo,	Should you see Nainaine Zabo,
Boyez dit li vini voir moin.	Send tell her, come see me.
Conduit moin la reine.	Lead me to the Queen.
Conduit moin dans château le roi.	Lead me to the King's Castle.
Conduit moin dans château le roi.	Lead me to the King's Castle.
Conduit moin dans palais mo roi.	Lead me to my King's Palace.

The varied native backgrounds and New World experiences of the Africans and their progeny yielded diverse religious beliefs and practices. Yet, observers and writers referred to all forms and expressions—traditional African religions, syncretized New World religions, and customs and traditional behaviors—as the same. Voices from within the circles at Congo Square that tell of the religious practices before the Civil War have not surfaced. Yet, as Mbiti affirmed, Africans did bring their religious beliefs and expressions with them to the gatherings. Those who provided interviews about the religious practices in Congo Square after the Civil War presented contrasting views depending on whether they were followers of Voudou or non-initiates. Consequently, answers to questions about religious practices, particularly Voudou, at the Sunday gatherings basically depended on how the person who provided the answer defined Voudou and the faith or belief of that person. The presence of gatherers in Congo Square, before and after emancipation, who perpetuated Voudou represented a conscious attempt to fulfill the dictates of their heritage by holding on to traditional beliefs and a continued embracement and celebration of African-derived culture and performance styles.

This celebration of culture and heritage on Sunday afternoons called for the best attire that the gatherers possessed. What constituted their "best," nevertheless, was as diverse as their labor specifications, the status and compassion of their owners, and their opportunity to earn money and purchase clothing for themselves. Generally, they wore the same type of clothing, or the same clothing, worn during the week—as most of them had neither options nor extras. Over the years, writers observed gatherers dressed in rags, torn and tattered clothing, only cloths about their loins, everyday regulation clothes, garments handed down from masters and mistresses, and "picturesque finery." Most writers, however, reported rags and the regulation clothing set under Spanish rule by Gov. Baron Hector de Carondelet in 1792.[38]

For enslaved males, Carondelet proposed that "masters" provide two brown cotton shirts, a woolen coat, a pair of pantaloons (pants), and two handkerchiefs each year. Regulation clothing for enslaved women included a suitable dress, a petticoat, and a handkerchief/bandana for the head known as a *tignon* (tēn-yon). During winters, seamstresses, usually enslaved women, used rough, heavy cloth to make pants, shirts, and dresses for the enslaved. The coats proposed by Carondelet, referred to as "blanket coats," had hoods that could be drawn over the head. In summers, men often wore short pants, and women wore dresses made out of thinner fabric such as calico.

For the feet, Carondelet proposed that "masters" provide foot coverings called grandiers—pieces of ox hide cut to fit the shape of the person's feet. With the oxen's hair turned inside, the person cushioned his or her feet with hay, wrapped them with rags, or wore woolen socks to keep them warm and dry. The grandiers, tied onto the feet with strips of ox hide, often proved to be so stiff and uncomfortable that those who received them frequently opted to go barefoot—as they did in summers and in the absence of such foot gear. Advertisements for regulation clothing appeared in newspapers under headings including: "Plantation Clothing," "negro [*sic*] Clothing," or "Shoes for Slaves."

Under American rule, the system of rules enacted by the territorial legislature (Act 33) in 1806, included similar clothing regulations. Each enslaved male was to receive one linen shirt and pantaloon in the summer, and a shirt, pantaloon, and greatcoat in the winter.[39]

Although Carondelet and American authorities proposed minimum clothing provisions, observers sometimes noted enslaved men at Congo Square clad in either a cotton shirt, tattered and torn pantaloons, or only a sash. In 1817, Johann Buechler, a traveler to New Orleans, observed males in Congo Square wearing what he referred to as "oriental and Indian" attire. Some wore Turkish turbans of various colors including red, yellow, blue, green, and brown. They wrapped a sash of the same sort around their bodies to cover themselves. Without the sash, he added, they would have been naked. In keeping with Buechler's observation, an *Item Tribune* article reported that for some, "their clothing was badly tattered from field work and some wore only clothes about their loins."[40]

A coarse *chemise* (shə-mēz), or straight loose dress, a petticoat, and a *tignon* completed the typical attire of enslaved women. Those who served in domestic roles commonly wore white aprons over their dresses. While African women wore head wraps—the *gélé* (gä-lā) and the *duku* (dü-kü) in some West African cultures—out of tradition, they wore *tignons* in Louisiana by law.[41]

Many free women of color, some of whom appeared to be white, adorned their hair with colorful feathers and other accessories. Although these accented their attractiveness and added to their appeal, Gov. Esteban Rodriguez Miró held that the attire indicated evidence of their misconduct and could lead to their punishment. In addition, the women of the ruling class objected to the stylish attire of those women of color. In 1786, Governor Miró issued a *Bando de Buen Gobierno* (Proclamation of Good Government) in which he listed civil and police regulations. Among the orders, he forbade women of pure or mixed African heritage to appear in public wearing feathers or curls in their hair. Instead, he ordered them to comb their hair flat or cover it with a handkerchief if it is combed high—as was the custom. The common term for this handkerchief or head covering became *tignon*; and this edict aimed to keep free women of color connected to enslaved women—in other words, "in their place." Nevertheless, the bright colors that the women selected and the creative ways in which they tied the *tignons* complimented their beauty. Red and yellow were popular colors as were the brightly striped and plaid ones.[42]

For the enslaved, Sunday was indeed a holiday, and when possible, the Afri-

Elderly woman with *tignon* head-wrap in Congo Square, February 1891.

cans dressed for the occasion. Buechler, in 1817, noted that some of the women at Congo Square wore the newest fashions in silk, gauze, muslin, and percale dresses with the gayest bandana kerchiefs upon their heads. Thirty years later, an 1846 *Daily Picayune* article reported similar attire. "Males and females . . . dressed in their holiday clothes, with the very gayest bandana kerchiefs upon the heads of the females."[43] Unlike adult women who, under orders, only wore *tignons*, some of the young girls at Congo Square sported brightly colored feathers and ribbons in their hair.[44]

One of the flashiest dressers at Congo Square, as noted by a *Daily Picayune* writer in 1846, was a "most distinguished individual" referred to as the master of ceremonies. On Sunday afternoons he operated his post dressed in a blue and white mixed suit with a black vest. His accessories included a pair of earrings and a large silver chain that hung from his vest. He topped off his outfit with a white hat around which he twisted a piece of black crepe. This businessman organized his own dance circle and surrounded it with posts and ropes to keep out uninvited and ordinary dancers. He admitted only the most distinguished dancers into his "magic ring." Spectators frequently tossed dimes to the dancers encouraging them to perform. Earning money by entertaining tourists had thus become a part of the activity at Congo Square.[45]

The Africans who gathered in Congo Square originated from varied locations as well as social and economic backgrounds, and their religious orientations and range of attire were equally diverse. Each dressed "according to his/her means" and worshipped according to his/her beliefs, but their participation knew no disparity, for in Congo Square they celebrated the holiday and their heritage equally and to the fullest.

Chapter 5

THE MUSICAL INSTRUMENTS

The gatherers used their memories and materials available to them to fashion the musical instruments that they played in Congo Square. They collected most of the materials from nature and modeled the instruments after prototypes from their homeland. Consequently, those instruments were visual representations of African cultural practices in New Orleans. The principal instrument among them was the drum, which musicians used to summon others to the Square. The drum also fused the music of each circle—laying the foundational beat, calling and answering, sending signals and cues, alerting other musicians and dancers to changes and breaks in the music, and responding to the constantly shifting improvisations of other participants.

Over the years, travelers and onlookers observed different sizes and several kinds of drums in Congo Square. The larger of these carried deep pitches, and their long, intense beats provided the underlying pulse for the other instruments. The smaller drums carried higher pitches and provided quicker, syncopated, and more intense beats. Christian Schultz, who observed a Congo Square gathering in 1808, wrote, "they [Africans] have their own national music, consisting for the most part of a long kind of narrow drum of various sizes, from two to eight feet in length, three or four of which make a band."[1]

Benjamin Latrobe entered several circles during his Sunday afternoon visit. In one circle, he observed a square, stool-shaped, frame drum, a wooden hollow gong that was struck with a stick, and a calabash with a round hole studded with nails and beat upon with two sticks sometimes referred to as a calabash drum. In a different circle, he witnessed a string instrument and two drums, one of which was cylinder-shaped and on which the drummer sat astride while playing with his hands and fingers.[2]

Latrobe along with other observers noted hollow drums, sometimes referred to as "gum stump dug-out drums," as they had been carved from logs. Animal skin, goat and sheep, stretched over one end constituted the head of these open-bottom drums. Long, as well as shorter, versions of them existed, and drummers held them between their knees as they played with hands and fingers. Reportedly, drummers also played with a combination of hands, sticks, and sometimes the bones of animals.[3]

James Thomas and other eyewitnesses noted that musicians played drums made from empty barrels (casks or kegs) with goat or sheepskin stretched over

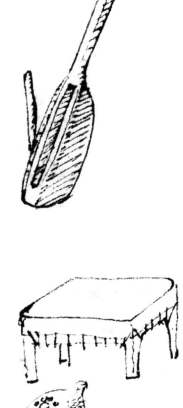

Illustrations, from the journal of Benjamin Latrobe, of the instruments that he observed
in Congo Square in 1819.

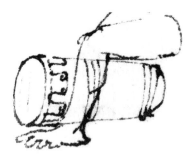

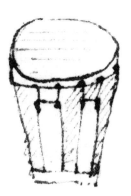

one end, often referred to as the tam tam (tom tom). Various sizes of these existed as the size of the barrel determined the size of the drum. Musicians played smaller versions of the tam tam by resting them between their knees and playing with hands and fingers.[4] During an interview with W.P.A. staff, ninety-four-year-old Wash Wilson, born and enslaved in Ouachita Parish, Louisiana, until around eighteen years of age when a Texas planter purchased him, recalled how they made drums and other musical instruments. These instruments fit the description of those played in Congo Square:

> Us take pieces of sheep's rib or cow's jaw or a piece iron, with a old kettle, or a hollow gourd and some horsehair to make de drum. Sometimes dey'd git a piece of tree trunk and hollow it out and stretch a goat's or sheep's skin over it for de drum. Dey'd be one to four foot high and a foot up to six foot' cross. In gen'ral two [people] played with de fingers or sticks on dis drum. Never seed so many in Texas, but dey made some. Dey'd take de buffalo horn and scrape it out to make de flute. Dat sho' be heared a long ways off. Den dey'd take a mule's jawbone and rattle de stick 'cross its teeth. Dey'd take a barrel and stretch a ox's hide 'cross one end and a man sat 'stride de barrel and beat on dat hide with he hand, and he feet, and iffen he git to feelin' de music in he bones, he'd beat on dat barrel with he head. 'Nother man beat one wooden side with sticks.[5]

Congo Square gatherers played a hand-held, pitched instrument for which many models and names exist in Africa including kalimba, mbira, and sanza. Cable referred to it as the marimba brett. To design this instrument, artisans placed pieces of reed in graduated lengths across a shallow box and attached the box to a backboard using a strand of wire. To play it, musicians plucked the ends of the reeds with their thumbs.

While no firsthand account of marimbas (also balaphons and xylophones) at Congo Square has surfaced, Maude Cuney Hare reported that marimbas were among the main instruments used to accompany Sunday dances there. Louisiana historian Edwin Adams Davis also noted that enslaved Africans in the New Orleans area played the marimbas, which they fashioned out of soft wood.[6] Meanwhile, the wind instruments observed at Congo Square included panpipes and large wooden horns shaped like a cow's horn. The musicians made panpipes, also known as "the quills," from joints of cane—usually three.[7] Bill Homer, born in 1850 on a plantation near Shreveport, reported that they also made quills from willow stalks. A staff member of the Texas Federal Writers' Project interviewed Homer when he was eighty-seven years old.

We plays de quill, make from willow stalk when de sap am up.

Drums typical of those that gatherers played in Congo Square.
The example above was made from a small handmade barrel.
The two examples below were carved in Africa from logs.

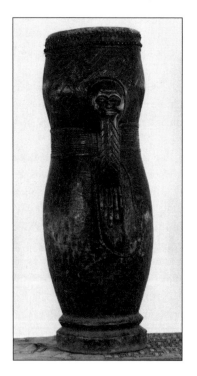

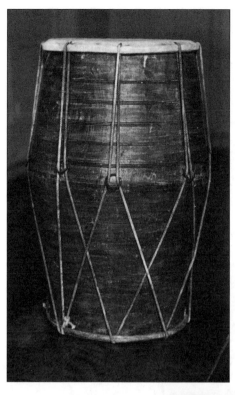

Drums made from barrels.

(Above, top) An example of a cata or log drum; (above, bottom) a cata, played in Rumba; (at right) a banza-style string instrument; (below) a mule's jawbone.

(Above, left) Examples of gourd rattles; (above, right) a gourd which has not yet been modified for musical use; (at left) a marimba, which is also known as a balaphon or xylophone; (below) two kalimbas.

Yous takes de stick and pounds de bark loose and slips it off, den split de wood in one end and down one side, puts holes in de bark and put it back on de stick. De quill plays like de flute.[8]

Blowing the quills.

Latrobe described and sketched a version of the banza (bania or banja), a string instrument that Africans fashioned from a calabash or gourd. At the top of its fingerboard was the carving of a man posed in a sitting position with his hands resting on his knees. During Latrobe's observation, a small, elderly man around the age of ninety played this instrument. Other observers, including Creecy, also witnessed the banza at Congo Square gatherings.

Technically referred to as a chordophone, the banza was the precursor to the banjo, and writers frequently referred to the two instruments interchangeably—occasionally referring to the banza as a "peculiar kind of banjo" or "crude banjo." While lutes and other string instruments of similar design existed throughout Africa, anthropologists credit enslaved Africans from the Senegambian region with bringing this model to the New World.[9] Moreau de Saint-Méry witnessed this instrument in St. Domingue (Haiti) and models existed in other parts of the West Indies including Jamaica. Latrobe's observation of this banza in the circle with a dance and drumming style of Kongo origin provided a concrete example of the exchange and intertwining of African cultures that existed at Congo Square and throughout the New World. Over the years, other eyewitnesses reported that the banza was one of the instruments used to accompany the Congo dance. For example, while traveling in Louisiana in 1829–30, Pavie observed enslaved Africans dancing a different dance with other musical instruments. However, upon the command to "dance the dance of the Congos," enslaved Africans brought out banjos and drums.

Along the same lines, Robert Farris Thompson's research links the carving atop the fingerboard of the banza that Latrobe sketched to the important Teke civilization in Kongo-Brazzaville.[10] Such combined Senagalese and Kongolese influence would establish this musical instrument as a visual representation of the

African cultural and material synthesis that occurred not only in New Orleans but throughout the African Diaspora.

In Congo Square, dancers used their bodies as instruments. Hand claps, foot stamps, chest and thigh pats, shouts and ululations accompanied the drums and other percussion instruments. Objects from nature, like shells and those that were otherwise useless, became musical instruments. Singers who encircled the dancers shook gourds filled with seeds, grain, or pebbles, and musicians beat ox, horse, and cow bones together as well as on empty barrels. Some male gatherers reportedly wore kneecaps with suspending metal nails that jingled when they danced. Gatherers shook, beat, and rasped the dried jawbones of horses or other animals with a stick or metal object like a key to make the loose teeth rattle and resonate.

In time, musicians added instruments that were not of African origin to the Sunday afternoon orchestras in Congo Square. These included the Jew's (jaw's) harp, triangle, tambourine, and violin (fiddle), also known as the cremona.[11]

Counterparts of the musical instruments played in Congo Square existed in Africa and many parts of the West Indies, including Haiti and Cuba. While this text refers to the musical instruments used in Congo Square during the pre-Civil War era, people of African heritage continue to play many of these today in Africa and throughout the African Diaspora. Drums are technically categorized as membranophones. Those made from hollowed logs existed throughout Africa as well as the New World, and those made out of barrels existed in all locations, including Africa, where European barrels were available. Artisans stretched animal skin over these open cylinders—hollowed logs and barrels—and secured the skin with rope, hoops or a combination of the two.

Latrobe's observation of the drummer sitting astride his drum while playing was also reported years later by Cable, who added that an additional drummer often sat on the ground at the open end of the drum and played on its side. This was a common practice throughout the Americas. In Martinique, Hearn observed that the drummer sat astride the drum and pressed the heel of his naked foot lightly or forcefully against the head of the drum to produce changes in the tone, a technique called "giving heel" to the drum. As was true in Wilson's description, another person simultaneously played on the side of the drum. Hearn published a sketch of two people playing a drum in this manner in his book *Two Years in the French West Indies*. He referred to the drum as a "Ka." In the Virgin Islands, the main drum used to accompany the Bamboula dance was also called a "Ka" and two drummers played it in the same manner.[12]

This style of drumming originated among people of Kongo-Angola heritage as observed in various parts of the Americas. In Haiti, the drum played in this manner called the Juba or Martinique was a variation of the Pétro drums which were associated with religious as well as secular Congo dances. Likewise in

Cuba, the djuka drums, which drummers laid horizontally and straddled as they played, accompanied a Congo secular dance called the Djuka (also Mani, Yuka, and Mula). Straddling the drum while playing was also common in South America where descendants from Kongo-Angola used this drumming style known there as Batuque to accompany the Bartuque, one of the oldest dances of Brazil. In Louisiana, this style of drumming accompanied the popular Congo dance; and in Puerto Rico, it accompanied the Bomba—both dances of Kongo origin. Today in Cuba, sitting astride the drum while playing remains a frequent feature of the Tumba Francesa societies.[13]

The stool-shaped drum that Latrobe observed existed in regions of the Kongo. Native of the Kongo, ethnomusicologist and professor Zawadi wa Mukuna explained that when seated—likely on the ground—the drummer situated the instrument so that his foot touched the head from underneath to alter the drum's pitch as he played with his hands.[14] Drums bearing similarity to this one existed in other parts of Africa and the West Indies, including the skin-headed Gome drum of Ghana and the wooden-headed Cajon, which is popular in Cuba. However, in contrast to the first model, drummers straddled the latter two instruments when playing them.

The practice of using a foot to alter a drum's tone, as drummers from West Central Africa demonstrated, continued in New Orleans' spasm bands. Here, using upside-down buckets, drummers hit the tops to produce high-pitched sounds and lifted the buckets with their foot then dropped them while hitting to produce deeper pitches. Thompson held that bands composed of such modified and homemade styles of musical instruments linked the practices of Congo Square to those of jazz. Although such trends in instruments gained popularity during the mid 1890s, eyewitnesses observed these practices much earlier. While in Louisiana during 1829–30, Pavie observed enslaved Africans beat an upside-down milk bucket to accompany a dance. In the early 1880s, Hearn witnessed African descendants beat a dry goods box with sticks or bones to accompany the Congo dance.[15]

Idiophones—instruments that do not require a string, reed, or membrane to produce their sound—were the most widely used instruments in Africa, second to the drums. Those played at Congo Square include the mbira, marimba (marimbula in Cuba), cowbells, rattles, scrapers, stick clappers, and wood blocks, all of which gatherers enhanced with bells around ankles, attached to belts and other garments. Gatherers also reinforced the music of these instruments by clapping their hands, patting their bodies, and stamping their feet. Drummers often wore rattle bracelets of nuts and seed pods around their wrists to accentuate the drum beats. Versions of all of these instruments and practices existed in Haiti, Cuba, and other areas of the Caribbean. The marimba emerged as a favored instrument for Haitian Méringues and in Cuban-style dances such as the Rumba. Gourd rattles were common in secular as well as religious music throughout the Caribbean, and singers who stood with or around musicians typically played them. Regarding the playing of these idiophones, J. H. Kwabena 'Nketia, the leading scholar on African music, wrote that "the Caribbean and Cuban traditions of persistent percussion—maracas, wood blocks, cowbells—are derived from Africa."[16]

The practice of scraping an animal jawbone with a stick, key, or other metal object was common in New Orleans as well as Haiti. Courlander stated that playing the burro's jawbone was familiar in Cuba as well. W.P.A. interviews of New Orleanians in 1940 showed that drummers often mounted the mule's skull (jawbone) on the top of their drums, which allowed them to scrape across the jawbone or rattle the teeth as they played. In his study *African-American Folksongs*, Henry Krehbiel reported that this concept had an African prototype in the form of a notched board that musicians rubbed with a stick. Scholar Rodney Livingstone referred to the instrument as a cassuto, a hollow piece of wood about a yard long covered with a board cut like a ladder, which embodies the same principle as the Chinese temple block instrument. While models undoubtedly exist in other locations, the cassuto scraper is known among the Kumbundu speakers of Angola.[17] The concept of striking and scraping a mule's jawbone, so widely practiced among black musicians in Louisiana from colonial times, is not unlike the contemporary practice of scraping washboards in zydeco music.

Flutes made of wood, the bark of cane, bamboo, or other materials with a natural bore as seen in Congo Square were common in Africa. In St. Domingue (Haiti), musicians made flutes and fife from rushes and bamboo as they also did in Jamaica where they were called bamboo fifes. Instruments in this category, referred to as aerophones, included panpipes, a set of single-tone flutes played by one person. These existed in West Africa, according to 'Nketia, and were also common in other parts of the continent.[18]

During an interview conducted in the 1930s by W.P.A. staff, New Orleanian Alexandre Augustin named the musical instruments that accompanied the Congo dance including the banza, animal jawbones, the boula, and the cata. Most of these instruments, as well as their names, still exist in the West Indies. In Haiti, the bula (boula) is the smallest of the three Arada drums used in Dahomean religious practices. In Puerto Rico, the instrument known as the cata in New Orleans and Cuba carries the name cuá and is commonly played in Bomba ensembles along with the boula (drum). The cata is a hollowed log or piece of bamboo, with openings at the top of both ends, which musicians lay in a crotch made from two Y-shaped sticks mounted in the ground and play like a drum using two sticks. It is a smaller version of a slit drum, a model of which exists among the Banda-Linda people of Central Africa. Augustin told interviewers that musicians played the cata with two spoons, a practice which master drummer Francisco Mora Catlett stated continues today in parts of Cuba.[19]

As 'Nketia noted regarding idiophones and the persistent percussion seen in the music of Cuba and other parts of the Caribbean, the instruments discussed here originated in Africa. Observers wrote about performances on these African-derived instruments in New Orleans into the 1880s. Interviews of New Orleanians under the Federal Writers' Project reveal that African descendants played variations of them well into the 1900s; and evidence of their influence continued to manifest itself in New Orleans and the nation. Some early jazz musicians played the banjo as well as drums made from barrels. Minstrel show bands consisted of the same orchestration witnessed at Congo Square—banjos, bones, and tambourines that resembled hand drums. In Haiti, the large-diameter shallow finger-drum that sometimes had metal disks that rattled, known elsewhere as the tambourine, was called the basse. The musical instruments played at the Congo Square gatherings were material evidence of African cultural practice and of the influence that African-derived instruments and orchestration had on indigenous New Orleans as well as American-born performance styles.[20]

Chapter 6

THE SONGS

The songs heard in Congo Square on Sunday afternoons diversified over the years resulting from and reflecting changes in the city's population of African descendants. As time passed, songs with a combination of African and Creole words, those in Louisiana Creole, and those in English joined and basically replaced songs of African origin. Although examples of songs representing each of these categories appear in this text, Louisiana Creole constitutes the majority of those included here as well as those documented in general. It was the common language of the Africans and their descendants who had originated from different nations in Africa and different parts of the New World. Despite the variations in language, underlying African performance practices continued including the integration of song, dance, and music. Certain songs accompanied certain dances, which called for certain rhythmic patterns. In keeping with sacred and secular practices, singers at Congo Square often encircled dancers and their songs took on various forms including call and response, solo and chorus, and unison.

Haitian historian Louis E. Elie wrote that Voudou initiates under the authority of Thélémaque Canga, one of the conspirators involved in a slave uprising, reportedly composed the following song in Haiti in 1734. The initiates, who were enslaved Africans, sang this revolutionary warrior's song of solidarity at ceremonies—particularly those involving Voudou:

> Eh! eh! Bomba!
> Heu! heu!
> Canga! fafio té!
> Canga, monne dé lé!
> Canga, do ki la!
> Canga li![1]

Ethnomusicologist and native of the Kongo, Professor Kazadi wa Mukuna stated that KiKongo words are readily recognizable in these lyrics although the spelling indicates that the song was not transcribed by a native speaker. The fact that followers of Voudou composed and sang this song was not surprising to Mukuna because of its reference to the devil, which in this song was the same as the white man. The lyrics exhort the gatherers to grab on, hold on, and tie him up. Adding to this, Ned Sublette found that one of the recognizable KiKongo terms is "Bomba," which means "secret." Accordingly, the lyrics admonished listeners to not only keep the secret from the white man, but also from domestic bondsmen and women, commonly known as house slaves. Alex LaSalle, a specialist in the music of Western Puerto Rico, reported hearing the lyrics to this song in Puerto Rico, which is where the Kongo-derived music and dance style known as Bomba originated.[2]

Moreau de Saint-Méry included the following version of this song in his writings on Haiti published in 1798.[3] Hélène d'Aquin Allain, who quoted Moreau, and Henry Castellanos who quoted Allain, as well as Charles Dudley Warner, all consequently printed the same spelling of the song in their works.[4] George Washington Cable published the subsequent version with modified spelling:

> Eh! eh! Bomba, hen! hen!
> Canga bafio té,
> Canga moune dé lé
> Canga do ki la
> Canga li.
>
> Eh! Eh! Bomba, hone! hone!
> Canga bafio tay,
> Canga moon day lay
> Canga do keelah,
> Canga li![5]

This song is an example of those in African languages that gatherers sang in Congo Square. The number of publications that included it and the variety of locations where African descendants sang it indicate its popularity. Although Allain never witnessed the dances or the songs in Congo Square, an interview with Lydia Delgado indicates that gatherers did sing this song there.[6] Travelers and local observers reported hearing songs in African languages in New Orleans as well as in Congo Square, including Benjamin Latrobe who wrote that the song he heard a man sing during a Sunday gathering was in an African language "for it was not French."[7] Observers gave similar reports long past the Civil War. In the early 1880s, newspaperman Lafcadio Hearn observed African descendants dancing the Congo and singing a purely African song.

As Louisiana Creole, also known as Creole and *patois*, was itself an Africanized form of French, songs with a combination of French and African languages as well as Creole and African languages existed. The following song is an example of such a combination. In a letter to Krehbiel, Hearn provided the following translation, although not a literal one, during the 1880s and wrote that African descendants still sang this song in New Orleans when he recorded it. The African words are italicized. "Ouendé" is pronounced "wenday," and "macaya" is pronounced "makkiyah:"

Ouendé, ouendé, macaya!	Go on! Go on! *eat enormously!*
Mo pas barrassé, *macaya!*	I ain't one bit ashamed—*eat outrageously!*
Ouendé, ouendé, macaya!	Go on! go on! *eat prodigiously!*
Mo bois bon divin, *macaya!*	I drink good wine! *eat ferociously!*
Ouendé, ouendé, macaya!	Go on! go on! *eat unceasingly!*
Mo mangé bon poulet, *macaya!*	I eat good chicken—gorging myself!
Ouendé, ouendé, macaya!	Go on! go on!
Mo pas barrassé, *macaya!*	Go on! Go on! *eat enormously!*
Ouendé, ouendé, macaya! – Macaya!	I ain't one bit ashamed—*eat outrageously!* [8]

Cable's article, *Creole Slave Songs*, also included bilingual songs of Creole and African languages. He referred to the song "Ah, Suzette" as having an African-Creole lyric. Singers told Cable that the song "Dé Zab," pronounced "des arbs," had a French title, but the rest was an African language.[9]

The following song, found in the Marcus Christian Collection and published in Cable's *Creole Slave Songs*, also contains African words the origins and meanings of which have not been identified. The observer described seeing an enslaved man singing it while chopping wood and noted that the song was a rhythmical, African tune that accompanied the Calinda, an African war dance. The singer sang it with a lifting, dancing motion, suiting the movements of his body to the rhythm of the tune as he chopped wood. Songs in African languages, those with a combination of African and French or Creole words, and those with all creolized words accompanied the Calinda dance, different versions of which existed in the Louisiana colony from its earliest days.

Heron mande
Heron mande,
Tigui li papa,
Heron mande,
Tigui li papa,
Heron mande,
Heron mande,
Heron mande,
Do se dan godo.[10]

As indicated, African descendants sang songs in African languages in New Orleans throughout and beyond Congo Square's existence. At the same time, particularly after the Louisiana Purchase in 1803, English-speaking African descendants joined the Congo Square gathering and consequently introduced additional songs and dances. *Norman's New Orleans and Environs* of 1845 reported that the gatherers danced to "Old Virginia Never Tire" or some other favorite air. A newspaper article of that same year reported that the gatherers sang "Hey Jim Along" and "Get Along Home You Yellow Gals."[11] The following version of "Old Virginia Never Tire," found in *Christy's Plantation Melodies*, may or may not be the version that African descendants sang. Originally published in 1851, the songbook resulted from the combination of three separate books and contains over 176 songs selected by E. P. Christy, the man credited as being the originator of Ethiopian Minstrelsy.

"Old Virginia Never Tire"

In Virginia's land, where corn-stalks grow,
    where the darkies [*sic*] are so gay,
With spade and hoe, and away they go to work
    till the close of day.
When work is done and night is come,
    'tis the darkies [*sic*] jubilee;
The girls so sweet, they look: so neat
    and merry as can be.

Chorus.
The fiddle sing, the banjo ding,
    Virginia never tire:
To laugh and sing is just the thing
    we darkies [*sic*] admire.
Oh, happy is the darkey's [*sic*] life, when,
    hunting for the coon,
He has the fun with the dog and gun
    to catch him very soon.[12]

The majority of the documented songs heard in Congo Square resulted from combined elements of different origins—a process known as syncretism. The songs consisted of African-based rhythms, French and Spanish influenced melodies, and Creole language—itself a product of syncretization. They bore various names including Creole songs, Creole Negro songs, Creole slave songs, and Creole folk songs—as they originated from Creole people. Some of the songs in this category originated in St. Domingue (Haiti) and came to Louisiana with Haitian immigrants who also spoke Kreyòl (Creole). The term Creole has developed different meanings over time; however historian Gwendolyn Midlo Hall's research shows the usage of the term when these songs evolved. She explained, "The word [Creole] simply meant people born in the Americas whose parents or more remote ancestors were Africans. This was the normal usage of the word

Creole everywhere in the Americas through the 18th century."[13] The language and songs of the people bore their identity—thus Creole language and Creole songs. Creole people used these songs to tell stories, impart history, express beliefs, and just "pass a good time."

As these songs reflected everyday life and experiences, composers commonly improvised or created verses on the spot; and the songs passed from person to person, place to place, and generation to generation. This mode of teaching or passing-on explains why different versions as well as different names existed for some of the same songs. Congo Square gatherers sang the following version of "Belle Layotte," a song about love, which was a common theme in Creole songs:

"Belle Layotte"   "Beautiful Layotte"

Mo déjà roulé tout la côte,   I have traveled all along the coast,
Pancor ouar pareil belle Layotte.   I haven't yet seen any like beautiful Layotte.
Mo déjà roulé tout la côte,   I have traveled all along the coast,
Mo roule tout la colonie;   I have traveled all over this land;
Mo pancor ouar griffonne la,   I haven't yet seen a light-skinned person,
Qua mo gout comme la belle Layotte.   Who suits me like the beautiful Layotte.
Mo déjà roulé tout la côte,   I have traveled all along the coast,
Pancor ouar pareil belle Layotte.   I haven't yet seen any like beautiful Layotte.

Mo déjà roulé tout la côte,   I have traveled all along the coast,
Pancor ouar pareil belle Layotte.   I haven't yet seen any like beautiful Layotte.
an Babét, mon ami,   Jean Babet, my friend,
Si vous couri par en haut,   If you go up that way/up there,
Vous mandé belle Layotte.   Ask beautiful Layotte
Cadeau la li té promi mouin.   For the gift she promised me.
Mo déjà roulé tout la côte,   I have traveled all along the coast,
Pancor ouar pareil belle Layotte.[14]   I haven't yet seen any like beautiful Layotte.

(translation by Tom Klingler, Ph.D.)

Creole slave songs have inspired the works of several nationally recognized musicians. Composer Henry Gilbert (1868–1928) chose the Creole song "Aurore Pradère (Bradaire)" as the theme for his symphonic ballet, *The Dance in Place Congo*, which the Metropolitan Opera Company performed in New York and Boston in 1918.[15] Prior to Gilbert, Louis Moreau Gottschalk (1829–1869) adapted a section of "Beautiful Layotte" for the theme of his *Ballade Creole*, and the following song, "Musieu Bainjo," inspired his composition "Banjo, Op. 15." African descendant Maude Cuney Hare translated and published the following version of that last song, "Gardé Piti Mulet Là (Musieu Banjo)." The satire and sarcasm in this song is a characteristic of many Creole songs:

"Musieu Bainjo"	"Mister Banjo"
Gardé piti Mulet là, "Musieu Bainjo,"	See the little mulatto, "Mister Banjo"
La com' li insolent!	Hasn't he a saucy air!
Chapeau sul' côté,	Hat cock'd on one side,
Soulié qui fait "cric-crac"	New shoes that go "cric-crac"
Gardé piti Mulet là, "Musieu Bainjo,"	See the little mulatto, "Mister Banjo"
La com' li insolent!	Hasn't he a saucy air!
Gardé piti Mulet là, "Musieu Bainjo,"	See the little mulatto, "Mister Banjo"
La com' li insolent!	Hasn't he a saucy air!
Foular á la pouche	Kerchief in his vest,
La canne á la main.	Walking-cane in hand.
Gardé piti Mulet là, "Musieu Bainjo,"	See the little mulatto, "Mister Banjo"
La com' li insolent!	Hasn't he a saucy air![16]

In 1902, Clara Gottschalk Peterson, Louis Gottschalk's sister, published a collection of Creole songs—several of which had inspired her then deceased brother's compositions. Acknowledging the source for the songs, she stated, "These melodies of the Louisiana Negroes . . . have served to rock whole generations of Southern children." Hall wrote that Louisiana Creole and its folklore, including Creole songs, became the preferred means of conversing among Louisiana's whites. This practice was particularly apparent among the elite, many of whom, as Peterson pointed out, learned the language and songs from their nurses of African descent.[17]

During interviews for the Federal Writers' Project, Black New Orleanians told staff members that gatherers sang "Lizette," "Celeste," "Suzette," "Missié d' Artaguette," and the song that follows, "Delaide Mo la Reine (Adelaide, My Queen)," in Place Congo:

Delaide, Mo la Reine	*Adelaide, My Queen*
Delaide, mo la reine,	Adelaide, My Queen,
Chimin-là trop longue pour allé—	The way is too long for me to travel—
Chimin-là monté dans les hauts:	That way leads far up yonder,
Tout, piti qui mo ye,	But, little as I am,
M'allé monté la haut dans courant.	I am going to stem the stream up there.
C'est moin, Liron, qui rivé	I, Liron, am come
M'allé di ye.	Is what I shall say to them.
Bon soir, mo la reine,	My queen, good night,
C'est moin, Liron, qui rivé.	'Tis I, Liron, who has come.[18]

Drumming and dancing were integral components of Creole songs, for the African rhythms in them called for African dance steps. One such dance was the Coonjai (Counjaille, Coonjine), the name and steps of which originated in Africa. Gatherers performed this dance when singing the popular love songs "Belle Layotte," "Remon," "Aurore Pradère," and "Caroline." The latter song "Caroline" held different names including "Aine, de' Trios," "Adeline," and "Azelie." Hare stated that "Belle Layotte" was probably also sung to a Calinda dance. The song "Dialogue d'Amour" and a Calinda dance reportedly ended some of the gatherings at Place Congo.

The popular song "Quan Patate-Latchuite" accompanied a Bamboula dance; and it was the song upon which Gottschalk based his famous composition "La Bamboula–Danse des Nègres, Op. 2":

"Quan Patate-Latchuite"	"When That Sweet Potato Will Be Cooked"
Quan patate-la tchuite.	When that sweet potato will be cooked.
Na nanan li, na nanan li.	We will eat it, we will eat it.
Quan même li dans sirop.	Even if it is cooked in syrup.
Quan même li dans la soupe.	Even if it is cooked in the soup.
Quan même li dans chaudiere.	Even if it is cooked in the pot.
Quan même li dans la cendé	Even if it is cooked in the ashes.
Na nanan li, na nannan li.	We will eat it, we will eat it.
Na nanan li, na nannan li.	We will eat it, we will eat it.[19]

Gottschalk learned this song, among many others, from his nurse, Sally, a native of Haiti, who moved to New Orleans with the Gottschalk family when they fled St. Domingue during the Haitian Revolution. Perhaps it is not coincidental that he wrote about Sally and her baking sweet potatoes in his autobiography entitled *Notes of a Pianist*. He stated:

> I again found myself before the large fireplace of our dwelling on the street 'des Ramparts' at New Orleans, where in the evening, squatting on the matting, the negroes [*sic*], myself, and the children of the house formed a circle around my grandmother, and listened, by the trembling fire on the hearth, under the coals of which Sally, the old negress [*sic*], baked her sweet potatoes, to the recital of this terrible negro [*sic*] insurrection.[20]

The melody of "Quan Patate-Latchuite" carried the African-derived habanera rhythm, which also provided the structure for the Congo dance. This rhythm shaped the melody of several Creole songs from Louisiana and the West Indies including "Tant Sirop Est Doux," which Hearn published in his book, *Two Years*

8
Quan' Patate La Cuite.

Quan' pa - tate la cuite. N'a va man - gé na va man - gé na va man - gé quan' pa - tate la cuite na va man - gé na va man - gé li

This melody is the basis of Gottschalk's "Bamboula" Op.2.

Quan' pa - tate la cuite. Na va man - gé na va man - gé na va man - gé quan' pa - tate la cuite na va man - gé na va man - gé li

When sweet potato is cooked
We shall eat it.

This melody is the basis of Gottschalk's "Bamboula" Op.2.

in the French West Indies. These are among the many songs that Haitian immigrants brought to Louisiana adding them to the existing repertoire. A newspaper article published in 1906 noted that nursery songs sung by the black nurses like "La Crocodile, Deux Canards" came to Louisiana from Haiti with the refugees. Cable implied that the song "Ah, Suzette," published in *Creole Slave Songs*, originated in St. Domingo.[21]

Gottschalk's memoirs state that he composed the "Bamboula" during his convalescence from typhoid fever. The song's four-bar melody, which was popular among Louisianans of African heritage, continued to run through his brain. Some sixty years later, African British composer and conductor Samuel Coleridge-Taylor (1875–1912) based his piano composition, "The Bamboula (African Dance)" on that same four-bar melody. Coleridge-Taylor published the melody at the top of his composition with credits to the collection of Henry Krehbiel and identified the West Indies as the place of origin. He included this composition in his collection entitled *Twenty Four Negro Melodies Op. 59*, for which Booker T. Washington wrote the preface. Washington praised Coleridge-Taylor for including and preserving African, Afro-American, and Afro-Caribbean musical elements in these compositions.[22] Coleridge-Taylor's use of the West Indian melody proved valuable for preserving and understanding New Orleans' culture and its connection to the West Indies during that time. Alice Nelson Dunbar wrote:

> Those who know the weird leit-motif of Coleridge-Taylor's Bamboula dance have heard the tune of the Congo dance, which every child in New Orleans could sing. Gottschalk's "Danse des Nègres [La Bamboula]" is almost forgotten by this generation but in it he recorded the music of the West Indians.[23]

Drums, along with other instruments, and a Calinda dance accompanied another popular song in Congo Square on Sunday afternoons, "Quand mo te jeune (Bal fini)," translated "When I was Young (The End of the Ball)." Reportedly, gatherers frequently sang this farewell song and performed the corresponding dance at sunset when police dispersed the crowd signaling the end of the Sunday celebrations. The lyrics summarized the sentiment of those who danced there. Life, pleasure, and good times pass away quickly, so enjoy them when you can:

"Quand Mo-té Jeune"	"When I was Young"
Quand mo-té jeun'	When I was young
Mo-té jonglé Michieu;	Merry was I, dear Sirs.
A c't'heur ma-pé vini vieux	And now when I am old
Mo-pé jonglé bon Dieu.	I still will merry be.

BAMBOULA
DANSE DE NEGRES

L. M. GOTTSCHALK Op: 2.
de la Louisiane.

THE BAMBOULA
(AFRICAN DANCE)

From the collection of
Henry E. Krehbiel

West Indies

Molto Allegro, quasi presto

S. COLERIDGE-TAYLOR
Op.59, No 8

Ma-pé jonglé bon temps passé,	I will be gay for pleasure flies.
Ma-pé jonglé bon temps passé,	I will be gay for pleasure flies.
Ma-pé jonglé bon temps passé,	I will be gay for 'good times' pass away,
Ma-pé jonglé bon temps qu'est passé.	I will be gay for 'good times' pass away.

Le bal fini, bonsoir, Messieurs,	The dance is done, Goodnight Messieurs.
Le bal fini, bonsoir, Mesdam'	The dance is done, Goodnight Madames.
M'al-lé parti,	I go, I go!
La, la, la, la, la	La, la, la, la, la[24]

Latrobe captured elements of African song structure and style in his statement about one of the songs that he heard in Congo Square: "The women squalled out a burthen to the playing, at intervals, consisting of two notes, as the Negroes [*sic*] working in our cities responded to the song of their leader."[25] African structural elements including call and response, improvisation, ornamentation, and slides from one note to another revealed themselves in this description. Traveler James Creecy also noted this singing style in Congo Square stating that the dancers "sing a second or counter to the music most sweetly."[26] New Orleans musicians continued to employ these elements when singing and when playing musical instruments as apparent in a variety of performance forms including jazz. Call and response singing as well as the unification of the song, drum, and dance are standard features of the Mardi Gras Indian performances.

Regarding the songs in general, the sentiments of the people embodied their lyrics, and African-derived poly-rhythms and syncopated beats provided their foundation. African languages, a combination of African and Creole languages, Louisiana Creole, and English framed their words. A French flair and the African-derived habanera rhythm influenced their melodies; and life, love, laughter, and longings typified their messages.

Songs with melodies built on the habanera rhythm and its derivatives, particularly "Quan Patate-Latchuite," were among the most popular at the gatherings. This song influenced the music of Gottschalk and Coleridge-Taylor whose compositions received national as well as international acclaim. It became a part of New Orleans popular culture into the twentieth century when reportedly every child in the city could sing its tune. Some of the Creole songs also reached national audiences. In 1884–85, George Washington Cable and Mark Twain (Samuel L. Clemens) toured the United States and Canada as a duo promoting their work, which for Cable included singing Creole slave songs that he had collected. Regarding Cable's performance of several "Creole African songs" for the Academy of Music in 1885, a reporter for the *Fort Wayne Daily Gazette* (Indiana) wrote, "The melody is weird but pleasing, and the words are a mixture of the Congo dialect and a French patois. He [Cable] then sang the words and music of a Congo dance, as performed by the Louisiana singers before the war."[27]

The reporter's reference to the weird melody indicated his unfamiliarity with the melodic structure of the songs. Musician/scholar Camille Nickerson's research revealed that while the diatonic scale was common in Creole songs, the African-based pentatonic scale was prevalent in more of the dance tunes,[28] some of which Cable sang on his tour. When singing those as well as other songs, people of African ancestry characteristically varied from the scale with what Hearn referred to as oddities of intonations and African characteristics of method. In other words, the written notations for the Creole songs did not fully represent how African descendants sang them. Hearn observed this fact when he enlisted Cable to write the notation for a Voudou song that a black woman sang for him. In the end, Hearn was unable to sing the song as she did because, as he put it, the musical notation was faulty.[29]

Henry Krehbiel, to whom Hearn sent songs and dance descriptions, also performed some of the Creole songs. Krehbiel, the music critic for the *New York Tribune* at the time, sang some of the songs in a lecture that he gave on Creole music. Cable's performances of the unfamiliar yet attractive melodies continually brought huge applause and requests for encores according to his letters to his wife during the year-long tour.[30] These songs clearly impacted local culture, and their influence reached the national level as well, particularly in the realm of entertainment.

A scene from the West Indies of a Calinda dance. The artist has more than likely opened what would have been a full-circle gathering for the benefit of the viewer. The female dancer holds a handkerchief in one hand and the end of her skirt with the other; while the drummer sits astride his drum, a common practice among drummers of Kongo heritage.

Chapter 7

THE DANCES

Several writers who witnessed African-derived dancing in early New Orleans—on the river's levee, in backyards, and in Congo Square—noted that participants gathered in circles or rings. The cultural practice of gatherers encircling dancers and musicians existed in many parts of West and Central Africa during sacred as well as social occasions. Those gatherers, however, did not constitute an audience of detached observers; for they joined the performers by clapping their hands, stomping their feet, patting their bodies, answering the calls of the chanters, adding improvised intonations and ululations (shrills in sometimes piercing pitches), singing songs that accompanied the dances, shaking gourd rattles, and replacing dancers who became fatigued. Also true to African cultural practice was the integration of dance, song, and drum/musical instruments. As Camille Nickerson affirmed in her study of the dances that occurred in Place Congo and continued other places long after slavery ended, none of the Creole dances, as she referred to them, were done exclusive of singing; and musical instruments accompanied them.[1]

Overtime, the repertoire of dances performed in those circles at Congo Square included European-derived styles accompanied by English-based songs; however, gatherers continued to perform African-derived dances there as well as in private settings. New Orleanians and travelers to the city observed derivatives of those African dances into the mid-1900s and their influences continue today lending evidence to the impact of cultural memory and African dancing on the city's culture.

Variations in the number of circles observed in Congo Square as well as the number of participants within the circles reflected the fluidity of the gatherings. These differences resulted from such variables as the weather, season of the year, and political circumstances. Several eyewitnesses who addressed the circles mentioned how many they saw. Christian Schultz observed twenty groups of dancers in the rear of town in 1808; and in 1819, Benjamin Latrobe entered four circles in the Square, but stated that there were more. James Creecy witnessed "groups of fifties and hundreds" in different sections of the Square in 1834.[2]

Regarding the composition of those circles, a *Daily Picayune* article stated that members of African nations danced among themselves and would not dance near certain other groups. On the contrary, the same article stated that fatigued dancers dropped out of circles and strolled off to groups of other nations in different sections of the Square suggesting that the circles may not have been or re-mained homogeneous—so to speak.[3] Commonalities that existed among African cultures facilitated the exchange and intertwining of practices. At the same time, some African-derived performances and cultural practices in the Congo Square descriptions remained distinct, identifiable, and traceable to an ethnic origin.

The myth that Africans haphazardly beat drums and extemporaneously made up dances reinforced the falsehood that they had no history. While room for improvisation and self-expression existed within performances, centuries-old practices continually passed from generation to generation. Songs in creolized languages basically replaced those in African languages to accompany dances in Louisiana and Congo Square. However, African-based choreography, musical in-struments, rhythmic patterns, and singing styles largely continued—despite the widespread interchange of names, multiple spellings of the names, and varied de-scriptions for each dance. The conditions of slavery—the uprooting of Africans from their homeland, the colonization and enslavement under rulers of different ethnic backgrounds and languages, the trafficking of enslaved Africans within and outside of regions and countries, and the documentation of information by people of different cultures and languages—all led to such discrepancies. The fact that African descendants of the same ethnic origin performed the same or very similar dances in different parts of the Americas, in many cases carrying the same name, indicated their agency in preserving their heritage and in perpetuating traditional culture wherever they were.

A standard feature of the circles at Congo Square was the musicians who sat, stood, or squatted inside as they played. The lead musicians were drummers, and the music of the circle rested on their rhythms. Other musicians who played percussive, melodic, string, and wind instruments added syncopated and impro-vised polyrhythms to the beat of the drums. The complex rhythms that resulted evoked equally complex steps and movements from the dancers. The dancers' feet may have kept one rhythm while their hips may have responded to another. The formation of the dancers inside each circle depended on the dance itself and included pairs, singles, lines, circles, semi-circles, and sets consisting of males and females.

In one circle, Latrobe observed a dozen women strutting around the in-side to the beat of percussion instruments. In the first circle that he entered, two women held handkerchiefs by the corners as they danced in slow fashion slightly moving their feet and bodies to the accompaniment of two drums and a string instrument. One of the drummers straddled his instrument as he played, and gatherers who encircled the performers sang an African song in the call and response style.[4] Although Latrobe provided a very brief description of this circle, key features suggest the ethnic origin of some of the performance practices. The drummer astride his drum is a characteristic of the Kongo nation; and the slow, slight movement of the feet and body in this brief description characterized a specific dance of Kongo origin widely performed in New Orleans during the time of Latrobe's observance. The absence of male dancers in this description suggests that they may not have entered the dance before he left that circle.

Some sixty years after Latrobe's observation, Lafcadio Hearn observed women performing similar dance movements in the backyard of a New Orleans residence. Referring to earlier years, Hearn's 1885 letter to New York music critic Henry Krehbiel mentioned that many other people had also witnessed this dance. He stated:

> I fear I know nothing about Creole music or Creole negroes [sic]. Yes, I have seen them dance; but they danced the Congo, and sang a purely African song to the accompaniment of a dry goods box beaten with sticks or bones and a drum made by stretching a skin over a flour-barrel. That sort of accompaniment and that sort of music, you know all about: it is precisely similar to what a score of travelers have described. . . . As for the dance—in which the women do not take their feet off the ground—it is as lascivious as is possible. The men dance very differently . . . leaping in the air.[5]

Hearn's comments about the Congo dance also appeared in his *Century Magazine* article, "The Scenes of Cable's Romances" and in Herbert Asbury's book, *The French Quarter: An Informal History of the New Orleans Underworld*. Asbury reported that Hearn asked several women to recite the words of the song that accompanied the dance. They replied that there was no use because he could never understand it. "C'est le Congo!—it is the Congo!" they explained.[6] Asbury quoted Hearn's commentary on the Congo dance:

> I observed that only a few old persons, who had probably all been slaves, knew how to dance it. The women did not move their feet from the ground. They only writhed their bodies and swayed in undulatory motions from ankles to waist. . . . The men leaped and performed feats of gymnastic dancing. . . . Small bells were attached to their ankles.[7]

African descendants performed the Congo dance outside of New Orleans in rural locations as well. In 1821, two years after Latrobe's observation, Isaac Holmes wrote:

> In Louisiana, and the state of Mississippi, the slaves have Sunday for a day of recreation, and upon many plantations they dance for several hours during the afternoon of this day. The general movement is in what they call the Congo dance; but their mu-

sic often consists of nothing more than an excavated piece of wood, at one end of which is a piece of parchment which covers the hollow part on which they beat; this, and the singing or vociferation of those who are dancing, and of those who surround the dancers, constitute the whole of their harmony.[8]

While in the rural area of Natchitoches in 1829–30, Theodore Pavie observed, that upon the command to "dance the dance of the Congos," a group of enslaved men used banjos and drums to accompany the African dance, which featured evolutions that he described as militaristic.[9]

Louisiana professor and folklorist Alceé Fortier, born in 1856, also witnessed an African-derived dance on a plantation in St. James Parish, where he grew up, with a description similar to that of Hearn's. The ball, the holiday event, was a well-established custom that took place on New Year's Day and involved several hours of playing musical instruments, singing, and dancing. Fortier referred to the dance as *Pilé Chactas*:

> The woman had to dance almost without moving her feet. It was the man who did all the work: turning around her, kneeling down, making the most grotesque and extraordinary faces writhing like a serpent, while the woman was almost immovable. After a little while, however, she began to get excited, and untying her neckerchief, she waved it around gracefully, and finally ended by wiping off the perspiration from the face of her danseur, and also the faces of the musicians. . . .
>
> The musical instruments were, first, a barrel with one end covered with an ox-hide—this was the drum; then two sticks and the jawbone of a mule, with the teeth still on it—this was the violin. The principal musician bestrode the barrel and began to beat on the hide, singing as loud as he could. He beat with his hands, with his feet, and sometimes, when quite carried away by his enthusiasm, with his head also. The second musician took the sticks and beat on the wood of the barrel. While the third made a dreadful music by rattling the teeth of the jawbone with a stick. Five or six men stood around the musicians and sang without stopping.[10]

The commonalities between and among these descriptions of Kongo-Angola-influenced dances in Louisiana are significant considering the span of years between observations, the fact that the observations took place in different parts of the state, and the fact that most writers only made brief journal entries or incidental observations, not detailed illustrations. It is important to distinguish between accounts of the dance as Holmes offered and the more descriptive reports of the dance as Latrobe, Hearn, and Fortier provided.

All four of these records addressed the singing that accompanied the dancing with Holmes and Latrobe calling attention to the fact that the singers surrounded the dancers. Latrobe and Hearn reported that the singing was in an African language, and Hearn specified its Kongo origin. Latrobe, Hearn, and Fortier noted the slight feet and body movements of the women, and Hearn pointed out the women's lascivious hip movements. Hearn, Fortier, and Pavie addressed the leaps, evolutions, and energetic movements of the males with Fortier also describing playful advances and flirting. Latrobe and Fortier noted that drummers straddled their drums while playing, Fortier stated that a second drummer played on the side of the drum, and Latrobe and Fortier both mentioned that women waved handkerchiefs during the dances. Of significance in the records of Holmes and Hearn is the fact that the gatherers named the dance themselves.

Descriptions of the Congo dance in Louisiana resembled a description of the Chica that Moreau de Saint-Méry recorded in St. Domingue (Haiti) in 1792. Moreau stated that the Chica carried the name Fandango in Spain and held the name Congo in other regions. He wrote:

> For the danseuse [female], who holds the corners of a handkerchief or the two ends of her apron, the art of this dance consists mainly in moving the lower part of the torso, while keeping the rest of the body almost motionless. To speed up the movement of the Chica, a dancer [male] will approach his danseuse, throwing himself forward, almost touching her, withdrawing, then advancing again, while seeming to implore her to yield to the desires which invade them.[11]

As in the description above and the one that follows, the opening phase of the dance sometimes featured a female holding a handkerchief or the ends of her apron and beginning with slow, sustained movements. This is likely the part of the dance that Latrobe witnessed in Congo Square. Edward Thorpe published the following description of the Chica in his study *Black Dance*:

> The dance began with a single female, holding the end of her skirt or a handkerchief; to a pronounced rhythm she would sway the lower part of her body while holding the torso relatively still; after a while a man would enter the arena, moving forward towards the woman, lunging provocatively, drawing back, throwing himself forward again precipitously until, to quote one chronicler of the time, "When the Chica reaches its most expressive stage, there is in the gestures and in the movement of the two dancers a harmony which is more easily imagined than described."[12]

Thorpe's suggestion that the Chica originated with the Kongolese received support from Lynne Emery who referred to the dance as the Chica-Congo due to the interchange of names. Reportedly, the Kongolese in particular performed this dance in the United States, which no doubt explains why the name of the dance became the "Congo" in some areas, including New Orleans. Cable, along with the author of the 1879 *Daily Picayune* article, "The Congo Dance," wrote that the name of the dance as well as the name "Congo Square" derived from the Kongo nation, which by 1803 represented the largest African ethnic group in New Orleans and the largest in the state by 1820.[13] The writer of the 1900 *Times Picayune Guide* noted the prevalence and popularity of the Congo dance in Congo Square when he wrote, "hundreds of the best class of whites used to promenade in the vicinity of the square to see the negroes [*sic*] dance Congo."[14]

People of African heritage in New Orleans did not restrict this dance to Congo Square. They performed it in the streets, backyards, and dance halls. Several years after Latrobe's observation, missionary Timothy Flint witnessed hundreds of African descendants, male and female, performing the great Congo dance during a street procession. They "have their own peculiar dress and their own contortions. They dance, and their streamers fly, and the bells that they have hung about them tinkle," he wrote.[15] Twenty-one years later, an 1843 news article reported a performance of the Congo dance in a backyard. This performance occurred during a period when the Sunday gatherings in Congo Square had reportedly ceased. Within two months of the previous article, another one stated that the Square "so long left free to loafers and cattle, is being put in chains."[16] Despite the bleak picture that the article presented, it was neither the end of the pre-Civil War Congo Square gatherings nor the end of the Congo dance in New Orleans.

The prevalence of the song that accompanied the Congo dance continued after Emancipation to the extent that in 1916, native New Orleanian Alice Nelson Dunbar (1875–1935) declared that every child in New Orleans could sing its tune. By that, she referred to the popular Creole song "Quan Patate-Latchuite." Yet, the song that accompanied the Congo dance that Latrobe and Hearn witnessed was in an African language. Were these the same dances or were there different versions of the Congo dance? The difference in languages may have resulted from the common trend of replacing songs in African languages with those in Creole to accompany African-derived drumming and dancing. It is also possible that Dunbar referred to another version of the Congo dance as different styles or versions of the dance existed throughout the West Indies. Haitian-born master dancer Peniel Guerrier identified seven versions of the Congo dance in Haiti— including religious and social forms. The names for some of these, from the research of Harold Courlander, are "Congo Pailette," "Congo Franc" (the African Congo), and "Congo Mazonne"—also known as "Congo Creole." Courlander believed the latter version also existed in Cuba, Martinique, and New Orleans.[17]

Different versions of the Congo dance also exist in Cuba, explained Danys Perez Prades "La Mora," a native of Santiago who specializes in the Afro-Cuban dances and songs from Eastern Cuba. Ranked as Primera Bailarina and Primera Profesora by the National Dance Commission in Cuba, La Mora explained that the Congo dance widely described in New Orleans during the time of the Congo Square gatherings was a social dance, a mating dance, where the man pursued the lady and tried to hypnotize and seduce her. The counterpart to this dance in Cuba is the Congo Layet.[18] Other Kongo-Angola-derived dances in Cuba include the Rumba Guaguancó and the Yuca. In the latter dances, male and female partners alternately advance toward each other, often with circling hips, and then they both push abdomens forward. This pelvic thrust or navel bumping, also known as the umbigada or the gesturing toward the partner's abdomen, initiates the retreat. It was also a feature of the Kongo-Angola-derived Batuque dance of Brazil.

This playful advance and retreat pattern was a feature of Haitian Congo dances as well, with a key characteristic being the circling hip movements. While such hip movements may have existed in dances that originated among other African nations, anthropologist and dance researcher Yvonne Daniel maintained that it is a distinctive feature of Kongo heritage; and when transported to the Americas from the Kongo-Angola region, it saturated new dance forms and became a characteristic legacy.[19] The influence of the Congo dance family or dance genre was extensive. While dances that carried the name Congo did not have identical descriptions throughout the New World, the ethnic origin, choreographic features, and cultural practices including drumming styles and rhythmic patterns revealed common links and family ties. In some parts of the Americas, the name Congo dance remained including Puerto Rico, Portobelo along the coast of Panama, and places previously mentioned. In other locations, including New Orleans, derivatives of this "advance and retreat" social dance with characteristic circular hip movements took on new names.

Native New Orleanian Florence Borders, born in 1924, observed an offshoot of the Congo dance in the city during the 1930s. "My aunt liked to do the Shake Babe," she stated. "She had a Shake Babe dress with a low band around the hips to accentuate her hip movements. During the dance the men would go up to the woman and back off, go up again and go around her. The men would do certain kinds of gyrations, certain little steps." Borders added that this dance was typical among common people. She noted that people danced in the streets then; and when they gave outstanding performances, they collected money from the people who watched. Borders observed her Aunt Bessie Richardson Gray dance the "Shake Babe" before 1935, the year that Gray moved to Chicago.[20]

While the movements of such offshoots or derivatives of the Congo dance bore similarities, often the names did not. Nationally recognized names of Congo-derived dances include the Shake and the Shimmy. Aline St. Julien, a native New Orleanian born in 1926, recalled the popularity of the Shimmy, another dance that characterized hip and lower torso movements. The dress suited for the Shimmy also had a long bodice and low waistline. "Sometimes pleats or fringes fell from the hip down," St. Julien stated. "All of it helped you move because the dress was working."[21] By the time Borders and St. Julien witnessed these dances, Mae West (1893–1980) and other performers had already taken them to the stage. Such performers included African American Earl "Snake Hips" Tucker (1905–1937) who, in the 1920s, built his stage career on the hip movements originally performed by Kongolese women.

The commonalities among descriptions of the Congo dance and its derivatives in New Orleans affirm the resilience of cultural memory and the influence of African performance styles on local culture. New Orleanians who gave interviews 120 years after the observations of Latrobe and Flint continued to indicate the dance's influence although they used the term "Congo" interchangeably to refer to the dance as well as to an event. In 1940, Alexandre Augustin, referring to earlier years, told Federal Writers' Project staff:

> One must not confuse the Congo dance with that of the voodoo. The Congo was danced by colored people in general. Dances were given on Sundays in the hall on Claiborne between Esplanade and Bayou Road (river side of the street).
>
> The music of the Congo consisted of a boula, a banjo and the cata. The boula was the skull of a mule. This skull was placed on top of an open barrel on which a piece of sheepskin had been tightly stretched. To keep the head from moving, hooks were driven on the sides of the barrel, and straps, drawn across the skull, were tied to the hooks, keeping the skull perfectly steady. Then two sticks were used to strike on the boula's teeth. The cata was played with two spoons that were struck on the knees. Thus you had the music of the Congo with banjo, boula and cata.
>
> Refreshments consisted of Creole beer (pine apple cider) [not "pineapple"] and baton zamandes (almond bars) then made by a colored man who lived on the corner of St. Philip and Treme Streets.[22]

Some of the same instruments in this description, drums and the banjo (banza), accompanied the Congo dance in the accounts of Latrobe. Other commonalities with the practices in Congo Square include the serving of Creole beer and the striking or scraping of a mule's skull to produce the rattling effect of loose teeth. Regarding the location of Augustin's observation, noted jazz musi-

cian Danny Barker (1909–1994) informed author and interviewer Tom Dent that
this area along Claiborne was an entertainment strip with gambling joints and old
black-owned businesses.[23]

In the following description, an interviewee used the term Congo dances
to refer to an event:

> The Congo dances were given in the hall of the Grand Army. At
> those balls, the men had bells on their pants. They would take a
> kerchief (madras) pass it around their dancing partner and hold
> the ends of the kerchief, pulling on the ends to force the woman
> to shake her posterior.[24]

The attachment of bells to men's pants for sound effects and ornamentation, the use of the handkerchiefs, and the women's hip movements in this account were present in descriptions of the Congo dance given in the early 1800s.
Regarding the location of the dances in the previous description, the Grand Army
of the Republic was an organization of Union veterans of the Civil War including
those who served with the Native Guards, a regiment of free men of color. New
Orleans City Directories of the 1800s listed several posts for the organization
as well as meeting locations, which the posts frequently shared. Among these
locations were: 25 Decatur Street (1880); 5 Commercial and 193 Gravier Streets
(1892); and 169 University Place (1896).

Based on shared features, Congo dances appear to have influenced another
dance event called Creole dances and the Creole dance. Several New Orleanians
who provided information for W.P.A. staff spoke about these dance events, which
sometimes took place in backyards and bar rooms as well as in Congo Square (after emancipation) and at Lake Pontchartrain in connection with Voudou activities. In 1940, at age seventy-two, Oscar Felix, a follower of Voudou, told writers
that after the religious portion of the ceremony, participants would engage in the
Creole dance. After the dance, everyone recited the "Our Father" on their knees,
then ate, drank, and had a good time. For the dance, Felix stated:

> One man would have two women on each side of him and they
> would put metal rings on their knees that would jingle and rattle.
> He would first turn one [woman] around then he would turn the
> other . . . then he would dance with one and then the other.[25]

Camille Nickerson (1888–1982) wrote that her father witnessed Creole
dances in backyards and side yards long after slavery ended and the dances in
Place Congo ceased. A different eyewitness provided a dance description that
contained similar features to those found in the dance that Latrobe and earlier
writers described, as well as to some Calinda dances.

The women formed a column, dancing gracefully from side to side, some with arms a-kimbo, and some holding bandana handkerchiefs by the corners behind their necks playing gracefully with them. After they dance in this manner for a while some man among the onlookers who decided that he wished to join with the dancers would suddenly leap into place, dancing opposite one of the women. This went on for a time, after which the man moved on to the next woman, and so continued until the entire column, sometimes quite long, had been completed, when another man would take his place.[26]

An 1887 news article presented yet another name for a dance that took place in conjunction with the Saint John's Day celebration—a Cungi dance. The performance featured dancers with bells and tin tubes fastened around their knees that created rattling sound effects like those once observed in Congo Square and in previous descriptions. The orchestra for the dance consisted of instruments previously played in Congo Square including the mule's jawbone, a drum made from a whiskey barrel, along with examples of instruments used in spasm bands like a cracker box. An article published the previous day in a different newspaper announcing this event presented a term that captured the essence of the event and illuminated the influence of African-derived dancing in New Orleans— "Congo-Creole-African dance."[27]

As demonstrated, the Congo dance was highly popular in Congo Square, New Orleans, and Louisiana, and its influence was broad. This was also true of the Calinda (Calenda, Kalenda, Kalinda, and Colinda), the first African-derived dance recorded in the Louisiana colony. Le Page du Pratz, who lived at different locations from 1718 to 1734, observed three to four hundred enslaved Africans dance a Calinda on Sundays. Although the origin of the word "Calinda" remains uncertain, the term refers to an African-derived dance of varied descriptions accompanied by African-based instruments and songs. Maude Cuney Hare, who provided an early definition of the Calinda in Louisiana, explained that it was a dance linked to songs of derision and accompanied by various instruments including a drum. Variations in the dance over the years led writers to interchangeably refer to the Calinda as a specific dance and a type of dance. When described as a type of dance, a Calinda characteristically involved circles, included songs, and employed rhythmical accompaniment—drums (typically a short one called a baboula and a longer one), calabashes filled with gravel, banzas, and handclapping.

Just as the Chica dance interchangeably carried the name Congo, Moreau acknowledged that the Chica carried the name Calinda in the northern islands of the West Indies known as the Leeward Islands. The Calinda's interchange of names with the Chica may explain why the bamboula drum accompanied Calinda dances in certain locations (see illustration on page 88), why some dance descriptions of Calindas approximated those for the Congo/Chica, and why some writers have suggested that the Calinda was of Kongo origin. One of the stanzas of an early song, "Chanson Negre," illustrated the association of the Calinda dance and the bamboula drum. Jean Jacques Rousseau used the song around 1740 to demonstrate a musical notation system that he invented. The song, which gained popularity in the West Indies and Louisiana, was later published under the name "Chanson Creole."

Dipo mo pêrdi Lizette,	Since I lost Lizette,
Mo pa batte Bamboula,	I have not played the Bamboula,
Bouche a moi tourné muette,	My mouth has turned mute,
Mo pa dansé Calinda.[28]	I haven't danced the Calinda.

(translation by Paulette Richards, Ph.D.)

The following description of a "Kalenda" [*sic*] dance is among the earliest that exists. Jean Baptiste Labat recorded it in 1698 while in Martinique:

> The dancers are arranged in two lines facing each other, the men on one side and the women on the other. Those who are tired of dancing and the spectators make a circle around the dancers and the drums. The more clever ones sing songs that they compose on the spot on whatever subject they judge appropriate while all the spectators sing the refrain accompanied by a lot of handclapping. With regard to the dancers, they hold their arms a little like those who dance while playing castanets. They jump, they turn about, they approach within two or three feet of each other and then withdraw in rhythm until the sound of the drum signals them to come together again, striking their thighs against each other—that is to say the men against the women. To see them, it seems that they are smacking their bellies together although it is only the thighs that receive these blows. In a moment they turn around and withdraw in order to start the same movement over again with gestures that are utterly lascivious as many times as the drum gives the signal which it does several times in succession. From time to time they link arms and take two or three turns still smacking their thighs together. One can see from this dance that it is the antithesis of modesty. Nevertheless it is so much to the taste of the Spanish Creoles of the Americas and so common among them that it is one of their most frequent amusements and even enters into their devotions. They dance it in their churches, and in their processions and nuns even dance

it Christmas Eve . . . It is true that they don't allow any men to
dance this devout dance with them.[29]

According to Labat, officials passed ordinances in the islands to forbid the
Calinda because of its indecency and lasciviousness perhaps referring to the striking of thighs. He pointed out that the ordinances intended more so to avoid the
numerous gatherings of African descendants who could initiate revolts, uprisings,
or parties of robbers. In Louisiana, Le Page du Pratz held the same fear about
the enslaved Africans who gathered to dance the Calinda, writing that "nothing is
more to be dreaded than to see the [negros] assemble together on Sundays under
pretence of Calinda or the dance."[30] Le Page, who witnessed the gatherings in
1726 on the King's Plantation when he moved there from another location in the
colony, abolished the assemblies and influenced other plantation owners to do
the same.

In 1792, nearly one hundred years after Labat's description, Moreau provided the following description of a Calinda as performed in Haiti:

> A dancer and his partner, or a number of pairs of dancers, ad-
> vance to the center and begin to dance, always as couples. This
> precise dance is based on a single step in which the performer
> advances successively each foot, then several times tapping heel
> and toe, as in the Anglaise. One sees evolutions and turns around
> the partner, who also turns and moves with the lady; while the
> partner moves his arms with the elbows rather near the body
> and the hands practically closed, the lady holds the ends of a
> handkerchief which waves.[31]

Congo Square gatherers reportedly performed different versions of the
Calinda dance on Sunday afternoons. The Creole songs that accompanied a Calinda included "Belle Layotte," "Dialogue d'Amour," and "Quand mo-té Jeune."
Reportedly, the final dance on Sunday evenings at Congo Square was a Calinda
and the last two songs sometimes accompanied it.[32] Nina Monroe published the
following dance description along with a collection of songs that she heard African descendants sing in New Orleans and on plantations in rural Louisiana. The
song "Heron Mande" was among those that accompanied this war-like version
of the Calinda. Monroe wrote:

> The Calinda was a war-dance in which men alone took part,
> stripped to the waist and brandishing sticks in a mock fight,
> while at the same time balancing upon their heads bottles filled
> with water from which one drop spilled put the participant *hors
> de combat* (out of the fight). Later the Calinda assumed more and
> more an objectionable character, until it was finally prohibited in
> the Place Congo in New Orleans about the eighteen-forties. But

I have it from the lips of an [elderly man of African descent] once an expert at the Calinda, that there was much sport in it at the stage of dancing with water-filled bottles, and that the last remaining dancer well deserved to have the water in his bottle replaced by good "tafia" (whiskey) celebrate his victory.[33]

African descendants performed a similar stick-fighting, all-male version of the Calinda in the West Indies, including Trinidad, Martinique, Haiti, Grenada, and St. Thomas.[34] Reports of the Calinda dance in one form or another also originated in Curaçao, Tobago, Carriacou, Jamaica, Cuba, Puerto Rico, Peru, Mexico, and Uruguay, among other locations.[35] There is speculation that restrictions were imposed on the Calinda in Louisiana, including Congo Square, during the 1840s, however no details of this have surfaced. Whether authorities in fact imposed a restriction, whether it involved one or all versions of the dance, whether the restriction targeted the association of Voudou and the Calinda, or whether writers and readers associated the restriction placed on the Calinda in the West Indies with Congo Square all remain in question.

The war-like version of the Calinda resembled a war dance called the Cadja, which a New Orleanian described in the late 1930s during an interview with Federal Writers' Project staff. This dance reportedly came from Africa, was popular during slavery, and continued many years afterwards. Only men performed the dance with each one balancing a bottle or jar of water on his head while singing and swaying his body, arms, and feet to the rhythm of beating drums.[36] The dancer who won by lasting the longest received a bottle of tafia.

The influence of the Calinda dance surfaced during interviews that W.P.A. staff conducted in New Orleans. They found that the African descendants called any dance with the movement of jumping up and down the Calinda. "Boudoum bou-doum," found in the refrain of songs that accompany the Calinda, was reportedly a sound word that meant to fall down. Thus, the catchphrase "Dansé Calinda, Boudoum Boudoum, Dansé Calinda Boudoum Boudoum!" served as an enticement to get children to leave their playthings and take a bath. Nurses invited children to make "Boudoum Boudoum" (to jump up and down) in the bath water. Some interviewees explained that the sound words, "Bou-doum, Bou-doum," mocked the cannon fire in Congo Square that announced the city's curfew for the enslaved. The following old New Orleans song included those words:

(Creole) / (English)

Mo té ain negresse, — I was a negress,
Pli belle que Metresse. — More beautiful than my mistress.
Mo té volé belle-belle — I used to steal pretty things
Dans l'armoire Mamzelle. — From Mamzelle's armoir.
Dansé Calinda, Bou-doum Bou-doum — Dansé Calinda, Bou-doum Bou-doum
Dansé Calinda, Bou-doum Bou-doum. — Dansé Calinda, Bou-doum Bou-doum.[37]

The Calinda dance also influenced Cajun culture as witnessed by the popular Cajun dance song "Allons Danser, Colinda." In the song, a young man urges a young woman named Colinda to come and dance with him while her mother is away. Shane Bernard and Julia Girouard, authors of the article "'Colinda': Mysterious Origins of a Cajun Folksong," found that prior to the twentieth century, Colinda strictly referred to a Black Creole dance; after the turn of the century, Colinda referred to both a Cajun song and Cajun dance. The popular two-step dance was once referred to as a Colinda; during those initial years, the lyrics meant "Let's dance the Colinda" (an African-derived dance), not "Let's dance, Colinda" (a young lady's name). The authors also presented an early Black Creole song "Anons au Bal Colinda," the tune of which reportedly showed a clear relationship to the traditional Cajun version of "Allons Danser, Colinda."[38]

In addition to the Congo (Chica) and Calinda, other dances performed in Congo Square included the Bamboula (Bámbula), Chacta (Cata), Counjaille, Juba, and the Carabine. As seen earlier in this chapter, Fortier's description of what he referred to as *Pilé Chactas* closely resembled that of the dance identified as the Congo dance, which may represent another example of name interchange. No other description has surfaced.

While reports existed of the Bamboula dance in New Orleans, a specific description that distinguished it from other dances, particularly the Congo dance, has not surfaced. A term used generically as well as specifically, "bamboula" referred to a drum, a dance, dancers, and a rhythm in some cases. In addition to New Orleans, the Bamboula dance was observed in numerous parts of the West Indies including Trinidad, St. Lucia, Guadeloupe, St. Domingue (Haiti), Puerto Rico, and the Virgin Islands (St. Thomas, St. Croix); and it remains prevalent in some of those locations today.[39] Moreau stated in his writings on St. Domingue (Haiti) that the bamboula drum received its name because it was sometimes made from a single piece of bamboo; however, Robert Farris Thompson, who traced the etymology of the word "bamboula," found that the Kikongo translation for bambula is "to remember" or "to remind."[40]

Camille Nickerson's brief report of the Bamboula dance reveals its relationship to the Congo dance. She stated that it was a dance of suggestive writhing and wild leaping and that is was the dance of Voudoo ceremonies. Ashbury's description of the Bamboula dance matched Hearn's description of the Congo dance and adopted a phrase from the Calinda dance. The phrase "Dansez Calinda!" became "Dansez Bamboula!" Asbury wrote:

> The movements of the Calinda and the Dance of the Bamboula are very similar, but for the evolutions of the latter the male dancers attached bits of tin or other metal to ribbons tied about their ankles. Thus accoutered, they pranced back and forth, leaping into the air and stamping in unison, occasionally shout-

ing "Dansez Bamboula! Badoum! Badoum!" while, the women, scarcely lifting their feet from the ground, swayed their bodies from side to side and chanted an ancient song as monotonous as a dirge.[41]

Asbury's account of the Congo dance under the title "Bamboula" finds support from an African cultural practice of assigning the same name to the drum and to the dance that it accompanied. One of the drums used to accompany the Chica/Congo was the baboula, which the drummer usually placed in a horizontal position and sat astride while another musician beat sticks against the drum's body. When discussing the Chica dance in St. Domingue (Haiti), Moreau mentioned that the drummer stood astride his drum.[42] This suggests that the Chica/Congo dance may have at times received the name Bamboula. Cross referencing and examination of dance descriptions show that writers and dancers used the names Congo dance and Bamboula dance interchangeably, while at the same time both names were used generically as well as specifically. Ashbury's description of the Congo dance under the title "Bamboula" dance was not unlike Cable's publication of the song "Quan Patate-Latchuite," which accompanied the Congo dance under the name "Bamboula."

Along the same lines, Alice Nelson Dunbar wrote that the tune for the Congo dance was that of the song, "Quan Patate-Latchuite," and New Orleanians who provided interviews for Federal Writers' Project stated that the same song accompanied the Bamboula dance. This song, which contains the four-note habanera/tango rhythm, further links the Congo dance and the Bamboula dance. In 1786, Bishop Cyrillo's complaint about the blacks dancing the Bamboula in Place Congo before the end of church service indicates the early presence of the dance and the rhythmic cell. Governor Miró replied to the complaint about the Bamboula by addressing the *tangos, o bailes de negros*. The word "tango" in this passage referred to the dances of the blacks, but it also carried multiple and layered meanings.

In the end, research indicates that although names and dance descriptions may have been interchanged in New Orleans at points, the Congo dance and the Bamboula dance were distinct dances that held shared practices and manifested themselves that way in various parts of the West Indies. While they were not the same dances, they were in the same family, explained Alex LaSalle, a specialist in the music of Western Puerto Rico where the two dances exist today along with their cousin the Bomba.[43] The long-term and widespread practice of the Kongo-derived dance in New Orleans under both names—Congo dance and Bamboula dance—illustrates the impact that people of the Kongo-Angola nation had on dance and music in New Orleans.

As mentioned, some writers used the term "bamboula" to refer to dancers. While some skilled, male dancers no doubt received recognition for their high leaps and powerful foot stamps, characteristic of the Congo and Bamboula dances, and some may have even received the name "bamboula dancer," folklore surrounding the bamboula dancer named Squire in Congo Square originated with writers Cable and Asbury. Local newspapers did tell of the real Squire, a legendary leader of the maroons who received the name Bras Coupé after he lost one of his arms as a result of a skirmish with police. Coupé reportedly formed bands of maroons that terrorized the city—re-entering it, stealing, and robbing residents. After his death in 1837 at the hands of fisherman Francisco Garcia, who received a monetary award, Bras Coupé's body lay exposed for some time on the public square.[44] Undoubtedly some of the maroons who reentered the city joined the gatherings in Congo Square, and Bras Coupé may very well have been one of them. His ability to repeatedly evade the law launched him into superheroic outlaw status—even before his death.

Another dance performed in Congo Square, the Counjaille (Counjai, Counja, Counjale, Coonjai, and Coonjine), carried different meanings as well as spellings, and the term referred to a dance as well as a dance tune. William Allen, author of *Slave Songs of the United States*, wrote that the Coonjai was a simple dance, a sort of minuet. Krehbiel added that while the minuet is in triple time, the Counjai is in duple. He suggested that both the name and dance originated in Africa. Songs that accompanied this dance included "Belle Layotte," "Remon," "Aurore Pradère," and "Caroline." Allen's description of the Counjaille revealed its relationship to the "Shout," a Christian-based dance that embodied elements of African religious expressions and that existed prevalently among African descendants in the low-country region of South Carolina and Georgia. The Shout, characterized by dancers stepping counterclockwise in a circle accompanied by a separate group of singers, also existed in regions of Louisiana.

> When the Coonjai is danced, the music is furnished by an orchestra of singers, the leader of whom—a man selected both for the quality of his voice and for his skill in improvising—sustains the solo part, while the others afford him an opportunity, as they shout in chorus, for inventing some neat verse to compliment some lovely dansuse [female], or celebrate the deeds of some plantation hero. The dancers themselves never sing, as in the case of the religious "shout" of the Port Royal Negroes; and the usual musical accompaniment, besides that of the singers, . . . barrel-headed-drum, the jaw-bone and key, or some other crude instrument.[45]

Music historian Rudi Blesh suggested that the term Counjaille referred to the rag dance of the levee boatmen who traveled up and down the Mississippi, Missouri, and Ohio rivers.[46] Noted musicologist Harold Courlander added that people in southern, waterfront cities like New Orleans associated the term with moving or loading cotton. He reported that African-American children along levees and docks sang:

> Throw me a nickel, throw me a dime
> If you want to see me do the Coonjine.[47]

Federal Writers' Project staff interviewed a New Orleanian who gave yet another version of this dance. Reportedly, dancers improvised steps and clapped their hands loudly on the first beat. The drum also gave one loud beat each time performers said the word "Counja." In this version, "Counja" was the evil spirit and was sometimes referred to as "Zombi":

"Dansé La Counjale"	"Dance of the Counjale"
Counja, Counja, Counja apé vini	Counja, Counja, Counja is coming
Cahé vous la tête lapé vini	Hide your head he is coming now
Fermé vous des jies pou pa ouare li.	Close your eyes so as not to see him.
Lapé vini, Hey…lapé vini…	He is coming…Hey…He is coming
Counja…Counja…Counja…apé vini	Counja…Counja…Counja…is a coming
Counja pae vini, Counja apé vini	Counja is coming, Counja is coming
Counja, Counja, Counja, Counja.	Counja, Counja, Counja, Counja.[48]

African descendant James Thomas, who witnessed gatherers dance the Juba at Congo Square wrote:

> All the country over, where there are any blacks, they were danc-
> ing "Rubin Rede," "Juba," and "Jumping Jim Crow." Judging
> from the antics of those blacks on the congo green in New
> Orleans, I judge their dances, Juber and Partner, were imported
> from Africa, modified slightly.[49]

Thomas was correct about the source of the Juba, which, according to Robert Farris Thompson, derived from nzuba, a thigh-slapping dance of Kongo origin. The name derived from the Ki-Kongo verb "zuba," which means "to slap."[50] Also called Giouba and Djouba, African descendants performed the Juba in Haiti and in Cuba. Along with the patting slap-dance step, the dance or a different version of the dance included counterclockwise movement in a circle accompanied by drums.

Descriptions of the Juba in Louisiana came from travelers who witnessed it in various parts of the state. Theodore Pavie witnessed a version of the Juba while visiting the Natchitoches area in 1829–30, although he did not name the dance. Musicians who accompanied the dance played a rough guitar fashioned from a gourd with strings made of wildcat gut and turned over a copper milking bucket to use as a drum. To dance, "they start a quick stomping, the dancers slapped their thighs and their hands in rhythm, turning and twisting or abruptly stopping in an attitude of surprise and pleasure, then a circle is formed."[51]

In 1852, another traveler named Shahmah witnessed a performance of the Juba at a Sunday afternoon gathering in rural Louisiana. Referring to the dance as "pat juber" he stated, "This is much the same thing we have seen among the Negroes [*sic*] of Nubia and the Upper Nile." Shahmah continued,

> One foot, resting on the heel, is brought a little in advance of the other, and the ball is made to strike, or pat in regular time; while, as an accompaniment, the hands are struck smartly together, and then upon the thighs . . . there is such perfect time.[52]

As Thomas indicated, African descendants across the country, particularly the South, danced the Juba, a derivative of which became known as Hambone. The Juba dance reportedly influenced hand-clapping games of young black girls, evolved into the Charleston in the 1920s, and influenced the step-show performances of African American male, and later female, Greek letter organizations. E. P. Christy and other minstrels performed a version of the Juba in New York on Broadway, using the same name. According to Christy's memoirs, published during his lifetime, Congo Square was the source of his show material lending evidence to Congo Square's influence on national popular culture.

Another dance performed at Congo Square was the Carabine. Scholar Alcee Fortier, who witnessed it on New Year's Day when growing up in Louisiana, provided a brief description. He recalled that the dance was quite graceful:

> The man took his danseuse by the hand, and made her turn around very rapidly for more than an hour, the woman waving a red handkerchief over her head, and every one singing,
>
> "Madame Gobar, en sortant di bal,
> Madame Gobar, tiyon li tombé."[53]
>
> [When Madame Gobar was leaving
> the dance, her tignon fell off.]

Some of the dancers in Congo Square decorated themselves with animal tails and fringes; and some wore belts made of small bells. Others attached sound makers such as shells, bells, bits of metal, and pieces of tin to ribbons and tied them around their arms and legs. When dancers performed outstandingly, spectators clapped and threw picallions (Spanish coins) into the circle.[54] Children danced in the Square as well, learning the dances by imitating adults. Reportedly, the young ones danced on the outskirts of the circles and added their laughter and playfulness to the Sunday event.[55] As English-speaking enslaved Africans with more acculturated backgrounds joined the gatherings, so did European-derived dance and song forms. *Norman's New Orleans and Environs* stated, "many an old inhabitant can remember [African descendants] dancing to 'Old Virginia never tire' or some other favorite air."[56]

Alongside European-derived dances, some African descendants continued to dance in the ways of their tradition. Several of the eyewitness accounts of Congo Square gatherings, given during the 1840s, indicate that the dance and the music were African. Dance descriptions given in the 1940s, around one hundred years after the gatherings ceased, show that black New Orleanians continued to employ those rhythms, dances, musical instruments, or other cultural practices. The use of handkerchiefs when dancing and the receiving of money for impressive, informal street performances became standards in New Orleans culture.

Jazz historian and musician Michael White affirms that a simplification of the types of rhythmic cells played in Congo Square became a part of indigenous New Orleans music. This is still heard in the second line and parade beats or rhythms of jazz and marching brass bands, which play in black social aid and pleasure club parades and jazz funerals. These rhythms were the predominant musical influences on Mardi Gras Indian dances and chants and a major influence on all early New Orleans jazz.[57] Thus, African-based rhythms that both stimulated and accompanied dance steps undergirded indigenous New Orleans' styles. Indeed, the music and the dance continuously influenced each other.

Chapter 8

The Economic Exchange

The economy of the Sunday gatherings in Congo Square resided largely in the hands of market women, which reflected a continuation of African marketing culture. Not only was this true of marketing in Congo Square, but of petty marketing throughout the city. Market women operated stalls in public markets, trudged sidewalks and alleys, called at doors of houses and businesses, and sold their goods on the levee, street corners, and public squares carrying their "shops" upon their heads, calling out their wares with melodic chants, and transacting sales in the language preferred by their customers.

While male vendors and marketers of African descent did exist, visitor Ellen Call Long stated that market women "in bright bandanas, and otherwise neatly dressed, presided over tables, and were evidently the popular traders." Thomas Nuttall, who visited the city in 1820, wrote, "The market . . . appeared to be tolerably well supplied, though singularly managed, and that entirely by negro [*sic*] slaves."[1] The observation of another traveler appeared in *The Bee* in 1835:

> In visiting the provision markets of New Orleans, an intelligent traveler must be surprised at seeing almost the whole of purchasing and selling the edible articles for domestic consumption, transacted by colored persons. Our butchers are negros [*sic*]; our fishmongers negroes [*sic*]; our venders of vegetables, fruit and flowers are all negroes [*sic*]—but what is worse, with very few exceptions the only purchasers that frequent the markets are negroes [*sic*]; and generally slaves. It is true that a few white women who keep boarding houses are occasionally seen; but it is too true that the responsible duty of purchasing every species of market provision for the use of families is confided to slaves.[2]

The fact that enslaved women in the city "dominated petty marketing was no accident," affirmed historian Virginia Gould. They "transported the knowledge of marketing with them from Africa to the New World."[3] This entrepreneurial spirit was also prevalent among free women of color as some of them had been previously enslaved and had managed to earn and save enough money to purchase their freedom. This was true of Rose Nicaud, reportedly the first coffee vendor in the city, who operated a stand in Jackson Square outside of the St. Louis Cathedral. An 1874 news article indicated that Nicaud was still operat-

109

ing her coffee stand and had done so for approximately twenty-five years when interviewed that year. Twenty years earlier, her business required eighteen gallons of pure milk per day, and her average daily profits from coffee sales by the cup ranged from fifty to sixty dollars. Although she continued to operate her stand after the Civil War, she reportedly could barely make a living.[4]

On Sunday afternoons, during the antebellum period, market women sold their goods around Congo Square "inside as well as out, in convenient localities."[5] Some walked with baskets balanced on their heads or trays connected to straps that hung from their necks, and some spread their wares on the ground. In later years, they set up along the edge of Congo Square and next to the fence surrounding the Square. Some market women used stands on wheels and tables screened with white cotton awnings that blocked the afternoon sun. Long streamers that hung from some of the awnings danced in the breeze.[6]

They arrayed their tables with pecan pies, roasted peanuts, cakes, molasses candy, coconuts and coconut candy, pralines made with pecans and with peanuts, popcorn, and croquettes. There was gingerbread called "estomac mulattre" or mulatto's belly—stage planks in American lingo. These were sometimes cut into the shape of men with the use of a mold. Calas, sometimes referred to as rice cakes, were also sold in the Square and at other locations in the city. Jessica Harris, noted food historian and cookbook author, found that the cala originated in Liberia, where it is traditionally sold by women street vendors. There, the rice fritter is called kala, which means rice in the Vai language of Liberia and its neighbor Sierra Leone.[7]

The market women also sold lemonade, a Louisiana rum called tafia, and pure, steaming coffee, the fragrance of which wafted through the air. The beverage of choice, however, was *la bierre du pays*, also called spruce beer and ginger beer. To make it, the women used fermented apples, ginger root, and mellow pines, and they plunged bottles of it in cold water at the Sunday gatherings. A *New Orleans Times* article presented yet another name for this beverage—Creole beer. The article stated that colored Creole women made this beer exclusively and held the recipe in secret. They sold it in the market at that time for five cents a glass or ten cents a bottle. The prohibition of strong liquors at the Sunday afternoon gatherings enabled the ginger beer to garner a significant profit. The beer was in such demand that it usually sold out before gunfire at sunset.[8]

Such a thriving economy existed at Congo Square because of the support of the enslaved who were hired-out and lived separately from their owners, free people of color, spectators of European descent, and enslaved Africans who earned wages on their free day. From the beginning of the colony, slaveholders frequently gave enslaved Africans plots of land on which to grow food for themselves. Some of the enslaved sold and traded the excess (with their owner's permission). The *Code Noir* further promulgated this practice by directing all inhabitants of the colony to refrain from work on Catholic holidays and Sundays.[9]

For many, this "free day" enabled them to acquire enough food and wages to simply supplement their survival. For others, it was an opportunity for business endeavors. Jean-Francois-Benjamin Dumont de Montigny, who came to the colony shortly after the founding of New Orleans, wrote about the early years. He recorded that:

> Most of the slaves clear grounds and cultivate them on their own account, raising cotton, tobacco, &c, which they sell. Some (owners) give their Negroes [sic] Saturday and Sunday to themselves, and during that time the master does not give them any food; they then work for other Frenchmen who have no slaves, and who pay them. Those who live in or near the capital generally turn their two hours at noon to account by making faggots (bundles of sticks) to sell in the city; others sell ashes, or fruits that are in season.[10]

A contemporary of Dumont's, Le Page du Pratz, in his *History of Louisiana*, admonished plantation owners to give the enslaved "waste ground" to cultivate for their own profit so that they may be able to dress a little better.[11] However, as historian James McGowan pointed out, the city's population of enslaved Africans in correspondence with the food shortage required that they work during their free time not only to clothe themselves but also to supplement their rations. Some Africans hired themselves out on their holidays, Saturday afternoons—which was later added as time off—and Sundays. During this time, with their slaveholder's permission, some of them marketed a variety of items including poultry, pigs, fish, and surplus rice and corn from their garden patches, driftwood found along the Mississippi River, moss—used to pad furniture and mattresses[12]—wild berries and nuts that they picked, and wild game that they hunted. The following song reveals some of their wares, many of which they found in nature:

Pitis sans popa,	Little ones without father,
pitis sans moman,	little ones without mother,
Qui ça 'ou' zut' fé pou' gagnein l'a'zanc,	What do you do to earn money?
No courri l'aut' bord pou' cercé patt c'at'	The river we cross for wild berries to search;
No tournein bayou pou' péc'é patassa;	We follow the bayou a-fishing for perch;
Et v'là comm ça no té fé nou' l'a'zanc.	And that's how we earn money.
Pitis sans popa,	Little ones without father,
pitis sans moman,	little ones without mother,
Qui ça 'ou' zut' fé pou' gagnein l'a'zanc,	What do you do to earn money?
No courri dans bois fouillé latanié	Palmetto we dig from the swamp's bristling stores
No vend' so racin' pou' fou'bi' planç'é;	And sell its stout root for scrubbing the floors;
Et v'là comm' ça no té fé nou' l'a'zanc.	And that's how we earn money.

Pitis sans popa,	Little ones without father,
pitis sans moman,	little ones without mother,
Qui ça 'ou' zut' fé pou' gagnein l'a'zanc,	What do you do to earn money?
Pou' fé di thé n'a fouillé sassaf'as,	The sassafras root we dig up; it makes tea;
Pou' fé di l'enc' no po'té grain' sougras;	For ink the ripe pokeberry clusters bring we;
Et v'là comm ça no té fé nou' l'a'zanc.	And that's how we earn money.
Pitis sans popa,	Little ones without father,
pitis sans moman,	little ones without mother,
Qui ça 'ou' zut' fé pou' gagnein l'a'zanc,	What do you do to earn money?
No courri dans bois ramassé cancos;	We go to the woods *cancos* berries to fetch,
Avé nou' la caze no trappé zozos;	And in our trap cages the nonpareils catch;
Et v'là comm ça no té fé nou' l'a'zanc,	And that's how we earn money.
Pitis sans popa,	Little ones without father,
pitis sans moman,	little ones without mother,
Qui ça 'ou' zut' fé pou' gagnein l'a'zanc,	What do you do to earn money?
No courri à soir c'ez Mom'selle Maroto,	At evening we visit Mom'selle Maroto,
Dans la rie St. Ann ou no té zoué loto;	In St. Ann's Street, to gamble awhile at keno;
Et v'là comm ça no té fé nou' l'a'zanc.	And that's how we earn money.

In *Creole Slave Songs*, Cable translated the second line of each stanza of this song as "how do you keep body and soul together," and the last line of each stanza as, "and that's how we keep soul and body together." Although he acknowledged that the Creole term, "l'a zanc" is derived from the French word, "l' argent," (la jarn) and means money, he failed to translate the sentence accurately.[13] Historian Gwendolyn Midlo Hall published the correct translation, printed here, in *Africans in Colonial Louisiana*. She explained, "Cable was under the false impression that the Creole slaves did not operate in a money economy and therefore changed the literal meaning of the song to reflect his mistaken impression."[14]

Enslaved people in English-ruled colonies commonly received Sundays as non-work days as well as plots of land to cultivate for themselves. However, one regulation set by Govenor Carondelet in the Louisiana Colony was not as common. In 1792, he declared that every Sunday should be exclusively for the enslaved without being compelled to work for his master unless he is paid. Under American rule, the Black Code of 1806 likewise entitled most of those enslaved to the fruit of their labors on Sunday at the rate of fifty cents per day if hired by their masters. Exceptions to this article of the Black Code existed for those serving in some domestic positions such as carriage drivers. While not all owners honored it, this law was in effect in 1845 when traveler S. Gleason Stevens encountered several enslaved men chopping logs to sell as firewood. The men informed Stevens that whatever they earned on Sundays was their own. Some of the enslaved also took advantage of their two hours for dinner, instituted by the Black Code, to earn money industriously and creatively.[15]

Some of the enslaved benefited economically when hired out by their owners. Sometimes the hired-out governed themselves and paid their owners for the privilege of hiring their labor. Historian Thomas Fiehrer concluded that "slaves habitually hired themselves out for other work and sometimes 'stole themselves' . . . as this was very often done on the owner's time." Eventually, some accumulated enough money to purchase their freedom.[16]

The economic status of many of the enslaved explained why, despite laws prohibiting them from visiting taverns, cabarets, balls, etc., newspaper articles and eyewitnesses reported that they continued to do so. Taverns that welcomed the money of the enslaved thrived and multiplied, and free people of color owned many of them. The prevalence and regularity of enslaved people at taverns was so great during the 1830s that an article published in *The Bee* in 1837 called for the city to regulate the large number of cabarets where "mobs and caucuses" of the enslaved assembled at night.[17]

The throngs of spectators contributed to the marketing that existed at the gatherings as did free people of color who attended. However, of significance is the fact that the foundation of the economic exchange consisted of enslaved merchants and customers. The economic status of the hired-out and the enslaved who hired themselves out on their day off along with the exchange and support among vendors influenced the financial success of the market women on Sunday afternoons. An 1864 *Picayune* article affirmed that the market women were "well patronized," and that the enslaved assembled in Congo Square by the hundreds to renew old loves, gather new friendships, talk over past affairs, make new plans, and "spend whatever surplus picayunes and dimes they may have acquired from their honest labors, or which came to them either as incentives or rewards for good conduct."[18]

As the marketing enterprises at the Sunday gatherings reflected African marketing culture, counterparts existed at events in other parts of the New World including the West Indies. Women merchants were on hand at social dances in Haiti, which were held Saturday nights, Sunday afternoons, or on holidays. Their goods included stocks of candies, liquor, tobacco, and other food items. The influence of this marketing culture continued to reveal itself in dance halls and at other social events in New Orleans. Some of the food items sold at Congo Square became a part of the city's food culture. W.P.A. interviews conducted in the 1940s reveal that Creole beer was a featured beverage in dance halls. In the early 1930s, Camille Nickerson wrote about the Creole dances that took place long after gatherings in Place Congo ended. She stated that calas, slices of Pains Patatte (sweet potato pudding), Creole pralines, and pineapple beer were among the food items served at those happy and enjoyable events.[19] Into the twenty-first century, the marketing of homemade pies and pralines remains a common practice at social aid and pleasure club parades, festivals in the city, and among home-based businesses.

Congo Square historical marker and circular patterned paving stones.

Chapter 9

CONCLUSION

Historians estimate that between nine and fifteen million Africans survived the wars of conquest, long marches to the coast of Africa, imprisonment in holding pens while awaiting ships of departure, and the ultimate horrors of the Middle Passage. This range represents the Africans who actually lived through those atrocities and who slave traders landed in the Americas. For those survivors, the opportunity to congregate in the ways of their traditions—to worship, sing, and dance—enabled them to fulfill cultural and religious dictates; but, not all of them received permission to do so. Out of fear of revolts and in an effort to promote Protestant faith, slaveholders in English territories of North America typically forbade Africans to assemble for traditional rituals or revelries in large numbers with those from different settings on a regular and long-term basis. Yet in the French, Spanish, and American-ruled, Catholic-based city of New Orleans, African descendants—enslaved and free—perpetuated African cultural practices and performance styles off and on in Congo Square for well over a century.

The significance of Congo Square's legacy and cultural impact is far-reaching. Its longevity as a gathering place for people of African descent extends from the early 1700s to within a decade of the city's occupation during the Civil War. These discontinuous Sunday events took place in the open and included African descendants irrespective of their legal status, labor category, or location in the city and surrounding areas. Eyewitness reports state that gatherers came by the hundreds and sometimes thousands. They came from diverse backgrounds with varying birthplaces, religious orientations, social adaptations, and musical influences. For them, Sunday afternoon was a holiday—a time for celebrating—and Congo Square back-of-town eventually became the only official gathering place for their festivities.

At Congo Square on Sunday afternoons, African descendants operated a thriving market, played African-derived rhythms and musical instruments, and engaged in African and African-based religious belief systems, songs, and dances. The performance styles and gatherings reflected those found in the parts of Africa and the French and Spanish West Indies, particularly Haiti and Cuba, where many of them had resided before landing in New Orleans. A study of Congo Square illustrates New Orleans' relationship with Caribbean countries and sheds light on its role in extending and perpetuating African music and dance in North America.

115

Over time, gatherers increasingly included creolized and European songs, dances, and musical instruments in the Sunday festivities. However, in spite of and alongside these styles, they continued to perpetuate African-derived practices fueled by a will to remember their traditional culture and heritage. The inevitable amalgamation of styles that African descendants performed in New Orleans, in and around Congo Square, influenced the evolution of new styles—New Orleans styles—African American styles. At the same time, onlookers like E. P. Christy, who were not of African heritage, adapted and modified those African performance styles and practices creating new styles—American music, theater, and dance styles. The careers of Christy, Gottschalk, and George Washington Cable provide examples of the national and international impact of the African-derived culture that emanated from Congo Square. While additional examples no doubt exist, they may never surface to provide due recognition of Congo Square's influence.

On the other hand, Congo Square's local influence in the form of African-derived performance practices and styles and in the cultural awareness and acknowledgement from Black New Orleanians is unquestionable. For many, Congo Square is more than a location. It represents African heritage and cultural consciousness. The name as well as the location is a reference for African cultural traditions in New Orleans; and Congo Square is mentioned in association with the beginning of jazz more than any other single site. Congo Square also played a peripheral roll in the emergence of rock n' roll music. During the 1950s black artists such as Fats Domino and Little Richard recorded their first hits—songs that captivated millions of white teenagers, a development that played a role in ending Jim Crow segregation—at Cosimo Matassa's J&M Record Shop, which was located directly across Rampart Street a few hundred feet from Congo Square.

Many local musicians have paid homage to Congo Square's cultural contribution and significance through their work. This recognition is evident in the numerous titles of musical compositions and recordings by New Orleans-based and native musicians along with their groups that bear the name Congo Square. These include Cyril Neville, the Neville Brothers, Donald Harrison, Los Hombres Calientes (Irvin Mayfield, Bill Summers, and Jason Marsalis), Percussion Inc., Terrence Blanchard, Bamboula 2000 (Luther Gray), and Wynton Marsalis. Internationally acclaimed, native New Orleans jazz musician Sidney Bechet, a bust of whom stands in the sculpture garden, claims in his autobiography, *Treat It Gentle*, that his grandfather was the legendary Bras Coupé, who played drums at the Sunday gatherings. One of the main stages, a market pavilion, a poster, and t-shirts at the annual New Orleans Jazz & Heritage Festival all bear the name Congo Square. Master drummer Luther Gray leads a percussion workshop that bears the name Congo Square, and the New Orleans Jazz and Heritage Foundation produces a festival that carries the name, The Congo Square Rhythms Festival. Such cultural recognition extends to dance as well. New Orleans' Kumbuka African Drum and Dance Collective, with Ausettua Amor Amenkum as founder and director, performs the Calinda as its signature dance. The Calinda was once a staple of the Sunday afternoon gatherings in Congo Square.

Such recognition also existed on the national level among musicians and cultural bearers who were not natives of New Orleans. Duke Ellington, percussionist Franciso Mora Catlett, and singer Teena Marie are just a few of the musicians who have included Congo Square in the titles of their work. Langston Hughes included Congo Square in some of his poems; and a market place in New York along with a theatrical company in Chicago also bear the name.

The African cultural practices—rhythmic cells, songs, dances, musical instruments, orchestration, styles of drumming, and marketing practices—perpetuated at Congo Square on Sunday afternoons during the eighteenth and nineteenth centuries clearly influenced the local New Orleans culture. The Mardi Gras Indian tradition of integrating drumming/rhythm, song and dance, the waving of handkerchiefs while dancing, and giving money to impressive dancers are among these. African-derived habanera rhythm and its derivatives, found in the most popular Creole slave songs and the correlating dances of Congo Square, are also found at the core of early New Orleans jazz compositions, second line or parade beat, jazz funeral music, and Mardi Gras Indians chants and rhythms. The dances witnessed in Congo Square continued in New Orleans and surrounding areas sometimes with modifications and sometimes retaining part of the original name. The Congo Dance, one of the most frequently performed dances in the Square, influenced derivatives in New Orleans including The Shake, Shake Babe, Twist, Shimmy, and Congo Grind, which Jelly Roll Morton also called the Hootchy-Ma-Cootch.

On the national level, at the root of the American performance form known as minstrelsy lay African cultural practices in the form of songs, dances, musical instruments, and instrumentation which are traceable to Congo Square. Musicians and cultural leaders around the world continue to be inspired by the legacy of the African descendants who gathered in their sacred space at Cogno Square. Like "African seeds planted in American soil," a phrase coined by writer Keith Medley, the cultural practices and performances that persisted in and around Congo Square bore fruit that continues to manifest itself and make New Orleans a distinct North American city.[1]

Children playing in the water spouts in Congo Square.

Chapter 10

Epilogue

The legacy left by the people of African descent who gathered in Congo Square beginning in the eighteenth century lives on. Three hundred years after colonizers brought the first Africans to the area and into the twenty-first century as well as the post-Katrina era, Congo Square continues to serve as a gathering place for all New Orleanians especially those of African heritage. Stones arranged in circular patterns reminiscent of the traditional dance formations adorn the ground once worn bare by dancing feet. Sculptures of legendary jazz musicians, as well as a native gospel singer, located within the Armstrong Park Complex stand as testaments to the Square's musical influence. African drum lessons, prayer vigils, political events, family gatherings, weddings, and community festivals that continue to take place there expand that influence and extend the Square's legacy as a place of political involvement, culture, religion, recreation, and revelry.

Over the years, various events and conditions precluded people of African descent from gathering or even entering the Square including the era of segregation. During those decades, the Square carried the official title of Beauregard Square although Congo Square remained a frequently used name. The location reclaimed the name of Congo Square during the early 1970s when city officials sought a meaningful use of the wasteland and blight that administrators created over a seventeen-year period when demolishing nine blocks of the Tremé neighborhood. Due to lack of funds, the initial plan to create a cultural center gave way to the decision to develop a park that honored native jazz musician Louis Armstrong, who had recently died. The plan, which aimed to provide a measure of redemption for the city as well as reflect Armstrong's cultural heritage and musical contribution, shed light on Congo Square and its premier influence on the beginning of jazz.

The revitalization of Congo Square included removing the large sculptured eagle that stood at the center of then Beauregard Square and replacing it with a circle of walk-in water spouts that sprang up from its floor, laying paving stones in circular designs on its floor, and adding park benches along with extensive landscaping. While this historic location regained its viability during this time, the New Orleans City Council never actually authorized the name change from Beauregard Square to Congo Square. As a result of the research for this book, city officials are currently in the process of drafting the ordinance that will officially recognize this location as Congo Square.

Now located within the Louis Armstrong Park Complex, with the Morris F. X. Jeff Municipal Auditorium at its immediate rear and the Mahalia Jackson Theater of Performing Arts in close proximity, Congo Square serves as a cultural center for citizens of all origins. During the last decades of the twentieth century and into the twenty-first century, numerous festivals found a home there including the first New Orleans Jazz & Heritage Festival, the first African Liberation Day Rally, Jazzin' in the Park, UMOJA, the Celebration of the African American Child, Rejoicin' in the Park, festivities hosted by All Congregations Together, the Juneteenth Celebration, the Congo Square International Festival, the Legacy Blues Festival, Caribbean Carnival Friends and Culture Festival, the White Buffalo Day Celebration, the Spanish Independence Day Festival, the Voodoo Festival, the Marcus Garvey Birthday Celebration, the Kwanzaa celebration, the New Orleans and South African Connection Culture and Music Festival, the Louisiana Black Heritage Festival, the "Satchmo" Louis Armstrong Festival, the International Middle Passage Rememberance Day—MAAFA Ceremony, some sessions of The Congo Square Symposium, the New Orleans Word Festival, and the Dr. Martin Luther King Day celebration.

Many of these events occurred annually in Congo Square before August 29, 2005, when Hurricane Katrina wreaked havoc on the city of New Orleans. During its aftermath, several breaches in the levee system that protected New Orleans from Lake Pontchartrain contributed to heavy and extensive flooding, which impacted eighty percent of the city. Rescue efforts and the security of New Orleans required full evacuation of the city's approximately 480,000 residents, sixty-seven percent of whom were African Americans. Some of them were descendants of those who once gathered in Congo Square during the eighteenth and nineteenth centuries. This drastic depopulation of the city, along with the extreme environmental, economic, social, and cultural changes that resulted from the hurricane's aftermath, created two distinct eras in the history of New Orleans—pre-and post-Katrina.

During the post-Katrina era, as New Orleanians returned to rebuild the city and their lives, Congo Square encountered a period of recovery as well. For over three years, city officials placed the Square along with the adjacent Louis Armstrong Park under lock and key only allowing entrance for pre-scheduled events. Notwithstanding, event planners pursued their location of preference. Organizations representing varied ethnic groups again sponsored political, spiritual, recreational, and cultural events in the Square indicating the continuation of Congo Square's legacy as a gathering place and the viability of the location as a cultural touchstone for all.

During the immediate post-Katrina era, Congo Square served as the starting point for the "Right to Return March" sponsored by the People's Hurricane Relief Fund. New Orleanians and supporters from across the country marched from the Square to city hall demanding proper conditions for safe return and a voice in the political rebuilding process. In 2006, the Square also served as the gathering place for the local march and rally held in conjunction with the nation-wide protest against the proposed immigration reform policy.

That same year, Congo Square hosted the unveiling of three "Bamboula" drums which drummer Luther Gray along with local artisans carved from a near-ly two-hundred-year old cypress log. Visual artist Douglas Redd embellished each drum with carvings of traditional symbols and designs to represent one of the three ethnic groups: the Bambara, Fon, and Kongo-Angola. Located in the Loui-siana State Museum in Baton Rouge and in New Orleans (Cabildo), the drums serve as interactive displays for museum visitors. That spring, native jazz musician Wynton Marsalis, the Lincoln Jazz Center Orchestra, and native Ghanaian Yacub Addy along with his percussion ensemble, Odadaa, presented the debut perfor-mance of their world premiere composition entitled "Congo Square" in Congo Square. In 2007, The New Orleans Jazz and Heritage Foundation presented the first annual Congo Square Rhythms Festival, which included a panel discussion, art exhibit, and a Sunday afternoon of music and dance in Congo Square.

In January 2009, city officials removed the locks from the gates of Louis Armstrong Park, including Congo Square, in conjunction with the reopening of the newly renovated and adjacently located Mahalia Jackson Theater of Perform-ing Arts, marking a milestone in the city's recovery. In the Spring of 2010, at the very end of his administration, Mayor C. Ray Nagin dedicated "The Roots of Music Cultural Sculpture Garden" in the Armstrong Park Complex and unveiled six new sculptures totaling eight within the area that showcase New Orleans' musical roots as well as some of its legendary musicians and indigenous musical styles. Shortly after this eventful occasion, city officials placed the entire complex, including Congo Square, under lock again, making it inaccessible to the public. Faulty construction of the concrete foundation during the sculpture garden's de-velopment resulted in lengthy and costly repairs, which fell into litigation and between the cracks of mayoral administrations.

The story of Congo Square continues to unfold, for it mirrors that of New Orleans and of the people who were essential to the city's survival, devel-opment, and cultural formation. The plot of land once designated as the only gathering place in the city for enslaved Africans emerged as the gathering place of preference for many New Orleanians, particularly those of African descent.

Prominent landmarks near Congo Square during the late nineteenth century included the turning basin of the Carondelet Canal (above) and the Orleans Parish Prison (below); both images are circa 1895.

Views of Congo Square by George François Mungier, circa 1890-95.

Views of "Beauregard Square" (Congo Square), circa 1917 (above); circa 1929 (below), note the upgraded lighting—this was just prior to the construction of the Municipal Auditorium. Also note the rail tracks in the top image; a mass rally was held nearby in May 1867 supporting efforts to desegregate the city's streetcars.

View of "Beauregard Square" (Congo Square), circa 1917; inset of "For White Only" sign.

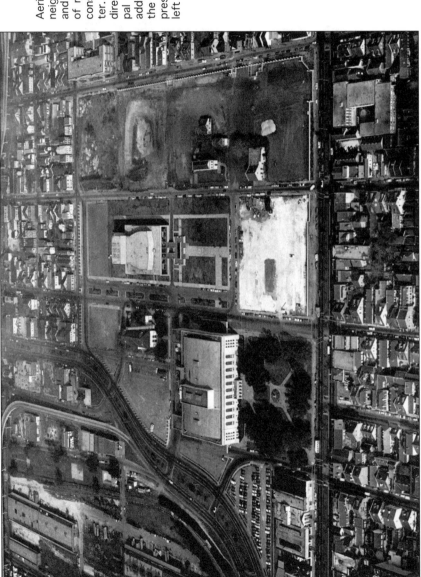

Aerial views of the Tremé neighborhood before (above) and after (left) the demolition of nine square blocks for the construction of a cultural center. Congo Square is located directly in front of the Municipal Auditorium. Note also the addition of the exit ramp from the newly constructed I-10 expressway (above and to the left of the auditorium).

Oscar "Papa" Celestin preforms with his band at the first New Orleans Jazz Club Jazz Festival, which was held at Congo Square in 1949 (above). Posters from the first New Orleans Jazz & Heritage Festival, which was also held at Congo Square in 1970 (below).

Images of Congo Square from the first New Orleans Jazz & Heritage Festival in 1970 (above and below). Since 2007 the New Orleans Jazz and Heritage Foundation has also produced the annual Congo Square Rhythms Festival.

In the wake of Hurricane Katrina during the Spring of 2006 internationally renown musician and New Orleans native Wynton Marsalis debuted his composition "Congo Square" before a wildly enthusiastic audience in New Orleans at Congo Square. Marsalis' composition featured numerous African musicians, including Ghanaian drum master Yacub Addy, who assisted in writing the piece. The composition was preformed in venues across the U.S and abroad.

"The Roots of Music Cultural Sculpture Garden": *Congo Square* by Adewale S. Adenle (above), *Mahalia Jackson* by Elizabeth Catlett (left), and *Sidney Bechet* by Abel Chretien (below).

"The Roots of Music Cultural Sculpture Garden":
Buddy Bolden by Kimberly Dummons (above),
French Opera House by Steve Kline (right), and
New Orleans Brass Band by Sheleen Jones-Adenle (below).

"The Roots of Music Cultural Sculpture Garden": *Louis Armstrong* by Elizabeth Catlett (left), and *Allison "Big Chief Tootie" Montana* by Sheleen Jones-Adenle (below).

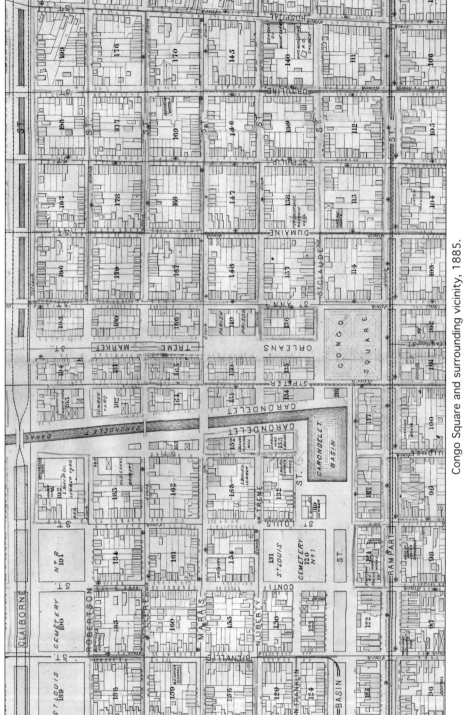

Congo Square and surrounding vicinity, 1885.

TIMELINE OF EVENTS
RELEVANT TO CONGO SQUARE

Pre-1699 Approximately thirty tribes of Native Americans inhabited the territory that became Louisiana.

Prehistoric Native American settlements existed near Bayou St. John and in the present French Quarter. Members of some of the nations celebrated their corn feasts in the vicinity of what is now Congo Square.

1699 **March 9:** A Native American guide showed Bienville and Iberville the Indian Portage along which they traveled to access the Mississippi River and the site where New Orleans would eventually rise.

Iberville founded a settlement for the colony at Biloxi.

1718 Bienville founded New Orleans.

1719 Two ships transporting 450 enslaved Africans arrived in the Louisiana colony and landed along the Mississippi Coast at Biloxi. Approximately twenty Africans previously resided in the colony.

1721 The headquarters of the Louisiana settlement was moved from the Mississippi Coast to New Orleans.

1724 Louisiana adopted the *Code Noir* (Black Code) from the slave codes of the French West Indies.

1726 Le Page du Pratz became overseer of the Company of the Indies Plantation in Algiers where he witnessed enslaved Africans dancing the Calinda and buying and selling goods on Sundays.[1] Those activities also occurred on other plantations.

1730 Officials constructed a fortification line along Dauphine Street to protect the city.[2]

1751 **February 18:** Police regulations: 1) forbade all inhabitants of the colony to permit the enslaved to assemble for any reason; 2) forbade free people of color to harbor the enslaved; 3) forbade tavern keepers to sell liquor to the enslaved; and 4) ordered all taverns closed on Sundays and holidays during worship and at nine o'clock every evening.[3]

1760   Officials redesigned and relocated the city's rear defense line and built a fort in the area now known as Congo Square.[4]

1762   **November 3:** Treaty of Fontainbleau provided for the cession of Louisiana to Spain.

1766   Louisiana became a Spanish colony.

1781   **January 19:** Because of the multitude of troops from the ships generated by the state of war between Spain and England and the large number of free and enslaved blacks in the city, the attorney general recommended that all kinds of masking and public dancing by blacks be prohibited during the carnival season.[5]

1786   Bishop Cyrillo de Barcelona, quoted by C. M. Chambon, who came to New Orleans around 1781, issued a pastoral letter in 1786 which denounced "Negroes who at the vespers hour, assembled in a green expanse called 'Place Congo' to dance the bamboula and perform the rites imported from Africa by the Yolofs, Foulahs, Bambarras Mandigoes, and other races."[6] The primary source has not been located.

        Governor Miro's *Bando de Buen Gobierno* (Proclamation of Good Government) prohibited labor on Sundays, ordered shops and business closed during the hours of Mass, forbade the tango or any other negro [*sic*] dance to occur before the end of Sunday evening services, and required women of mixed African heritage to comb their hair flat or cover it with a handkerchief [*tignon*].[7]

1792   Carondelet's Codes, issued by Governor Carondelet, proclaimed that Sundays belonged exclusively to the enslaved who should not be compelled to work for his master unless he is paid.[8]

1794   Officials reconstructed the city's rear fortification line and fort and named it Fort San Fernando (Ferdinand).[9]

1795   A city ordinance restricted amusement for the enslaved to Sundays.

        Workers unearthed coffins at the site of Fort St. Ferdinand when digging the Carondelet Canal.[10]

1796   James Pitot, whose writings on New Orleans cover from 1796 to 1802, wrote that hundreds of licensed taverns openly sell to the enslaved, and public balls, organized by the free people of color, admit the enslaved who elude their owner's surveillance.[11]

Workers completed digging the Carondelet Canal, a man-made waterway that extended Bayou St. John bringing it into the city, with the open space of Congo Square's uptown side serving as part of the basin's terminus.

1797   Francis Baily, a visitor to New Orleans, recorded his observance of the Sabbath:

> Scarcely had the priest pronounced the benediction, ere the violin or the fife struck up at the door, and the lower classes of people indulged themselves in all the gaiety and mirth of juvenile diversions. Singing, dancing, and all kinds of sports were seen in every street . . . the negroes [*sic*] . . . are suffered to refrain from work on that day. Here, arrayed in their best apparel, . . . they would meet together on the green, and spend the day in mirth and festivity.[12]

Governor Carondelet reinforced the city forts and placed Capt. Noel Carriere, a free man of color, in charge of Fort San Fernando.[13]

1798   Claude Tremé designed streets and sold subdivided property as house plots between 1798 and 1810 beginning the development of the Tremé neighborhood in the vicinity of Congo Square.

1799   **February 24:** Fortescue Cuming published the journals kept by a traveler to New Orleans and included accounts of a Sunday afternoon walk: "On our way to the upper fort we saw vast numbers of negro [*sic*] slaves, men, women, and children, assembled together on the levee, drumming, fifing, and dancing, in large rings." Around 4:00 p.m. the following Sunday, the traveler observed, "upwards of one hundred negroes [*sic*] of both sexes assembled on the levee, fiddling, dancing, and singing."[14]

April: The ballroom of Bernando Coquet and Jose Boniquet received its first official permit to hold dances for free people of color and the enslaved, who were admitted with permits from owners. These balls had been held prior to this permit; and although Coquet and Boniquet received this permit exclusively, small taverns offered similar dances.[15]

1800   Spain agreed to cede Louisiana back to France.

1802   Berquin-Duvallon, a traveler, observed "tippling houses" at every cross street, which were crowded day and night: "The low orders of every colour, white, yellow, and black, mix indiscriminately. . . . To dancing there is no end . . . here slaves, free people of colour of both sexes, and sailors in jacket and trowsers hopping and capering to the sound of a fiddle. . . ." The orchestra at a public carnival ball which he attended was "half a dozen gypsies, or else people of color," playing their fiddles.[16]

1803   **April 30:** The United States purchased Louisiana from France.

November 30: Spain transferred Louisiana to France.

December 20: France transferred Louisiana to the United States.

1804   John Watson, who resided in New Orleans from 1804 to 1805, witnessed enslaved Africans, "assemble in great masses on the levee on Sundays, and make themselves glad with song, dance, and merriment."[17]

City officials demolished Fort Ferdinand.[18]

1808   While on a Sunday afternoon walk, Christian Schultz witnessed:

> in the rear of the town . . . the sight of twenty different dancing groups of . . . Africans, collected together to perform their *worship* after the manner of their country. They have their own national music, consisting for the most part of a long kind of narrow drum of various sizes, from two to eight feet in length, three or four of which make a band. The principal dancers or leaders are dressed in a variety of wild and savage fashions, always ornamented with a number of the tails of the smaller wild beasts. . . . These amusements continue until sunset, when one or two of the city patrols show themselves with their cutlasses, and the crowds immediately disperse.[19]

May 18: The police code of 1808 restricted the enslaved from attending public balls of free people of color and forbad Africans and free people of color from assembling at nights except for funerals of their relatives.[20]

1809   Approximately 3,226 enslaved Africans, 3,201 free people of color, and 2,731 whites entered New Orleans from Cuba as Haitian refugees.[21]

1810   **May 8:** City Council members ordered the police and watchmen to patrol the streets, public squares, and levees at dusk and arrest vagrants and runaways as well as disperse all gatherings of enslaved people especially in the meat market and at the doors of cabarets.

May 16: The mayor referred to the place for the sports and dances of the enslaved in a city council discussion about the location of Charity Hospital, on or near Basin Street, destroyed by fire in 1809.[22]

June 23: Officials executed a man of African descent in Congo Square, the first such case in the city under the Black Code as adopted by the Americans.[23]

The city purchased property from Claude Tremé, annexed it, and sold it as house plots, furthering the development of the Tremé neighborhood in the vicinity of Congo Square.

1811   **January 8:** Charles, the Louisiana-born enslaved property of Deslondes, and others, led over five hundred enslaved Africans in a revolt during which they marched toward New Orleans from nearby St. Charles Parish.[24]

January 9: *New Orleans Montiteur De Louisiana* reports: "All cabarets in the city and suburbs of New Orleans are ordered to be immediately closed, and no male Negro is to be permitted to pass the streets after 6 o'clock."[25]

January 16: Officials passed the Ordinances of 1811, which forbade the enslaved to sleep in a house other than that of his owner, rent a house, assemble except for pre-approved funerals, or dances and sports, and restricted their meetings for the recreational purposes to Sundays, until sundown, at places designated by the mayor.[26]

January: Officials executed a man of African descent named Gilbert, who was one of the lieutenants in the 1811 Slave Revolt, at Congo Square.[27]

1812   **February 15:** A house ball given for enslaved persons and for which invitations were sent continued until three or four o'clock in the morning despite two visits made by patrols around ten o'clock and midnight when they arrested sixteen of the dancers. Some dancers fled to a nearby residence where another such ball was underway. Dancers who attended arrived from different parts of the city including the area of Bayou Road. The mayor, in his response, stated that the ordinance of January 16, 1811, needed to be amended.[28]

April 30: Louisiana gained statehood.

November 2: The City Council forbade the previously tolerated games and dances of the enslaved stating that those who shall be gathered together on Sunday or any other day of the week for purposes other than a funeral will be arrested by the police, constables, watchmen, or any other white person and taken to jail to receive fifteen to thirty lashes.[29]

November 3: In response to the council's ban on enslaved Africans gathering and dancing on Sundays and holidays, Mayor Girod agreed that dancing should not take place in scattered areas of the city. However, he advocated for gatherings to continue in customary places under public notice and police watch. The mayor felt that seldom in the midst of entertainment will the enslaved find the quietness, surrounding, and composure necessary to plant a conspiracy. He wrote that:

> all necessary precautions must be taken to protect the public, but, on the other hand, we cannot take heed of any measure which may prove a betrayal of our uneasiness and fear . . . would it not be a form of injustice to deprive them of this pleasure just at a time when the balls for the white and free people of color are about to be given? At least such is my opinion and I believe that a suppression of the balls on the one hand and a display of favoritism on the other, are apt to engender a desire for complaint and a feeling of discontent.

> Therefore, I should be pleased if you will have your resolution so amended as not to interfere with the dances when held at the customary places, or which you may designate as such both as regards to the City and the Faubourgs, provided, of course, they be watched by a few additional men from the city police, with orders that they have those dances stopped if they became too boisterous or too riotous.[30]

1813   **January 14:** Mayor Girod wrote to the council regarding its opinion that the balls to which he had already addressed should be suppressed at once.

> Let us attempt, at least in the interest of harmony and for maintenance of good morals, to have them discontinued gradually by measures of such a precautionary nature that no one might attribute it to any thing but a desire to enforce the public peace. With that aim in

view, I suggest that you henceforth declare the license
to be $25.00; in the case of those who shall give the
balls without the Mayor's permission a fine of $50.00
is to be charged and a fine of $100.00 inflicted against
those same persons who would be responsible for quar-
rels, arguments, or fights. This will afford us a double
advantage in accomplishing our purpose and likewise
overcome disorder without causing any murmur or
complaint from the public. This has reference only to
the balls given by white men and colored women—be
they public or given under the misleading guise of social or subscription balls. As regard to the balls given by
colored people among themselves, I recommend that
you fix the license at $10.00 and for ball given by ne-
groes [*sic*] a license of $5.00.[31]

January 16: Mayor Girod wrote to the council, "I would like you to look
into the matter of permitting the negroes [*sic*] to give dances. . . . I think
a permit can and should be issued to them, to apply to three different
locations which could be assigned to them: namely, Faubourg Ste. Marie,
near Fort St. Ferdinand, and Faubourg Marigny. I should like to have this
permit granted to them tomorrow."[32]

December 30: Mayor Girod appealed to the city council to repeal the
resolution that forbade enslaved people to gather and dance on Sundays
stating that:

when they are dancing, they cannot conspire against
us. . . . If, in denying them every form of amusement
and dissipation, you took away from them all means
of meeting, I might refrain from offering opposition
to your resolution, but it does not produce that effect.
. . . The slaves see each other and have social contacts
with the same facility as heretofore, and you shall never
stop them, no matter what you may do. . . . If it be true
that you can not stop them from meeting, in spite of
your orders, stop enforcing these orders which, to say
the least are useless, for if you take away from them the
privilege of meeting to dance, you should also fear that
they meet to form a conspiracy, if they wish, since they
can. . . . One fact not to be overlooked and which proves
the contradiction of the measure of which I have just
spoken with that which I propose, is the order against
dances given by slaves and the public authorization of

the balls of white men and women of color. In all the colonies the first were allowed for political reasons, the others forbidden as being a violation of good morals. However, you must recall that when I proposed to stop these balls one of the members of the Council arose and spoke at length against this proposal, which he had the temerity to characterize as despotic and tyrannic. But the only tyranny I find is, I repeat, to deprive the slaves of a privilege which they enjoyed under all other governments of the colonies, and which sound judgment would have them granted.[33]

1814   **January 8:** Mayor Girod called the council's attention to a New Year's dance given at night for enslaved persons, which openly violated their ordinance regarding such activity. The mayor added that if complaints have risen against the enslaved dancing from three o'clock in the afternoon to sunset in public, what will they say about a nocturnal gathering in an isolated location?[34]

1815   **January 8:** Jordan B. Noble, fourteen years old and enslaved, served as Andrew Jackson's drummer during the Battle of New Orleans.

March 22: Referring to inquiries made by a number of citizens regarding the matter, Mayor Girod requested the city council to repeal the ordinance that prohibited dancing and other entertainment for those enslaved.[35]

April 2: The mayor agreed to frequently send a policeman and one or more watchmen to disperse the enslaved people who gathered all hours of the day at the public square which was previously Fort St. Louis as well as the neighboring streets.[36]

July 23: City officials resolved to clear and level the public square where Fort St. Louis formerly stood.[37]

1816   **April 16:** Cayetano Mariotini opened Cayetano's Circus in Circus Square. Referred to in folklore as Congo Circus, it came from Havana, and according to sources had previously set up in New Orleans.[38]

1817   **April 11:** J. G. Flugel, a traveler to New Orleans, witnessed a Negro dance in Faubourg Ste. Marie around four o'clock on Sunday:

I saw today among the crowd Gildemeister of Bremen, clerk or partner of Teetzmann. He told me that three

of the negroes [*sic*] in the group closest to us were formerly kings or chiefs in Congo. I perceive in them a
more genteel address. They are richly ornamented and
dance extremely well. As I was looking on a sailor told
me that a few months ago he had come from Havana
where he had sailed with some slaves from the coast of
Guinea. Among them was the son of Pepin, a King of
Congo, who had been recommended to a merchant-
house, Fernandez Fernando of Havana, who were [*sic*]
to expedite him to Port au Prince, St. Domingo, where
he now lives.[39]

May 15–June 13: Traveler Johann Buechler observed enslaved Africans
dancing behind the city on Sundays starting at four o'clock in the evening
at large open places at different locations. Some of the dancers were
practically naked. Buechler later traveled to Cuba where he witnessed
the same kind of dancing every Sunday after supper. In the countryside,
many of the dancers did not have on clothing. In the city of Havana,
they danced inside a garden and were dressed, at least those he could
see.[40]

October 15: Ordinances passed by the City Council: 1) forbade the
enslaved to assemble for any purpose except worship (in a church or
temple, at designated hours), funerals, sports, and dancing; 2) restricted
dancing and other merriment of the enslaved to Sunday afternoons ending at sunset, at one public place appointed by the mayor; 3) forbade any
white person or free person of color to admit the enslaved to balls; and
4) prohibited the enslaved from whooping, hallowing, or singing aloud
an indecent song.[41]

1818   **June:** Estwick Evans, a traveler to New Orleans, recorded, "the Sabbath is devoted to recreation. On this day the negroes [*sic*] assemble and
amuse themselves and spectators by dancing."[42]

        August 1: Property owners near the Carondelet Canal drew up a petition
asking for the immediate demolition of the Circus.[43]

1819   Henry Cogswell Knight (Arthur Singleton), a traveler to the city, wrote:
"On Sabbath evening, the African slaves meet on the green,[44] by the
swamp, and rock the city with their Congo dances."[45]

        February 21: Benjamin Latrobe, architect and engineer, described Sun-
day afternoon activities in Congo Square:

My accidentally stumbling upon the assembly of Negroes which I am told every Sunday afternoon meets
on the common in the rear of the city. . . . Approach-
ing the common I heard a most extraordinary noise,
which I supposed to proceed from some horse Mill, the
horses trampling on a wooden floor. I found however
on emerging from the houses, onto the common, that it
proceeded from a crowd of 5 or 600 persons assembled
in an open space or public square. I went to the spot and
crowded near enough to see the performance. All those
who were engaged in the business seemed to be *blacks*. I
did not observe a dozen yellow faces [mulattoes]. They
were formed into circular groups in the midst of four
of which, which I examined (but there were more of
them) was a ring, the largest not 10 feet in diameter.
In the first were two women dancing. They held each
a coarse handkerchief extended by the corners in their
hands, and *set* to each other in a miserably dull and slow
figure, hardly moving their feet or bodies. The music
consisted of two drums and a stringed instrument. An
old man sat astride of a cylindrical drum about a foot in
diameter, and beat it with incredible quickness with the
edge of his hand and fingers. The other drum was an
open staved thing held between the knees and beaten
in the same manner. They made an incredible noise.
The most curious instrument however was a stringed
instrument which no doubt was imported from Africa.
On the top of the finger board was the rude figure of
a man in a sitting posture, and two pegs behind him to
which the strings were fastened. The body was a Calabash. It was played upon by a very little old man, apparently 80 or 90 years old.

The women squalled out a burthen to the playing, at
intervals, consisting of two notes, as the Negroes working in our cities respond to the song of their leader.
Most of the circles contained the same sort of dancers. One was larger, in which a ring of a dozen women
walked, by way of dancing, round the music in the center. But the instruments were of different construction.
One, which from the color of the wood seemed new,
consisted of a block cut into something of the form
of a cricket bat with a long and deep mortise down
the Center. This thing made a considerable noise, being
beaten lustily on the side by a short stick. In the same

orchestra was a square drum looking like a stool, which made an abominably loud noise: also a calabash with a round hole in it, the hole studded with brass nails which was beaten by a woman with two short sticks.

A man sung an uncouth song to the dancing which I suppose was in some African language, for it was not French, and women screamed a detestable burthen on one single note. The allowed amusements of Sunday, have, it seems, perpetuated here, those of Africa among its in habitants. . . . Continuing my walk about a mile along the canal, and returning after Sunset near the same spot, the noise was still heard. There was not the least disorder among the crowd, nor do I learn, on enquiry, that these weekly meeting of the Negroes have ever produced any mischief.[46]

1820   City officials planted young sycamore and elm trees in Circus Square, constructed sidewalks, and enclosed the area with wooden railings and two turnstile gates for circuses that located there.[47]

February 18 Thomas Nuttall, a traveler, witnessed a Sunday market which he said,

> . . . at this season . . . appeared to be tolerably well supplied, though singularly managed, and that entirely by negro [*sic*] slaves, who spread out the different articles in petty quantities, like the arrangement of an apple stall, charging, however, at the rate of about 100 per cent for the trouble. Superfine flower [*sic*] now sold at the low rate of six dollars per barrel; bacon and cheese at 10 cents the pound, salt butter at 25 cents; sugar at seven dollars per cwt.; coffee 25 to 30 dollars per cwt,; rice seven dollars per cwt. Fresh beef, however, and that by no means good, sold at 25 cents per pound. As in the West Indies, the principal market appears to be on Sunday in the forenoon. In the afternoon the negroes [*sic*] assemble in the suburbs of the city,[48] and amuse themselves by dancing. When thus assembled by the common friendship, if they have any reflection, they must be convinced of the efficient force which they posses to emancipate themselves; they are, however, strictly watched by the police, and the sole object of their meeting appears to be amusement.[49]

August 16: Police arrested several people (enslaved, white, and free people of color) in the suburb Tremé at a house where people repaired at night to practice idolatrous rites, dance, and carouse.[50]

1821   Issac Holmes observed a performance of the Congo dance while traveling in Louisiana.[51]

1822   The 1822 and 1823 editions of Norman Paxton's *New Orleans Register & Directory* recorded that Congo Square was "very noted on account of its being the place where the Congo and other negroes [*sic*] dance, carouse, and debauch on the Sabbath."[52]

John Lay, a Buffalo merchant, recorded that "on a Sunday, he witnessed a Congo dance attended by 5,000 people and at a theater, saw 'The Battle of Chippewa' enacted."[53]

Missionary Timothy Flint, who arrived in New Orleans toward the end of 1822, witnessed hundreds of African descendants perform the great Congo dance during a street procession.

1823   Welcome Arnold Green, a traveler, wrote about the Sabbath in New Orleans:

> A majority of the retail stores are kept open and during the morning a space around the market is much more alive, with a host of the slave and coloured population exhibiting a variety of articles for sale, than any other day in the week.
>
> This and their assembling on a back square of the city for the purpose of joining in what they term their Congo dances in the afternoon is excusable, or more so in those who have no other day they can consider their own for business or amusement. In short, though there is little appearance of a northern Sabbath.[54]

1829   **March 30:** A city council ordinance prohibited the exposure or lodging of any enslaved person in the city squares to sell them or hire them out. The city squares addressed included those within Canal, Rampart, Esplanade, and Levee streets. Offenders of the ordinance would receive a fine; however, the resolution excluded the sale of enslaved persons made by public officers of the state.[55]

Theodore Pavie witnessed versions of the Juba and the Congo dances while visiting the Natchitoches area near the Ouachita River in 1829–30.[56]

1830   Officials moved the signal gun/cannon, which fired nightly at 9:00 p.m. to indicate the curfew for the enslaved, from Place d'Armes to Congo Square.[57]

March: Traveler James Stuart wrote, ". . . on one of the last days of March, while I was at New Orleans a slave was hung for some trifling offense, but none of the newspapers took the slightest notice of the execution."[58] During this time, executions took place at Congo Square.

1831   **May–June:** Traveler P. Forest reported that on Sundays, blacks gathered in large numbers and distinct groups (indicated by flags) in *The Camp*, a huge green field on the bank of a lake about three leagues from New Orleans. Indian families that settled nearby joined the music, songs, dance, and festivities.[59]

September 24: Those engaged in cock fighting were obliged to go to the Congo ground.[60]

1832   **April 18:** The First Municipal Council authorized the use of Congo Square to exhibit pleasure carriages on railroads.[61]

1833   **February 19:** The enslaved attend balls with their masters.[62]

June 13: In a letter dated Georgetown, D.C., 1833, a traveler to New Orleans wrote:

> The negroes [*sic*] here are better off than any I have seen in the Southern States. They dress on the Sabbath like princes. Many of them, slaves as they are, are the first dandies in the city—in the best of broadcloth and the finest of hats. Such buy their time, for six or seven dollars a week—and not unfrequently earn a dollar before breakfast. . . . They feel more independent. They are more their own masters. Remember, I speak not of slavery in the city . . . .[63]

1834   James Creecy, during a visit to New Orleans, recorded a detailed scene of Congo Square:

> North of Rampart Street, about its center is the celebrated Congo Square, well enclosed containing five or six or perhaps more acres, well shaded, with grav-

eled walks and beautiful grass plats, devoted on Sunday afternoons to negro [*sic*] dances and amusements. The Creoles of Louisiana—Spanish, French and negroes [*sic*]—are Catholics, with but few exceptions. . . . The holy mass is not neglected . . . but the afternoons and evenings of the Lord's day are spent in amusements, fun, and frolic of every description—always with an eye to much sport for a little expense.

The "haut ton" attend opera, theaters, masquerades, &c. The quadroons have their dashing fancy balls, dances, &c.; and the lower order of colored people and negroes [*sic*], bond and free, assemble in great numbers in Congo Square, on every Sunday afternoon in good weather, to enjoy themselves in their own peculiar manner. Groups of fifties and hundreds may be seen in different sections of the square, with banjos, tom-toms, violins, jawbones, triangle, and various other instruments. . . . The dancers are most fancifully dressed with fringes, ribbons, little bells, and shells, and balls, jingling and flirting about the performer's legs and arms, who sing a second or counter to the music most sweetly. . . . Young and old join in the sport and dances. One will continue the rapid *jig* till nature is exhausted; then a fresh disciple leaps before him or her and "cuts out" the fatigued one, who sinks down gracefully on the grass, out of the way, and is fanned by an associate with one hand, while water or refreshments are tendered by the other.

When a dancer or danseuse surpasses expectation, or is particularly brilliant in the execution of "flings" and "flourishings" of limb and body, shouts, huzzas, and clapping of hands follow, and numerous picallions are thrown in the ring to the performers by (strange) spectators. . . . . The gaieties continue till sunset; and at the "gun-fire" the whole crowd disperse, disappear . . . until the next blessed Dimanche.[64]

1835   Joseph Holt Ingraham recorded a visit to the city:

Leaving the basin, we passed a treeless green, which we were informed by a passer-by, was dignified by the classical appellation of "Congo Square." Here our obliging informant gave us to understand, the coloured "ladies and gentlemen" are accustomed to assemble on gala and saints days, and to the time of outlandish music, dance, not the Romaika, alas! But the "Fandango;" . . . As the Congoese *elite* had not yet left their kitchens, we, of course, had not the pleasure of seeing them move in the mystic dance . . . to the dulcet melody of the Congo banjo.[65]

Henry Didimus who traveled to the city during the winter of 1835–36 wrote that the Sabbath in New Orleans is the noisiest day of the week. A drum and fife suddenly stuck up "Yankee Doodle" played by two black men in full regimentals performing to an audience of their own colour.[66]

March 21: The Mayor authorized Congo Square to be enclosed with an iron fence.[67]

August 5: Although the plan never developed, the Municipal Council offered Congo Square to the state of Louisiana to build a capitol and court house.[68]

November 30: The city council was requested to support the mayor and regulate the mask balls of colored women.[69]

1836 **February 17:** The municipal council resolved to construct an iron fence around Congo Square.[70]

New Orleans was divided into three municipalities under one mayor with Congo Square located in the First Municipality.

1837 **May 17:** The First Municipal Council granted Congo Square to the Orleans Theater Company for erecting a theater thereon.[71]

August 28: First Municipal Council member "Wiltz, with permission of the council, presented a resolution authorizing free Negroes and slaves to give balls on Circus Square (Congo Square) from 12'o clock until sun set under surveillance of the police."[72]

November 8: The city was asked to regulate the large number of cabarets where "mobs and caucuses" of enslaved Africans gather.[73]

1839 **January 1:** "Slaves' Ball Room in Suzette Street":

Almost every Saturday night there is a ball held by slaves in the above street, near Levee St. and kept up until daylight on Sunday morning. The noise and the disturbance is very disagreeable to the citizens of that neighborhood, although it may be very profitable to the proprietors. Perhaps if there were a few more ball rooms of the above description opened with a few of the northern abolitionists as managers they might be very successful, as the slave gentry might have an opportunity of stealing, and carrying on their villainy on a more extensive scale.[74]

November 5: Large numbers of enslaved Africans congregated in cabarets at night.[75]

1840 **September 24:** Cabaret owners persist in selling liquor to the enslaved.[76]

November 19: "Negro Audacity"—Police found a suspect on the levee engaged in a Congo dance along with thirty African descendants."[77]

1841 **January 12:** "Leading off the Dancers"—thirty-four enslaved persons were arrested for unlawful assembly at a "negro [*sic*] ball" that was being held at 2:30 Sunday morning at a house in the Second Municipality:

> In one part of the room a cotillion was going on, and in a corner a fellow was giving a regular old Virginia "break down" on his own account. A genteel looking (man), with Devonshire brown mustachios, was acting as master of ceremonies, and the music consisted of a clarinet, three fiddles, two tambourines, and a bass drum. In the refreshment room, an elderly (man) was strumming a sickly banjo, to which (another) was dancing "Jim Along Josey."[78]

July 22: "Assemblages of Slaves"—two cabaret owners, in separate cases, received fines for allowing the enslaved to congregate on their premises.[79]

August 19: "Giving Certificate of Freedom to Slave"—officials arrested James Charlott for giving a free pass to an enslaved person.[80]

1843 **January 2:** An ordinance prohibited strolling musicians, organ players, and other musicians from practicing their trade without a mayor's permit.[81]

January 9: An ordinance authorized the mayor to give licenses for the

enslaved to hold balls (dances) on a special day only, as indicated on licenses.

September 23: *Daily Picayune* reports:

> The natives of China are located in the neighborhood
> of Congo Square, where you may see, any day that the
> wind is high enough, Hong-Kong, Choo-Loo, Pom-
> Poo, and several other celestials, flying pretty, parti-
> colored paper kites.[82]

October 18: "The Congo Dance":

> We (the reporters) never saw this dance until last Sun-
> day. . . . This ball—this black ball, was a public one, and
> was held in the yard of a house in the Third Munici-
> pality. The company was numerous and ranged from
> ebony black to quarteroon yellow. The orchestra was
> full . . . a long neck banjo, the head of which was orna-
> mented with a bunch of sooty parti-colored ribbands
> . . . another musician beat the jawbones of an ass with
> a rusty key . . . a third had the end of a butter firkin,
> covered with a tightly drawn sheep skin—a kind of à
> la petit tambour, on which he kept time with his digits,
> and the fourth beat most vehemently an old headless
> cask that lay on its side, ballasted with iron nails. To
> these . . . efforts were given a general chorus.
>
> The dancers were three, (one male and two females) . . .
> the latter danced with an air of . . . modesty . . . their
> male partner had on a pair of leather knee caps from
> which were suspended . . . metal nails, which made a
> jingling noise that timed with his music. He indulged in
> sundry extra shines which ministered to his own self-
> esteem and to the gratification of the audience. . . . Such
> is a negro [*sic*] Congo dance in New Orleans.[83]

December 10: "Congo Square"—We yesterday noticed that this old
common, so long let free to loafers and cattle, is being put in chains. Do
the authorities fear that it would go away?[84]

A resolution allowed free people of color to reside in the First Municipality.

1844   July 15: "Dancing Under Difficulty"—on Sunday afternoon as early as four o'clock the writer observed a grand dress black ball in the "full tide of successful operation" near Lake Pontchartrain. The writer added that the difficult conditions of a ninety-six degree temperature and little circulation in the dance room, showed a devotion to the dance.[85]

1845   Benjamin Moore Norman's *New Orleans & Environs* referred to Congo Park as the place where Negroes in olden times customarily met.[86]

April 28: First Municipal Council restored dancing (sometimes referred to as balls) for the enslaved in Congo Square from May 1 to August 21, from 4:00 to 6:30 p.m. with written consent from owners and police supervision. Dances must not have been offensive to public decency.[87]

June 24: "Scenes in Congo Square – Regular Ethiopian Break Down":

> Thousands of Africans and their descendents congregated in and about Congo Square on Sunday afternoon where they played instruments of their own contrivance and danced upon the green sward. Such songs as *Hey Jim Along* and *Get Along Home You Yallow Gals* were heard.[88]

July 15: "Sunday Rioting":

> Police and owners are requested to check the licentious and riotous conduct of the enslaved especially on Sundays, particularly in the First Municipality—without curtailing their innocent enjoyments upon that day. "You will meet hundreds on a Sunday afternoon, clad in garments more costly than their masters can afford to wear, promenading with loaded sticks and bludgeons in their hands and even with pistols and dirks about their persons."[89]

1840s   James Thomas, African descendant, visited "Congo Green" while in New Orleans:

> In the forties I used to go on Sunday to see the blacks dance. They were given a (what is now a park) large Square called Congo green where they indulged in dancing with music made by thumping on the head of a barrel with skin stretched over it. The performer would thump on it and carry on a chant. Another would beat the sides with two cobs or sticks. The dancers used to wear pieces of tin or some substitute on their legs to

make a sort of jingle. I judged it was African music.
The people looked as they, most of them, were the imported article.[90]

City officials planted more sycamore trees in the square.

1846   **February 23:** The masquerade on Mardi Gras Day dispersed at Circus
Square.[91]

March 22: "Congo Square – The Master of Ceremonies":

Congo Square festivities including the "beau ideal" of a
master of ceremonies were described:

In various parts of the square a number of male and female Negroes assemble, dressed in their holiday clothes,
with the very gayest bandana handkerchiefs upon the
head of the females, and, accompanied by the thump-
ing of a banjo or drum, or the squealing of a greasy
cremona, perform . . . African dances.[92]

During 1846 and 1847, A. Oakey Hall wrote the majority of the sketches
about New Orleans that are found in *The Manhattaner in New Orleans*.
Included is a description of Circus Street (Rampart Street), the scraggy
trees, and the park (Congo Square) with primitive posts and consumptive
grass:

The stranger asks is it hallowed ground? so solemnly
still is everything about it. . . . It is not hallowed ground;
and you will believe this well, if you come on Sunday afternoon and witness crowds of happy servants shaking
the swampy soil with dancing and jumping, or fright-
ening, with the noise of clattering bones, and barrel-
headed drumming. . . . So too, if you will come when
a huge tent covers the corner of it, and the noise of
four trombones, and one drum of astounding power
and endurance, that blow and thump all the beauty out
of the Star-spangled Banner. . . .[93]

April 27: "Unlawful Assemblage of Slaves"—police arrested "a batch"
of enslaved people at a cabaret on the corner of Bienville and Dauphine.
Shortly after, they arrested another group in a cabaret on the corner of
Customhouse and Bourbon. Each enslaved person received five lashes
and each cabaret owner received a $50 fine.[94]

June 12: "Unlawful Assembly"—police arrested dozens of enslaved and free people of color in a building on the Bayou Road where they often assembled for prayer and preaching.[95]

1847   **March 1:** The First Municipal Council granted permission for a pavilion to be built in the square.[96]

1848   **December 11:** The First Municipal Council granted permission to hold circus performances in the square.[97]

December 31: "Public Squares":

> . . . look at Congo Square or Circus Place . . . how neglected!—the walks are overgrow—the sod worn into holes and bare in large patches—the fine old trees filled with dead branches, that rattle mournfully in the wind, as if chiding the city fathers for so neglecting those under whose branches they have sported in youth. The negroes [*sic*] are the only ones who patronize it, and for them the old blue walls of the parish prison, seen so plainly, with the innumerable windows, queer gables and oddly constructed towers, have no terrors—no, though they have assembled there full many a time, crowded into Orleans street [*sic*] too, in front of the old prison, to see human beings deprived of their existence by the rope. There the spot, that niche between the two large buildings, where many a victim of the hangman has been thrust forth and struggled in the choking embraces of death all countered for the grave in felon's shroud, in the presence of gaping thousands. It may be these scenes have caused Congo Square to be deserted; but we imagine not—such associations would only make the place more popular. Circuses exhibit here, and under a canvas awning spangle bedecked men and lightly costumed women perform strange antics on horseback, while the clown drives care away with quips and quiddities and rare old jokes whose age should cause more solemn reception—for age should be venerated and respected, not laughed at.[98]

1849   **January 15, March 19, April 30:** The First Municipal Council granted permission to use Congo Square for circus performances.[99]

1850   **July 31:** "Unlawful Assemblies"—for the second time this week, police arrested a group of enslaved people at a house on Burgundy Street kept by Joseph English. "Voudou"—police arrested eleven free women of color at a house on Burgundy Street for engaging in the rites of Voudou and fined them each $20 or a month in prison.[100]

October 15: "The Place d'Armes & Its Vicinity"—plans to improve the Place d'Armes (in front of the Cabildo, Cathedral and Presbytere) call for an ordinance to transfer the military drills to Congo Square. A request is also made to reduce the sidewalks on two sides of Congo Square from twelve to nine feet in order to widen St. Peter and St. Ann streets.[101]

November 11: The First Municipal Council ordered the wrought iron fence and gates, along with the cannon, located at the original Place d'Armes to be transferred to Congo Square, which was appropriated for salutes, the evening gun, and military drills on Sundays.[102]

1851   **January 25:** "The First Municipal council renamed the Place de'Armes, Jackson Square, and designated Congo Square as the new Place d'Armes where the militia would drill on Sundays."[103]

February 1: "Globe Ball Room"—the public was informed of the opening of the Globe Ball Room on Saturday, February 19 at the corner of St. Peter and St. Claude within Congo Square.[104]

July 20: "Voudou Again"—police arrested a free man of color for engaging in Voudou practices at a house on Burgundy near Conti.[105]

July 25: "Voudou"—police arrested about a dozen women and charged them with practicing Voudou.[106]

July 26: "The Voudou People"—police arrested a dozen women (one enslaved and eleven free) in a house on Burgundy Street for practicing Voudou. The Recorder fined each one ten dollars.[107]

1852   The city returned to one governing body upon resolving the three municipalities.

November 20: New Orleans City Ordinance 395 C.C. changes the former Circus Street to Rampart Street.

1853   **February 16:** The Board of Assistant Aldermen passed a resolution granting the site of Place d'Armes (Congo Square) for erection of a capitol building.[108]

February 22: "Soirée African"—police arrested seventy-two enslaved

Blacks at a carnival party Sunday night on Terspichore Street. Those arrested were to either receive fifteen stripes or pay a third of fifteen dollars.[109]

March 5: City Council donated Congo Square or Place d'Armes to the state for the State House or Capitol.[110]

June 15: "Negro Insurrection Suppressed!"—police identified six or eight females with the insurrectionary movement.[111]

July 4: Fourth of July celebration held in Place d'Armes, formerly Congo Square, included fireworks and balloon ascensions.[112]

Traveler named Julian, who arrived in New Orleans in 1853, attended a "Negro Ball" where participants dance a most extravagant bamboula and the polka.[113]

1854   **October 21:** The City Council granted private citizens permission to exhibit fireworks in Congo Square.

         November 3: "Voudous Dance"—On Wednesday night five "Voudous," four black and one white, two women and three men, were found by the efficient and vigilant police.[114]

1855   James Thomas, who visited Congo Square in earlier years, attended an opera, *The Barber of Seville*, at the Theatre d'Orleans while on one of many trips to New Orleans. The audience included free people of color and several hundred enslaved people.[115]

1856   **December 2:** The City Council declared, "It shall not be lawful for any person or persons to beat a drum, or blow a horn, or sound a trumpet, in any street or public place within the limits of the city. Provided that his provision shall not apply to any militia or other procession, or to those cases in which auctioneers are permitted to beat drums."[116]

         December 8: A city ordinance required the mayor's permission for all public balls, dances, and entertainment.[117]

1857   **January 7:** The city council revised and approved a series of ordinances for the reunited city government. The enslaved were allowed to assemble on the commons for the purpose of dancing, or playing ball or cricket, with permission from the mayor for that specified day only expiring at sunset.[118]

1858   **February 16, March 23, March 30:** Balloon races between "Wells and Moral" took place in Congo Square.[119]

        April: A city ordinance prohibited all persons of color, bond and free, from assembling for religious or other purposes, without white supervision.[120]

1859   **October 9:** "The First Fancy Dress Ball of the Season"—a private ball for the enslaved was given by their slave holders.[121]

1860   **October 2:** The *Daily True Delta* reports that "in past years, Congo Square was linked with the practice of Voudou."[122]

1861   **February 20:** A mass political meeting was held in Congo Square.[123]

        April 29: New Orleans surrendered to Union forces.

        May 1: General Benjamin Butler took control of the city.

        May 8: "Renting of Premises to Slaves"—the Grand Jury recommended an ordinance to the existing laws regarding renting property to those enslaved.[124]

        Federal authorities ordered the nine o'clock curfew for the enslaved and the signal of cannon fire to discontinue.[125]

        July 30: Police arrested enslaved Africans for unlawful assembly while attending a meeting of the Morning Star Benevolent Association on Delord Street.[126]

        August 14: "Armed Slaves"—police arrested seven armed enslaved blacks.[127]

1863   **June 3-5:** Citizens of New Orleans and Jefferson rallied by the thousands in Congo Square in support of the Union and liberty.[128]

        July 11: The funeral procession of deceased Union Capt. Andre Cailloux, the first black hero of the Civil War, passed through Congo Square. It included members of thirty-seven black societies and the Forty-Seventh Massachusetts Regiment of the Union Army.[129]

1864   **February 20:** "Another Enthusiastic Demonstration"—a mass gubernatorial campaign meeting took place in Congo Square.[130]

May 11: Slavery abolished in Louisiana. A mass meeting was held in Congo Square to celebrate the Louisiana State Constitutional Convention's adoption of the article abolishing slavery.[131]

June 12: "Emancipation Celebration:"

> On June 11th twenty thousand freedmen along with clergy, General Banks, Governor Hahn, Mayor Hoyt, and other Union officers attended an emancipation celebration in Congo Square. In the Square a large platform, rising in the form of an amphitheater, had been erected, with a stand for the speakers. The platform was decorated with flags and evergreens. . . . The speaker's stand was covered by a large awning, underneath which we found a number of ladies, teachers of the colored schools established by General Banks. Among those on the platform, we noticed old Jourdan [Jordan Noble] and fifteen or sixteen colored veterans of 1815. . . . About 12:00, Captain Pearson's battery fired a salute of one hundred guns, and one hundred taps were struck by the Alarm Telegraph on the city bells. . . . The procession began to file out of the square on Rampart Street.[132]

December: Seth B. Howe's circus set up and operated in Congo Square.[133]

December 11: "Congo Square"—a synopsis of the Congo Square gatherings concludes that the "dancing days in Congo Square are over; the banjo and the violin are heard there no more. The deserted Square has become a Place d'Armes—a sober retreat for the care-worn citizen, a playground for young children—and the once mirthful slave is having his "break-down" on the wide, wide world.[134]

December 13: "Congo Square"—Congo Square is agog. What Negro in New Orleans does not know Congo Square, and immediately reflect on his face a broad grin at the mere idea of it? It is a small section of Paradise to him. There he feels that he is not a [N word], but Negro. The article continued by announcing the circus that had come to Congo Square and the anticipation surrounding it.[135]

1865   **April 21:** "Mass Meeting in Congo Square"—New Orleanians mourned the death of President Abraham Lincoln at a mass meeting in Congo Square.[136]

October 23: De Haner's Circus set up in Congo Square.[137]

December 2: Policemen held their drill in Congo Square.[138]

1866   **August 6:** *New Orleans Daily Crescent* published "The Environs of New Orleans," a description of early life in New Orleans including Congo Square and the Indian ball game called "raquette."[139]

1867   **May 7:** "The Negroes and the City Railroads"—African descendants engaged in a mass effort to desegregate the city railroad cars on Rampart Street near Congo Square.[140]

1868   **September 11:** "The Levee"—the Negroes have mostly deserted it [the levee] and now congregate on Dryades Street.[141]

1869   **August–September:** German citizens proposed to erect a monument to Humboldt in Place d'Armes or Congo Square and change the name of the Square to Humboldt Square.[142]

        September–October: Mayor Conway vetoed the ordinance to change the name of Place d'Armes (Congo Square) to Humboldt Square. "The original name of the square was Circus. It was however, always known as Congo, even after it was called Place d'Armes by the city."[143]

1870   **March 11:** "A Murder in Congo Square"—one Sicilian shoots another in the square.[144]

        June 17: Police Superintendent Badger ordered Congo Square and Washington Square closed in the evenings at 10:00 p.m. Although the article does not explain why, the history of crime in the two locations, including murder, no doubt contributed to these closings.[145]

1879   **October 12:** *Daily Picayune* publishes "The Congo Dance," a synopsis of the old square on a Sunday afternoon sixty years prior is included.[146]

1880   "The old gathering ground actually ceased as a playground for Negroes around 1880."[147]

1881   **June 17:** "Marie Lavaux"—Death of the Queen of the Voudous Just Before St. John's Eve.[148]

        New Orleans City Council Ordinance 7126 provided for the appointment of Commissioners of Congo Square.

July 8: "Congo Square"—seldom used for any purpose, the Square's dilapidated appearance led to beautification plans: remove the old rusty railing, lay out and gravel the walks, trim and whitewash the trees, and cut and trim the grass. A different advertisement, "Sealed Proposals," published in the same paper, offered the iron railings around the Square for sale.[149]

1882   **August 5:** "In Congo Square"—Footpads Applying Their Work Under the Shadow of the Parish Prison. Assailants called "footpads" attacked and badly beat a man of African descent under the motive of robbery.[150]

1884 - Congo Square received grooming for the Cotton Exposition World's
1885   Fair. Officials removed the fence and gateways, made new graveled walks, whitewashed the tree trunks, and installed a fountain at its center. The fountain was completed in 1885.[151]

Writer Charles Dudley Warner visit New Orleans during the Cotton Exposition and witnesses singing and dancing near Congo Square.[152]

1887   **June 23:** "St. John's Eve"—the celebration on the 24th will feature a Congo-Creole African Dance.[153]

June 24: "A Cungi Dance – The Congo Reed At West End": Attracted by a newspaper announcement, several hundred people gathered to celebrate Saint John with an old-time Cungi dance. The orchestra consisted of the "jawbones of an ass, bound together with colored ribbon, a half whiskey barrel with a drum head in one end and a cracker box." The musician struck the jaw-bones against a small stool, on which he sat, and rapidly drew an iron key up and down the teeth, which were still in the sockets, producing a sharp rattling noise. A dozen or more singers accompanied the instruments and the dancers, one of whom fastened straps of bells trimmed with tin tubes around each knee.[154]

1891   **March 14:** "The Scene at the Prison"—of the eleven Italians involved in the assassination of Police Chief David Hennessy, an angry mob shot nine in jail, hung one from a corner lamp post and one from a tree in Congo Square.[155]

1892   **June 19:** The *Times Democrat* publishes the article "A Congo Priest – A Legend of St. John's Eve."[156]

1893   **March 30:** New Orleans City Council Ordinance 7351 CCS changed the name of Congo Square to Beauregard Square in honor of Confederate Civil War hero, Gen. P. G. T. Beauregard. Renovations made in conjunction with the name change included whitewashing oak trees, planting new trees, and adding new benches.[157]

1906   **March–August:** Beauregard Park Commissioners stopped blacks from walking through the park on Saturday nights on the way to a dance hall that had existed for some time in the vicinity.[158]

1917   The city purchased thousands of dollars of playground equipment for Beauregard Square.[159]

       New Orleans City Council Ordinance 4221 CCS made it unlawful to play music in parks, squares, etc. without permit.

1923   Beauregard Square received a swimming pool.

1928   **April 15:** "Ghosts of 'Congo Square': Prison Structures Doomed in the March of Progress"—proposed Beauregard Square Site for Auditorium Rich in Legends of Negro Voodoo Practices, Early Mystic Beliefs."[160]

       October 14: "New Orleans Auditorium Site in Old Days"—retelling of Sunday afternoon gatherings.[161]

1930   City officials completed and dedicated the Municipal Auditorium, now known as the Morris F. X. Jeff Auditorium, on the rear side of Congo Square.[162]

1945   **June 28:** "Rose Dirman a Hit at Pop Concert"—Summer "Pop" Concert Orchestra performed open-air concert at night in Congo Square.[163]

1949   **August 2:** "Bonano's Band to Open Jazz Concert Here"—the New Orleans Jazz Club sponsored a series of eight open-air jazz concerts at night in Congo Square featuring Sharkey Bonano and his Kings of Dixieland, two African American dancers introduced as Pork Chops and Kidney Stew, and the African American trumpeter "Papa" Celestin and his band.[164]

       August 3: "Jazz Festival is Loudly Applauded by Hep Crowd."[165]

1953   The New Orleans Creole Fiesta Association, members of African heritage, performed dances including the quadrille, schottische, and the cake walk at a Pop Concert in Congo Square.

1956   The city began demolishing sections of the Tremé neighborhood adjacent to the Square with plans to create a Cultural Center.

1963   **October–November:** "Group Protest Plan for Square"—Landmark Society protests $21 million plan that will allow street cutting through a portion of the square, surface parking, and building construction.[166]

1968   **May:** The parade for the International Jazz Festival, held in conjunction with the 250th Anniversary of the founding of New Orleans, began at Congo Square.

1970   **April 22-26:** The first New Orleans Jazz & Heritage Festival was held at Congo Square.

1971   **July 6:** Louis "Satchmo" Armstrong died at the age of seventy.

1973   After seventeen years, the city completed the demolition of a nine-block section of the Tremé neighborhood adjacent to Congo Square with no definite plans for its development.

1974   With support from the mayor, the city council authorized funds to develop the 31.2 acre property which included the Municipal Auditorium, the Theatre of Performing Arts, Congo Square, and sections of the demolished Tremé neighborhood into the Louis Armstrong Park Complex in honor of the native jazz musician.

1977   Archaeological investigations of the Congo Square area in 1977–78 by a team of archaeologists from the University of New Orleans uncovered a variety of artifacts including ceramic fragments, metal, glass fragments, whole bottles, pieces of leather, buttons, coins, and bones. Most of the items had been manufactured in the nineteenth and early twentieth century with a few 18th century exceptions.[167]

1980   **April:** "Jazz Fest – A Memorial to Satchmo": After more than $10 million of renovations and seven years of work, Louis Armstrong Park opened April 15 in conjunction with the opening of the New Orleans Jazz & Heritage Festival. Armstrong's widow, Lucille Armstrong, unveiled the park's twelve-foot sculpture of Armstrong crafted by renowned artist Elizabeth Catlett and funded by more than a thousand donations from twenty-six countries around the world. Louis Armstrong Park and Congo Square are located within the 31-acre Louis Armstrong Park Complex.[168]

The renovation of Congo Square included paving stones laid in circular patterns and a circle of water spouts at its center.

1990   **October 11:** Cofounders Luther Gray and Jamilah Peters-Muhammad incorporated The Congo Square Foundation.

1990s   Renewed interest in Congo Square prompted the emergence of several community festivals some of which became annual events.

1993   **January 28:** Congo Square listed on the National Register of Historic Places.

1997   **May:** A bust of famous jazz musician Sidney Bechet (1897–1949), who boasted of his African ancestry, was mounted at one of the entrance points to Congo Square (relocated to the Sculpture Garden in 2010).

         November 28: A historic marker funded by community organizations and coordinated by the Congo Square Foundation was unveiled at the site of Congo Square.[169]

2005   In the wake of Hurricane Katrina, which hit New Orleans on August 29, city officials closed Congo Square for a period of recovery and restoration.

2007   **September 30:** 1st Annual Congo Square Rhythms Festival held in Congo Square.

2009   **January:** Congo Square reopened to the public after Hurricane Katrina in conjunction with the reopening of the adjacent Mahalia Jackson Theater.

2010   **April 28:** Renovations in Congo Square and Armstrong Park included the restoration of the water spouts at the center of the Square and the dedication of "The Roots of Music Cultural Sculpture Garden." Renowned sculptor Elizabeth Catlett unveiled her twelve-foot sculpture of Mahalia Jackson at the event.

NOTES

Foreword

1. Langston Hughes, *The Big Sea: An Autobiography* (New York: Hill and Wang, 1940), 10.
2. Willie Anku, "Principles of Rhythm Integration in African Drumming," *Black Music Research Journal* 17, no. 2 (Autumn 1997): 211-38.
3. Melville J. Herskovits, *The Myth of the Negro Past* (New York: Harper and Brothers, 1941).

Chapter 1: Introduction

1. Edward Durell [Henry Didimus, pseud.], *New Orleans As I Found It* (New York: Harper and Bros., 1845), 34.
2. Henry Cogswell Knight [Arthur Singleton, pseud.], *Letters from the South and West* (Boston: Richardson and Lord, 1824), 127.
3. Benjamin H. Latrobe, *The Journals of Benjamin Latrobe, 1799-1820 From Philadelphia to New Orleans*, ed. Edward C. Carter, John C. Van Horne, and Lee W. Formwalt (New Haven: Yale University Press, 1980), 3:204.
4. Earl F. Birden, "Kemble's 'Speciality' and the Pictorial Countertext," in *A Case Study in Critical Controversy: Adventures of Huckleberry Finn*, ed. Gerald Graff and James Thelan (New York: Bedford Books, 1995), 383-406.
5. Gilbert Chase, *America's Music from the Pilgrims to the Present* (Chicago: University of Illinois, 1987), 65.
6. Hélène d'Aquin Allain, *Souvenirs D'Amérique Et De France, Par une Créole* (Paris: Bourguet Calas, 1883); Carolyn Morrow Long, *Spiritual Merchants* (Knoxville: University of Tennessee Press, 2001), 40-41.
7. William Edward Farrison, *Wells Brown, Author and Reformer* (Chicago: University of Chicago Press, 1969), 446.
8. In this text, Kongo spelled with a "K" and Kongo/Angola will refer to the huge West Central African region and the people who originated there. Congo spelled with a "C" will refer to the dance and the location Congo Square.
9. John Smith Kendall, *History of New Orleans* (New York: Lewis Publishing Co.), 2:679; C. M. Chambon, *In and Around the Old St. Louis Cathedral of New Orleans* (New Orleans: Phillippe's Printery, 1908), 33.

Chapter 2: The Legacy of the Gatherings

1. Daniel H. Usner, Jr., "American Indians in Colonial New Orleans," in *Powhatan's Mantle: Indians in the Colonial Southeast*, ed. Peter H. Wood, Gregory A. Waselkov and M. Thomas Hatley (Lincoln: University of Nebraska Press, 1989), 105.
2. Ibid., 114; Shannon Lee Dawdy, *Building the Devil's Empire: French Colonial New Orleans* (Chicago: University of Chicago Press, 2008), 78.
3. John Smith Kendall, *History of New Orleans* (New York: Lewis Publishing Company,

1922), 2:679; LeBlanc de Villeneufve, *The Festival of the Young Corn or The Heroism of Poucha-Houmma*, trans. and ed. Mathé Allain (Lafayette: University of Southwestern Louisiana, 1964), preface, 6.

4.   Marc de Villiers, "History of the Foundation of New Orleans (1717-1722)," *Louisiana Historical Quarterly* 3, no. 2 (April 1920): 161-251.

5.   Gwendolyn Midlo Hall, *Africans in Colonial Louisiana* (Baton Rouge: Louisiana State University Press, 1992), 3, 14-15; Daniel H. Usner, Jr., *Indians, Settlers, and Slaves in a Frontier Exchange Economy* (Chapel Hill: University of North Carolina Press, 1992), 193-94.

6.   Hall, *Africans in Colonial La.*, 5.

7.   James D. Hardy, Jr., "The Transportation of Convicts to Colonial Louisiana," in *The Louisiana Purchase Bicentennial Series in Louisiana History*, vol. 1, *The French Experience in Louisiana*, ed. Glenn R. Conrad (Lafayette, La.: Center for Louisiana Studies, 1995), 117-120; Edwin Adams Davis, *Louisiana: A Narrative History*, 3rd ed. (Baton Rouge: Claitor's Publishing Division, 1971), 57; Hall, *Africans in Colonial La.*, 5-6.

8.   Glenn R. Conrad, "Emigration Force: A French Attempt to Populate Louisiana," in *The Louisiana Purchase Bicentennial Series in Louisiana History*, vol. 1, *The French Experience in Louisiana*, ed. Glenn R. Conrad (Lafayette, La.: Center for Louisiana Studies, 1995), 133.

9.   Davis, *Louisiana*, 57-58.

10. Hall, *Africans in Colonial La.*, 7; Thomas N. Ingersoll, *Mammon and Manon in Early New Orleans: The First Slave Society in the Deep South, 1718-1819* (Knoxville: University of Tennessee Press, 1999), 12, 107; Daniel H. Usner, Jr., "From African Captivity to American Slavery: The Introduction of Black Laborers to Colonial Louisiana," *Louisiana History* 20, no. 1 (Winter 1979): 30.

11. Hall, *Africans in Colonial La.*, 57; Ingersoll, *Mammon and Manon*, 70.

12. Davis, *Louisiana*, 80; Hall, *Africans in Colonial La.*, 57, 60.

13. Antoine Simone Le Page du Pratz, *Histoire de la Louisiane*, (Paris: De Bure, l'aine, 1758), 3:226-7.

14. Thomas M. Fiehrer, "The African Presence in Colonial Louisiana: An Essay on the Continuity of Caribbean Culture," in *Louisiana's Black Heritage*, ed. Robert MacDonald et. al. (New Orleans: Louisiana State Museum, 1979), 10.

15. Ibid., 10; Davis, *Louisiana*, 72; Hall, *Africans in Colonial La.*, 122; Jessica Harris, *Iron Pots and Wooden Spoons: Africa's Gifts to New World Cooking* (New York: Simon and Schuster, 1999), 19; Jessica Harris, *Beyond Gumbo: Creole Fusion Food from the Atlantic Rim* (New York: Simon and Schuster, 2003), 51.

16. Hall, *Africans in Colonial La.*, 124.

17. J. Carlyle Sitterson, "The Savior of Louisiana," in *The Louisiana Purchase Bicentennial Series in Louisiana History*, vol. 16, *Agriculture and Economic Development in Louisiana*, ed. Thomas A. Becnel (Lafayette, La.: Center for Louisiana Studies, 1995), 212; Fiehrer, "The African Presence," 10.

18. Joseph E. Holloway, "The Origins of African-American Culture" in *Africanisms in American Culture*, ed. Joseph E. Holloway (Bloomington: Indiana University Press, 1990), 14-15; Usner, "From African Captivity," 34; Ingersoll, *Mammon and Manon*, 107; Friehrer, "The African Presence," 11; Hall, *Africans in Colonial La.*, 37, 51, 124,

126, 133, 137.

19. de Villiers, "History of the Foundation of N.O.," 161-251.

20. Le Page du Pratz, *Histoire de la Louisiane*, 227.

21. Roulac Toledano and Mary Louise Christovich, *New Orleans Architecture*, vol. 6, *Faubourg Treme and the Bayou Road* (Gretna: Pelican Publishing Company, 1980), 7; Richard J. Shenkel et. al., *Archaeology of the Jazz Complex and Beauregard (Congo) Square, Louis Armstrong Park, New Orleans, Louisiana: Research Report* (New Orleans: University of New Orleans, 1980), 162; Brenda Marie Osbey, "Faubourg Tremé: Community in Transition—Part I: Early History," *New Orleans Tribune*, (1990).

22. "Congo Square," *New Orleans Democrat*, July 8, 1881; James Wobble, "New Orleans Auditorium Site in Old Days," *Item Tribune*, October, 14, 1928; *Times-Picayune*, February 21, 1936.

23. Toledano and Christovich, *Faubourg Treme*, 64-65; Shenkel, *Archaeology of the Jazz Complex*, 162.

24. Osbey, "Faubourg Tremé."

25. John Pope, "Progress Mislaid Many Meant to Rest in Peace," *Times-Picayune*, August 18, 1985; Henry Castellanos, *New Orleans As It Was*, ed. George Reinecke (1895; reprint, Baton Rouge: Louisiana State University Press, 1978), 158-60, 298.

26. *Historical Sketch Book & Guide to New Orleans* (New Orleans: Will H. Coleman, 1885), 297; Castellanos, *New Orleans As It Was*, 157; *Daily Picayune*, December 10, 12, 1864.

27. New Orleans City Council Ordinances & Resolutions, October 21, 1854, No. 1795, Louisiana Division/City Archives, New Orleans Public Library; *New Orleans Tagliche Deutsch Zeitung*, February 16, March 28, 30, 1858, December 2, 1866; New Orleans City Council Ordinances & Resolutions, April 18, 1832, Louisiana Division/City Archives, New Orleans Public Library; "A Kaleidoscopic View of New Orleans," *Daily Picayune*, September 23, 1843; "Fireworks," *Louisiana Courier*, June 28, 1813.

28. First Municipal Council Ordinances & Resolutions, November 11, 1850, January 25, 1851, Louisiana Division/City Archives, New Orleans Public Library; Wobble, "New Orleans Auditorium Site."

29. *The Era*, June 3, 5, 1863; *New Orleans Times*, February 20, 1864; *Daily True Delta*, June 12, 1864; *The Black Republican*, April 29, 1865; Shenkel, *Archaeology of the Jazz Complex*, 26; Wobble, "New Orleans Auditorium Site;" Marie Goodspeed, "Rose Dirman a Hit at Pop Concert," *New Orleans States*, June 29, 1945; Marie Goodspeed, "Jazz Festival is Loudly Applauded by Hep Crowd," *New Orleans States*, August 3, 1949.

30. Loren Schweninger, ed., *The Autobiography of James Thomas: From Tennessee Slave to St. Louis Entrepreneur* (Columbia: University of Missouri Press, 1984), 109, 49; Henry Cogswell Knight [Arthur Singleton, pseud.], *Letters from the South and West* (Boston: Richardson and Lord, 1824), 127; C. M. Chambon, *In and Around the Old St. Louis Cathedral of New Orleans* (New Orleans: Phillippe's Printery, 1908), 33; Francis Baily, *Journal of a Tour in Unsettled Parts of North America in 1796-1797* (Carbondale: Southern Illinois University Press, 1969), 173; *The Times Picayune Guide to New Orleans*, 4th ed. (New Orleans: The Picayune, 1900), 62; Marcus Christian, "Negro Dances," in *A Black History of Louisiana*, Louisiana and Special Collections, Earl K. Long Library, University of New Orleans [(unpublished), 3]; Federal Writers' Project, folder 118B, Cammie G. Henry Research Center, Watson Memorial Library, Northwestern State

University of Louisiana; Benjamin Moore Norman, *Norman's New Orleans and Environs*, ed. Matthew J. Schott (1845; reprint, Baton Rouge: Louisiana State University Press, 1976), 182; Timothy Flint, *Recollections of the Last Ten Years in the Valley of the Mississippi*, ed. George R. Brooks (1826; reprint, Carbondale: Southern Illinois University Press, 1968), 219.

31. John Smith Kendall, "Notes on the Criminal History," *The Louisiana Historical Quarterly* 34, no. 1 (1951): 149; *Louisiana Gazette*, June 23, 1810; Albert Thrasher, *On to New Orleans! Louisiana's Heroic 1811 Slave Revolt* (New Orleans, Cypress Press, 1995), 64, 239; Castellanos, *New Orleans*, 159; Albert Phelps, *Louisiana: A Record of Expansion* (New York: Houghton Mifflin and Co., 1905), 76-77; Davis, *Louisiana*, 67.

32. Walter Johnson, *Soul by Soul: Life Inside the Antebellum Slave Market* (Cambridge: Harvard University Press, 1999), 1-2, 7; Davis, *Louisiana*, 212.

33. Usner, "From African Captivity," 28; Eugene Berjot, *Un Voyage à la Nouvelle-Orléans. Par le Dr. E. Berjot* [N.P., 18--], 16; George W. Cable, *Dance in Place Congo and Creole Slave Songs* (New Orleans: Faruk von Turk, 1974), 12; *Times Picayune Guide*, 62.

Chapter 3:   The Significance of the Gathering

1. "Congo Square," *New Orleans Democrat*, July 8, 1881; Jerah Johnson, *Congo Square in New Orleans* (New Orleans: Louisiana Landmarks Association, 1995), 39, 9.

2. Charles Blockson, *African Americans in Pennsylvania: A History and Guide* (Baltimore, Md.: Black Classic Press, 1994), 96.

3. John Watson, *The Annals of Philadelphia* (Philadelphia: Historical Society of Pennsylvania, 1830), 483, http://books.google.com/books?id=51YQ0TzReWMC&pg=PA483&dq=fanning+%22more+than+one+thousand+of+both+sexes,+divided+into+numerous+little+squads%22&ei=u6FgSsjDJ6mCyAS3qsiWCw

4. Dena J. Epstein, *Sinful Tunes and Spirituals* (Chicago: University of Illinois Press, 1977), 84-8.

5. Paul LaChance, "The 1809 Immigration of Saint-Dominque Refugees," in *The Road to Louisiana: the Saint-Domingue Refugee, 1792-1809*, ed. Carl A. Brasseaux and Glenn R. Conrad (Lafayette, La.: Center for Louisiana Studies, 1992), 247.

6. Felix Flugel, ed., "Pages from a Journal of a Voyage Down the Mississippi to New Orleans in 1817," *Louisiana Historical Quarterly* 7, no. 3 (1924): 432.

7. James Creecy, *Scenes in the South* (Philadelphia: Lippincott and Company, 1860), 45.

8. Henry A. Kmen, "The Roots of Jazz and the Dance in Place Congo: A Re-Appraisal" *Inter-American Musical Research Yearbook* 8 (1972): 11; Joseph G. Tregle, Jr., *Louisiana in the Age of Jackson* (Baton Rouge: Louisiana State University Press, 1999), 309; Johnson, *Congo Square*, 44.

9. *True American*, August 6, 1835; *New Orleans Observer*, January, 2 1836; Albert Fossier, *New Orleans: The Glamour Period, 1800-1840* (New Orleans: Pelican Publishing Company, 1957), 379-80.

10. *True American*, August 12, 1835; *The Bee*, August 17, 19, 1835; Edward F. Haas, ed., *Louisiana's Legal Heritage* (Pensacola: The Perdido Bay Press, 1983), 74-75.

11. *Journal of the First Municipality of the City of New Orleans*, May 17, 1836–May 20, 1850, Special Collections, Howard-Tilton Memorial Library, Tulane University.

12. *Daily Picayune*, January 12, 1841, October 18, and December 10, 1843.

13. First Municipal Council Ordinances & Resolutions, April 28, 1845, Louisiana Division/City Archives, New Orleans Public Library; *Daily Picayune*, June 24, 1845.

14. *Daily Picayune* March 22, 1846; A. Oakey Hall, *The Manhattaner in New Orleans* (New Orleans: J. C. Morgan, 1852), 106.

15. *Daily Picayune*, December 31, 1848.

16. Maude Cuncy Hare, *Six Creole Folk Songs* (New York: Carl Fischer, 1921), 3.

17. New Orleans City Council Ordinances & Resolutions, December 2, 8, 1856, Louisiana Division/City Archives, New Orleans Public Library; *Daily Picayune*, March 5, 1856.

18. Henry Jefferson Leovy, *Laws and General Ordinances of the City of New Orleans: Revised and Digested* (New Orleans: E. C. Wharton, 1857), 258.

19. "Unlawful Assemblies," *Daily Picayune*, July 31, 1850.

20. *Daily True Delta*, July 20, 25, 26, 1851; November 3, 1854.

21. St. James African Methodist Episcopal Church, 222 N. Roman Street, was founded by free men of color who first held services in the Wesley Chapel of the Methodist Episcopal Church. Members entered the present church site in 1848 although construction was not completed until 1851. The building is considered the oldest church building in continuous use in New Orleans as well as Louisiana, and is the denomination's "Mother Church" in the area. Col. James Lewis, Sr. recruited the first Negro Company of soldiers in this area of South at this church. See *Times-Picayune*, January 24, 1970.

22. Ibid.; Caryn Cosse Bell, *Revolution, Romanticism, and Afro-Creole Protest Tradition in Louisiana, 1718-1868* (Baton Rouge: Louisiana State University Press, 1997), 84.

23. Marcus Bruce Christian, "Voodooism and Mumbo Jumbo," in *A Black History of Louisiana*, Louisiana and Special Collections, Earl K. Long Library, University of New Orleans [(unpublished), 14].

24. Federal Writers' Project, folder 25, Cammie G. Henry Research Center, Watson Memorial Library, Northwestern State University of Louisiana.

25. Mayor Martin Behrman's Administration, Park Commissioners' Reports, 1906, Louisiana Division/City Archives, New Orleans Public Library.

26. First Municipal Council Ordinances & Resolutions, October 15, 1817, Louisiana Division/City Archives, New Orleans Public Library; First Municipal Council Ordinances & Resolutions, April 28, 1845, Louisiana Division/City Archives, New Orleans Public Library; Frederick L. Olmsted, *The Cotton Kingdom*, ed. Arthur Meier Schlesinger (1861; reprint, New York: Modern Library, 1984), 592.

27. Benjamin H. Latrobe, *The Journals of Benjamin Latrobe, 1799-1820 From Philadelphia to New Orleans*, ed. Edward C. Carter, John C. Van Horne, and Lee W. Formwalt (New Haven: Yale University Press, 1980), 3:203.

28. "The African Slave Trade," Review of *Captain Canot, or Twenty Years of an African Slaver*, by Brantz Mayer, *De Bow's Review* (1855): 20.

29. Frank H. Severance, *The Journeys and Journals of an Early Buffalo Merchant [John Lay]* (Buffalo: Buffalo Historical Society, 1896).

30. *Daily Picayune*, June 24, 1845; Henry Castellanos, *New Orleans As It Was*, ed. George. Reinecke (1895; reprint, Baton Rouge: Louisiana State University Press, 1978), 157-158.

31. Latrobe, *The Journals of Benjamin Latrobe*, 204.

32. Harrison Barnes, interview by Bill Russell and Richard B. Allen, January 24, 1959, reel 2, Hogan Jazz Archives, Howard-Tilton Memorial Library, Tulane University.

33. Grace King, *New Orleans: The Place and the People* (New York: Macmillan Co., 1899), 340.

34. Acts and Deliberations of the Cabildo, 1769-1803, January 10, 1772, Louisiana Division/City Archives, New Orleans Public Library.

35. Antoine Simon Le Page du Pratz, *The History of Louisiana*, ed. Joseph G. Tregle, Jr. (1758; reprint, Baton Rouge: Louisiana State University Press, 1975), 387; *Daily Picayune*, December 11, 1864.

36. Creecy, *Scenes in the South*, 20.

37. Ibid.

38. Ned Sublette, *Cuba and Its Music: From the First Drums to the Mambo* (Chicago: Chicago Review Press, 2004), 133.

39. Ibid., 134

40. Samuel A. Floyd, "Black Music in the Circum-Caribbean," *American Music* 17, no. 1 (Spring 1999): 1-38; Bill Summers, interview by author, August 27, 2008.

41. Michael Skinkus, interview by author, August 16, 2008.

42. Christopher Washburn, "The Clave of Jazz: A Caribbean Contribution to the Rhythmic Foundation of an African-American Music," *Black Music Research Journal* 17, no.1 (Spring 1997): 59-80.

43. Lester Sullivan, interview by author, April 13, 2010.

44. Edwin P. Christy, *Christy's Plantation Melodies, No. 4* (Philadelphia: Fisher and Bros., 1854), vi.

45. Observation made by author at funerals and church services at African Methodist Episcopal and Baptist churches in and around Charleston, South Carolina.

46. Floyd, "Black Music," 30.

47. Timothy Flint, *Recollections of the Last Ten Years in the Valley of the Mississippi*, ed. George R. Brooks (1826; reprint, Carbondale: Southern Illinois University Press, 1968), 103.

48. *Daily Picayune*, October 18, 1843, and March 22, 1846; Loren Schweninger, ed., *The Autobiography of James Thomas: From Tennessee Slave to St. Louis Entrepreneur* (Columbia: University of Missouri Press, 1984), 109; Hall, *The Manhattaner in New Orleans*, 106; Charles Dudley Warner, *Studies in the South and West* (New York: Harper and Brothers, 1889), 64-71.

49. *Times Democrat*, June 6, 1887; Lafcadio Hearn, "The Scenes in Cable's Romances," *Century Magazine* (November 1883): 43; Henry E. Krehbiel, *Afro-American Folksongs* (New York: G. Schirmer, Inc., 1914), 3; Federal Writers' Project, folder 25, Cammie G. Henry Research Center, Watson Memorial Library, Northwestern State University of Louisiana.

50. Christy, *Christy's Plantation Melodies*, v, vi.

51. Ibid., vi.

52. "Authenic Memoir of E. P. Christy," *The Age* (New York), April 16, 1848.

53. Ibid.; H. P. Grattan, "The Origin of the Christy's Minstrels," *The Theatre: A Monthly Review of the Drama, Music, and the Fine Arts* 5 (1882): 120-134.

54. Annemarie Bean, James Hatch, and Brooks McNamara, *Inside the Minstrel Mask,*

Readings in Nineteenth Century Blackface Minstrelsy (London: Wesleyan University Press, 1996), 69.

55. "Authentic Memoir of E. P. Christy."

56. "The Circus in New Orleans," *Times-Picayune*, November 20, 1955; "The European Circus," *Daily Picayune*, December 10, 1864; "The Great Circus Pageant," *Daily Picayune*, December 16, 1864.

57. "The E. P. Christy Will," *New York Times*, May 5, 1865.

58. Christy, *Christy's Plantation Melodies*, v.

Chapter 4:   The Gatherers

1. Gwendolyn Midlo Hall, *Africans in Colonial Louisiana* (Baton Rouge: Louisiana State University Press, 1992), 29, 34-35, 41, 159.

2. Ibid., 284-86; Gwendolyn Midlo Hall, *Slavery and African Ethnicities in the Americas* (Chapel Hill: University of North Carolina Press, 2005), 70-74.

3. Ibid., 75-76.

4. George W. Cable, *Dance in Place Congo and Creole Slave Songs* (New Orleans: Faruk von Turk, 1974), 6; James S. Zacharie, *New Orleans Guide, With Descriptions of the Routes to New Orleans* (New Orleans: The New Orleans News Company, 1895), 116.

5. Felix Flugel, ed., "Pages from a Journal of a Voyage Down the Mississippi to New Orleans in 1817," *The Louisiana Historical Quarterly* 7, no. 3 (1924): 432; "The Congo Dance," *Daily Picayune*, October 12, 1879.

6. African descendant James Thomas, who visited the city between 1839 and 1861, noted the huge sign on the St. Charles Hotel that read "Maryland and Virginia Negroes for Sale." See Loren Schweninger, ed., *The Autobiography of James Thomas: From Tennessee Slave to St. Louis Entrepreneur* (Columbia: University of Missouri Press, 1984).

7. "The Congo Dance," *Daily Picayune*, October 12, 1879.

8. Hebert Asbury, *The French Quarter: An Informal History of the New Orleans Underworld* (St. Simons Island: Mockingbird Books, 1964), 185; Daniel H. Usner, Jr., "From African Captivity to American Slavery: The Introduction of Black Laborers to Colonial Louisiana," *Louisiana History* 20, no. 1 (Winter 1979): 40; Gary A. Donaldson, "A Window on Slave Culture: Dances at Congo Square in New Orleans, 1800-1862," *Journal of Negro History* 69 (1984): 70.

9. James Creecy, *Scenes in the South* (Philadelphia: Lippincott and Company, 1860), 20.

10. Médéric-Louis-Elie Moreau de Saint-Méry, *A Civilization That Perished: The Last Years of White Colonial Rule in Haiti*, ed. Ivor Spencer (Lanham, Md.: University Press of America, 1985), 57; Médéric-Louis-Elie Moreau De Saint-Méry, *Dance* (1796; reprint, Brooklyn: Dance Horizon, 1975), 50.

11. Joseph Tregle, "Early New Orleans Society: A Reappraisal," *Journal of Southern History* 18, no. 1 (February 1952): 33; *The Bee*, June 13, 1833.

12. *Daily True Delta*, May 8, 1863.

13. New Orleans City Council Ordinances & Resolutions, January 16, 1811, Article 2, Louisiana Division/City Archives, New Orleans Public Library; James Stuart, *Three Years in North America* (New York: J. and J. Harper, 1833), 2:194-5; Loren Schweninger, "A Negro Sojourner in Antebellum New Orleans," *Louisiana History*

20, no. 3 (Summer 1979): 311.

14. Tregle, "Early New Orleans Society," 33; "From the United States Telegraph," *The Bee*, June 13, 1833; Werner A. Wegener, *Negro Slavery in New Orleans* (M.A. thesis, Tulane University, 1935), 59.

15. Creecy, *Scenes in the South*, 20.

16. *Daily Picayune*, December 11, 1864; "New Orleans Auditorium Site in Old Days," *The Item Tribune*, October 14, 1928; Eleanor Early, *New Orleans Holiday* (New York: Rinehart and Company, Inc., 1947), 217; Joe Gray Taylor, *Negro Slavery in Louisiana* (Baton Rouge: Louisiana Historical Association, 1963), 131; *New Orleans Crescent*, August 6,1868; Salomon de Baron Rothschild, *A Casual View of America: The Home Letters of Salomon de Rothschild, 1859-1861*, trans. and ed. Sigmund Diamond (London: Cresset Press, 1962), 112.

17. Creecy, *Scenes in the South*, 22-23.

18. Schweninger, *Autobiography of James Thomas*, 109.

19. Georges J. Joyaux, ed. and trans. "Forest's Voyage aux Etats-Unis de l' Amérique en 1831," *Louisiana Historical Quarterly* 39, no. 4 (January 1956): 468; Johnson, *Congo Square*, 38.

20. John Mbiti, *African Religions and Philosophy* (Oxford: Heinemann Educational Publishers, 1969), 2.

21. Alcée Fortier, *History of Louisiana, 1512-1768*, (New York: Goupil and Company of Paris, 1904), 2:87.

22. Hall, *Africans in Colonial La.*, 162-63, 302; Robert Farris Thompson, *Flash of the Spirit* (New York: Vintage Books, 1984), 107.

23. Hall, *Africans in Colonial La.*, 286; Kimberly A. Hanger, *A Medley of Cultures: Louisiana History at the Cabildo* (New Orleans, Louisiana Museum Foundation, 1996), 28; Francois X. Martin, *The History of Louisiana* (1882; reprint, Gretna, La.: Pelican Publishing Company, 1963), 257-58.

24. Abraham P. Nasatir and Ernest R. Liljegren, "Materials Relating to the Mississippi Valley, From the Minutes of 1795, The Spanish Supreme Councils of State, 1787-1797," *Louisiana Historical Quarterly* 21, no. 1 (1938): 62.

25. Edwin Adams Davis, *Louisiana: A Narrative History* (Baton Rouge: Claitor's Publishing, 1971), 80.

26. Paul LaChance, "The 1809 Immigration of Saint-Dominque Refugees," in *The Road to Louisiana: the Saint-Domingue Refugee, 1792-1809*, ed. Carl A. Brasseaux and Glenn R. Conrad (Lafayette, La.: Center for Louisiana Studies, 1992), 257.

27. *New Orleans Montiteur De La Louisiana*, January 12, 1811; Thomas Thompson, "National Newspaper and Legislative Reactions to Louisiana's Deslondes Slave Revolt of 1811," *Louisiana History* 33, no.1 (Winter 1992): 5-6; also see: Albert Thrasher, *On to New Orleans! Louisiana's Heroic 1811 Slave Revolt* (New Orleans, Cypress Press, 1995).

28. *Code de Police* (New Orleans: Renard Printer, 1808); Ordinances of the City Council of New Orleans, Article 7, January 16, 1811, Louisiana Division/City Archives, New Orleans Public Library.

29. Ordinances of the City Council of New Orleans, October 15, 1817, Louisiana Division/City Archives, New Orleans Public Library. The 1810 census indicated that of the 17,242 people, 28.7 percent were free people of color and 34.6 percent were

enslaved. The 1820 census indicated that of the 27,176 people, 23.0 percent were free people of color and 27.1 percent were enslaved. See Joseph Logsdon and Caryn Cossé Bell, "The Americanization of Black New Orleans, 1850-1900," in *Creole New Orleans: Race and Americanization* ed. Arnold R Hirsch and Joseph Logsdon (Baton Rouge: Louisiana State University Press, 1991), 206.

30. Christian Schultz, *Travels on an Island Voyage* (New York: Issac Riley, 1810), 2:197.

31. Robert Farris Thompson, "When the Saints Go Marching In: Kongo Louisiana, Kongo New Orleans," in *Resonance from the Past: African Sculpture from the New Orleans Museum of Art*, ed. Frank Herreman (New York: Museum of African Art, 2005), 139; Jason R. Young, *Rituals of Resistance* (Baton Rouge: Louisiana State University Press, 2007), 112.

32. *New Orleans Commercial Bulletin*, July 5, 1869.

33. Federal Writers' Project, folder 25, Cammie G. Henry Research Center, Watson Memorial Library, Northwestern State University of Louisiana.

34. "A Voodoo Tree: Haunted Sycamore of Congo Square," *Times-Democrat*, August 1, 1891.

35. Ibid.

36. Marcus Christian, "Voodooism and Mumbo-Jumbo" in *A Black History of Louisiana*, Louisiana and Special Collections, Earl K. Long Library, University of New Orleans [(unpublished), 40, 40-A].

37. Zora Neale Hurston, *Mules and Men* (New York: Harper Perennial, 1935), 193.

38. Henry Castellanos, *New Orleans As It Was* ed. George Reinecke (1895; reprint, Baton Rouge: Louisiana State University Press, 1978), 158; *Daily Picayune*, March 22, 1846; Cable, *Dance in Place Congo*, 6; Charles Gayarre, *The History of Louisiana* (1866; reprint, Gretna: Pelican Publishing Company, 1974), 3:313; Martin, *History of Louisiana*, 57; James Wobble, "New Orleans Auditorium Site in Old Days," *Item Tribune*, October, 14, 1928; Davis, *Louisiana*, 80; Grace King, *New Orleans: The Place and the People* (New York: Macmillan Co., 1899), 335.

39. Francis Burns, "The Black Code: A Brief History of the Origin, Statutory Regulation and Judicial Sanction of Slavery in Louisiana," in *The Louisiana Purchase Bicentennial Series in Louisiana History*, vol. 13, *An Uncommon Experience: Law and Judicial Institution in Louisiana 1803-2003*, ed. by Judith K. Schafer and Warren M. Billings (Lafayette, La.: Center for Louisiana Studies, 1997), 309.

40. *Daily Picayune*, October, 12, 1879; "New Orleans Auditorium Site in Old Days," *Item Tribune*, October 14, 1928; Johann Buechler, *Land-und Seereisen eines St.Gallischen Kantonsburgers nach Nordamerika und Westindien uber Amsterdam nach Baltimore, Pitzburg, Gallipoli Sensanetta, Neu-Vevay, die Gegend Wabasch am Ohio, Natschet, Battonrouge und Neu-Oleans am Mississippi etc., 1816, 1817 und 1818*, quoted in Dena Epstein, *Sinful Tunes and Spirituals* (Chicago: University of Illinois Press, 1977), 95.

41. Davis, *Louisiana*, 121; Cable, *Dance in Place Congo*, 6.

42. King, *New Orleans*, 342, 334; Beatrice Washburn, "First & Last Nights: I" in *The New Orleanian*, (December 1930): 16.

43. Buechler, *Land-und Seereisen*, quoted in Epstein, 95; *Daily Picayune*, March 22, 1846.

44. Asbury, *The French Quarter*, 184.

45. "Congo Square: The Master of Ceremonies," *Daily Picayune*, March 22, 1846.

Chapter 5:   The Musical Instruments

1. Christian Schultz, *Travels on an Island Voyage* (New York: Issac Riley, 1810), 2:197.
2. Benjamin H. Latrobe, *The Journals of Benjamin Latrobe, 1799-1820 From Philadelphia to New Orleans*, ed. Edward C. Carter, John C. Van Horne, and Lee W. Formwalt (New Haven: Yale University Press, 1980), 204.
3. Ibid.; *Daily Picayune*, October 12, 1879.
4. A. Oakey Hall, *The Manhattaner in New Orleans* (New Orleans, J. C. Morgan, 1851), 106; Loren Schweninger, ed., *The Autobiography of James Thomas: From Tennessee Slave to St. Louis Entrepreneur* (Columbia: University of Missouri Press, 1984), 109.
5. Wash Wilson, Texas Slave Narratives, Federal Writers' Project.
6. George W. Cable, *Dance in Place Congo and Creole Slave Songs* (New Orleans: Faruk von Turk, 1974), 3; Maude Cuney Hare, *Six Creole Folk Songs* (New York: Carl Fischer, 1921), 3; Edwin Adams Davis, *Louisiana: A Narrative History* (Baton Rouge: Claitor's Publishing, 1961), 226.
7. Cable, *Dance in Place Congo*, 4-5.
8. Yetman, Norman, *Life Under the "Peculiar Institution:" Selections from the Slave Narrative Collection* (New York: Robert Krieger Publishing Company, 1976), 168.
9. Latrobe, *Journals of Benjamin Latrobe*, 204; James Creecy, *Scenes in the South* (Philadelphia: Lippincott and Company, 1860), 21; *Daily Picayune*, October 12, 1879; Philip F. Gura and James Bollman, *America's Instrument, The Banjo in the Nineteenth Century* (Chapel Hill: University of North Carolina Press, 1999), 12.
10. Robert Farris Thompson, "When the Saints Go Marching In: Kongo Louisiana, Kongo New Orleans," in *Resonance from the Past: African Sculpture from the New Orleans Museum of Art*, ed. Frank Herreman (New York: Museum of African Art, 2005), 136-143.
11. *Daily Picayune*, March 22, 1846; Creecy, *Scenes in the South*, 21; Cable, *Dance in Place Congo*, 3.
12. Lacadio Hearn, *Two Years in the French West Indies* (New York: Harper, 1923), 148; Ayesha Morris, "The Power of Dance: Bamboula Has Deep and Strong Ties to African Heritage, Island History and Freedom Fight," *The Virgin Island Daily News*, February 25, 2006: http://www.virginislandsdailynews.com/index.pl/article?id=13672670 (accessed December 2009).
13. Harold Courlander, "Musical Instruments of Haiti," *The Musical Quarterly* 27, no. 3 (July, 1941), 371-383; Harold Courlander, "Musical Instruments of Cuba," *The Musical Quarterly* 28, no. 2, (April, 1942): 227-240; Gehard Kubik, "Drum Patterns in the 'Batuque' of Benedito Caxias," *Latin American Music Review/Revista de Música Latinoamericana* 11, no. 2 (Autumn–Winter, 1990): 115-181; Myriam Evelyse Mariani, *African Influences in Brazilian Dance* in *African Dance: An Artistic, Historical and Philosophical Inquiry*, ed. Kariamu Welsh Asante (Trenton, N.J.: African World Press, Inc., 1996), 79-97. A feature of the Bartuque dance in Brazil was the umbigada where one dancer advances and touches his/her belly (navel) against that of another person. Tumba Francesa are cultural performance groups that feature the dances, songs and drumming styles that enslaved Haitians brought to Cuba.
14. Kazadi wa Mukuna, interview by author, September 3, 2009.
15. Thompson, "When the Saints," 136-143; Theodore Pavie, *Souvenirs Atlantiques. Voyage*

aux Etats-Unis et au Canada, par Theodore Pavie trans. F. Peterson (Paris: Roret, 1833), 319-20; Elizabeth Bisland, ed., *The Life and Letters of Lafcadio Hearn Including the Japanese Letters* (New York: Houghton Mifflin Company, 1923), 1:331.

16. Courlander, "Musical Instruments of Haiti," 380; J. H. Kwabena `Nketia, "Drums, Dance, and Song," *Atlantic Monthly* 203 (April 1959): 69-72.

17. Courlander, "Musical Instruments of Cuba," 240; Schweninger, *Autobiography of James Thomas*, 109; Creecy, *Scenes in the South*, 21; Henry Edward Krehbiel, *Afro American Folksongs: A Study in Racial and National Music* (New York: G. Schirmer, Inc., 1914), 121; Ruth Stone, ed., *The Garland Handbook of African Music* (New York: Routledge, 2008), 346-47.

18. J. H. Kwabena `Nketia, *The Music of Africa* (New York: W. W. Norton and Company, 1974), 92-94; Courlander, "Musical Instruments of Haiti," 383.

19. Federal Writers' Project, folder 25, Cammie G. Henry Research Center, Watson Memorial Library, Northwestern State University of Louisiana; Francisco Moro Catlett, interview by author, July 9, 2008.

20. Courlander, "Musical Instruments of Haiti," 377.

Chapter 6: The Songs

1. Louis E. Elie, *Histoire d'Haiti* (Port-au-Prince: Droits de Traduction, de Reproduction, 1945), 184.

2. Kazadi wa Mukuna, interview by author, September 3, 2009; Ned Sublette, Tom Dent Lecture Series, New Orleans Jazz & Heritage Foundation, November 14, 2009; Alex LaSalle, interview by author, November 14, 2009.

3. Médéric-Louis-Elie Moreau de Saint-Méry, *Description Topographique, Physique, Civile, Politique, et Historique de la Partie Française de l'isle Saint-Domingue* (Philadelphia: Chez l'auteur, 1797), 49.

4. Hélène d'Aquin Allain, *Souvenirs d'Amerique et de France par une Créole* (Paris: Bourguet-Calas, 1883), 149; Henry Castellanos, *New Orleans As It Was*, ed. George Reinecke (1895; reprint, Baton Rouge: Louisiana State University Press, 1978), 94; Charles Dudley Warner, *Studies in the South and West* (New York: Harper and Brothers, 1889), 71.

5. George W. Cable, *Dance in Place Congo Square and Creole Slave Songs* (New Orleans: Faruk von Turk, 1974), 28.

6. An elderly New Orleanian, Lydia DeCastro, passed down this song to Ausettua Amor Amenkum (founder and director of Kumbuka African Dance & Drum Collective) and stated that gatherers sang it in Congo Square on Sunday afternoons. Ausettua Amor Amenkum, interview by author, July, 12, 1998.

7. Benjamin H. Latrobe, *The Journals of Benjamin Latrobe, 1799-1820 From Philadelphia to New Orleans*, ed. Edward C. Carter, John C. Van Horne, and Lee W. Formwalt (New Haven: Yale University Press, 1980), 3:204.

8. Henry E. Krehbiel, *Afro-American Folksongs* (New York: G. Schirmer, Inc., 1914), 39-40; Elizabeth Bisland, ed., *Life and Letters of Lafcadio Hearn Including the Japanese Letters* (New York: Houghton Mifflin Company, 1923), 1:352-353.

9. Cable, *Dance in Place Congo*, 32.

10. Marcus Christian Collection, Mss 11, box 33, Louisiana and Special Collections, Earl

K. Long Library, University of New Orleans.

11. Benjamin Moore Norman, *Norman's New Orleans and Environs*, ed. Matthew J. Schott (1845; reprint, Baton Rouge: Louisiana State University Press, 1976), 182; *Daily Picayune*, June 24, 1845.

12. Edwin P. Christy, *Christy's Plantation Melodies* (Philadephia: Fisher and Bros., 1851).

13. Gwendolyn Midlo Hall, "Myths about Creole Culture in Louisiana," *Louisiana Cultural Vistas* 12 (Summer 2001): 81.

14. Maude Cuney Hare, *Six Creole Folk Songs* (New York: Carl Fischer, 1921), 11.

15. Ibid., 4; *Who's Who in America* (Chicago: Marquis Publications, 1968), 1:453.

16. Hare, *Six Creole Folk Songs*, 7.

17. Clara Peterson, *Creole Songs from New Orleans in the Negro Dialect* (New Orleans: L. Grunewald, ca. 1909), preface; Gwendolyn Midlo Hall, *Africans in Colonial Louisiana* (Baton Rouge: Louisiana State University Press, 1992), 194.

18. Federal Writers' Project, folder 118B, Cammie G. Henry Research Center, Watson Memorial Library, Northwestern State University of Louisiana.

19. William Francis Allen, *Slave Songs of the United States* (New York: A. Simpson and Co., 1867), 113; Hare, *Six Creole Folk Songs*, 4, 11, 18, 21; Federal Writers' Project, folder 4, Cammie G. Henry Research Center, Watson Memorial Library, Northwestern State University of Louisiana.

20. Louis M. Gottschalk, *Notes of a Pianist* (Philadephia: J. B. Lippincott and Co., 1881), 104.

21. Lafcadio Hearn, *Two Years in the French West Indies* (New York: Harper, 1923), 428-29; "Lafcadio Hearn Consort of Negress," *Daily News*, August 6, 1906; Cable, *Dance in Place Congo*, 18.

22. Gottschalk, *Notes of a Pianist*, 36; Samuel Coleridge-Taylor, *Twenty Four Negro Melodies*, Op 59 (Boston: O. Ditson, ca. 1905), 39-43.

23. Alice Nelson Dunbar, "People of Color in Louisiana: Part II," *The Journal of Negro History* 1, no. 4. (October 1916): 361-376.

24. Hare, *Six Creole Folk Songs*, 14.

25. Latrobe, *Journals of Benjamin Latrobe*, 204.

26. James Creecy, *Scenes in the South* (Philadelphia: Lippincott and Company, 1860), 21.

27. "Twain-Cable," *Fort Wayne Daily Gazette*, February 6, 1885.

28. Camille Nickerson, *Afro-Creole Music of Louisiana* (M.A. thesis, Oberlin Conservatory, 1932).

29. Bisland, *Life and Letters of Lafcadio Hearn*, 319, 332.

30. Ibid., 319; "Twain-Cable," *Fort Wayne Daily Gazette*, February 6, 1885.

Chapter 7: The Dances

1. Camille Nickerson, *Afro-Creole Music of Louisiana* (M.A. thesis, Oberlin Conservatory, 1932), 60.

2. Christian Schultz, *Travels on an Island Voyage* (New York: Issac Riley, 1810), 2:197; Benjamin H. Latrobe, *The Journals of Benjamin Latrobe, 1799-1820 From Philadelphia to New Orleans*, ed. Edward C. Carter, John C. Van Horne, and Lee W. Formwalt (New Haven: Yale University Press, 1980), 3:204; James Creecy, *Scenes in the South* (Philadelphia: Lippincott and Company, 1860), 20-21.

3.   "The Congo Dance," *Daily Picayune*, October 12, 1879.
4.   Latrobe, *Journals of Benjamin Latrobe*, 204.
5.   Elizabeth Bisland, ed., *The Life and Letters of Lafcadio Hearn Including the Japanese Letters* (New York: Houghton Mifflin Company, 1923), 1:331.
6.   Lafcadio Hearn, "The Scenes of Cable's Romances," *Century Magazine* 27, no. 1 (November 1883): 43; Hebert Asbury, *The French Quarter: An Informal History of the New Orleans Underworld* (St. Simons Island: Mockingbird Books, 1964), 191-92.
7.   Asbury, *French Quarter*,192.
8.   Isaac Holmes, *An Account of the United States of America* (London: H. Fisher, 1823), 332.
9.   Theodore Pavie, *Souvenirs Atlantiques: Voyage aux Etats-Unis et au Canada, par Theodore Pavie*, trans. F. Peterson. (Paris: Roret, 1833), 319-20.
10. Alceé Fortier, "Customs and Superstitions in Louisiana," *The Journal of American Folklore* 1, no. 2 (1888): 136-40.
11. Médéric-Louis Elie Moreau de Saint-Méry, *The Dance* (1796; reprint, Brooklyn: Dance Horizon, 1975), 60-61.
12. Edward Thorpe, *Black Dance* (New York: The Overlook Press, 1990), 16.
13. Ibid., 15; Lynn Fauley Emery, *Black Dance in the United States from 1619 to 1970* (Palo Alto, Calf.: National Press Books, 1972), 164; "The Congo Dance," *Daily Picayune*, October 12, 1879.
14. *The Times Picayune's Guide to New Orleans* (New Orleans: The Picayune, 1900), 63.
15. Timothy Flint, *Recollections of the Last Ten Years in the Valley of the Mississippi*, ed. George R. Brooks (1826; reprint, Carbondale: Southern Illinois University Press, 1968), 103.
16. "Negro Audacity," *Daily Picayune*, November 19, 1840; *Daily Picayune*, October 18, December 10, 1843.
17. Harold Courlander, *Haiti Singing* (New York: Cooper Square Publications, 1973), 72, 156-157.
18. Danys Perez Prades "La Mora," interview by author, July 9, 2008. In 1994 La Mora was evaluated as Primera Bailarina and Primera Profesora by the National Dance Commission in Cuba.
19. Peniel Guirrier, interview by author, July 8, 2008; Yvonne Daniel, *Dancing Wisdom: Embodied Knowledge in Haitian Vodou, Cuban Yoruba, and Bahian Candomble* (Chicago: University of Chicago Press, 2005), 113.
20. Florence Borders, interview by author, November 6, 2007.
21. Aline St. Julien, interview by author, November 20, 2007.
22. Federal Writers' Project, folder 25, Cammie G. Henry Research Center, Watson Memorial Library, Northwestern State University of Louisiana.
23. Danny Barker, interview by Tom Dent, March 18, 1987, in *Tremé Oral History Project*, Collection #494, folder 1/7, Amistad Research Center, New Orleans.
24. Ibid.
25. Federal Writers' Project, folder 25, Cammie G. Henry Research Center, Watson Memorial Library, Northwestern State University of Louisiana.
26. Nickerson, *Afro-Creole Music*, 62.
27. "A Cungi Dance," *Times Democrat*, June 24, 1887; "St John's Eve," *Daily States*, June 23,

1887.

28. Dena Epstein, *Sinful Tunes and Spirituals: Black Folk Music to the Civil War* (Urbana: University of Illinois Press, 1977), 94.

29. Jean Baptiste Labat, *Nouveau Voyage Aux Isles de L'Amérique* (Paris: La Haye P. Husson, 1724), 52.

30. Antoine Simon Le Page du Pratz, *The History of Louisiana*, ed. Joseph G. Tregle, Jr. (1758; reprint, Baton Rouge: Louisiana State University Press, 1975), 387; Labat, *Nouveau Voyage*, 52.

31. Moreau de Saint-Méry, *The Dance*, 54-55.

32. Maude Cuny Hare, *Six Creole Folk-Songs* (New York: Carl Fischer, 1921), 3, 11, 21.

33. Nina Monroe, *Bayou Ballads, 12 Folk Songs from Louisiana* (New York: G. Schirmer, Inc., 1921), vii.

34. Thorpe, *Black Dance*, 15; Susanna Sloat, ed., *Caribbean Dance from Abakua to Zouk* (Gainesville: University Press of Florida, 2002), 259; Harold Courlander, *Drum and Hoe: Life and Lore of the Haitian People* (Berkley: University of California Press, 1960), 133.

35. Julian Gerstin, "The Allure of Origins: Neo-African Dances in the French Caribbean and the Southern United States" in *Just Below South: Intercultural Performance in the Caribbean and the U.S. South*, ed. Jessica Adams, Michael P. Bibler and Cécile Accilien (Charlottesville: University of Virginia Press, 1977), 127-146.

36. Federal Writers' Project, folder 4, Cammie G. Henry Research Center, Watson Memorial Library, Northwestern State University of Louisiana.

37. Ibid.

38. Barry Jean Ancelet, "Zydeco/Zarico: Beans, Blues and Beyond," *Black Music Research Journal* 8, no. 1 (1988): 33-49; Shane Bernard and Julia Girouard, "'Colinda': Mysterious Origins of a Cajun Folksong," *Journal of Folklore Research* 29, no. 1 (January-April 1992): 37-52.

39. Ayesha Morris, "The Power of Dance: Bamboula Has Deep and Strong Ties to African Heritage, Island History and Freedom Fight," *The Virgin Island Daily News*, February 25, 2006: http://www.virginislandsdailynews.com/index.pl/article?id=13672670 (accessed December 2009).

40. Danys La Mora, interview by author, July 9, 2008; Robert Farris Thompson, "Kongo Carolina, Kongo New Orleans: A Transatlantic Art Tradition" Mary Schiller Myers School of Art, Video Lecture (2007): http://art.uakron.edu/visiting-artists/kongo-carolina-kongo-new-orleans-a-transatlanti/

41. Asbury, *French Quarter*, 184.

42. Emery, *Black Dance*, 26; Médéric-Louis Elie Moreau de Saint-Méry, *A Civilization That Perished: The Last Years of White Colonial Rule in Haiti* ed. Ivor D. Spencer (1797-98; reprint, Lanham, Md.: University Press of America, 1985), 55.

43. Alex LaSalle, interview by author, November 14, 2009.

44. "Death of Squire," *The Bee*, July 20, 1837; Asbury, *French Quarter*, 185-86; Henry Castellanos, *New Orleans As It Was*, ed. George Reinecke (1895; reprint, Baton Rouge: Louisiana State University Press, 1978), 158; Bryan Wagner, "Disarmed and Dangerous: the Strange Career of Bras Coupé" *Representations* 92, no. 1 (Fall 2005): 117-51.

45. William Francis Allen, *Slave Songs of the United States* (New York: A Simpson and Co., 1867), 113; Henry E. Krehbiel, *Afro-American Folksongs* (New York: G. Schirmer, Inc., 1914), 121.

46. Rudi Blesh and Harriet Janis, *They All Played Ragtime* (New York: Oak Publications, 1966), 84.

47. Harold Courlander, *Negro Folk Music, United States of America* (New York: Columbia University Press, 1963), 191.

48. Federal Writers' Project, folder 4, Cammie G. Henry Research Center, Watson Memorial Library, Northwestern State University of Louisiana.

49. Loren Schweninger, ed., *The Autobiography of James Thomas: From Tennessee Slave to St. Louis Entrepreneur* (Columbia: University of Missouri Press, 1984), 49.

50. Ibid.; also see Thompson, "Kongo Carolina."

51. Pavie, *Souvenirs Atlantiques*, 319-20.

52. Frances H. Green, *Shahmar in Pursuit of Freedom* (New York: Thatcher and Hutchinson, 1858), 276-77.

53. Fortier, "Customs and Superstitions," 137.

54. Creecy, *Scenes in the South*, 22.

55. Asbury, *French Quarter*, 184.

56. Benjamin Moore Norman, *Norman's New Orleans and Environs*, ed. Matthew J. Schott (1845; reprint, Baton Rouge: Louisiana State University Press, 1976), 182.

57. Michael White, interview by author, March 23, July 25, 2005.

Chapter 8:   The Economic Exchange

1. Ellen Call Long, *Florida Breezes or Florida, New and Old* (Jacksonville: Ashmead Bros., 1883), 26; Thomas Nuttall, *A Journal of Travels into the Arkansas Territory* (Philadelphia: T. H. Palmer, 1821), 245.

2. *The Bee*, October 13, 1835.

3. Virginia M. Gould, "'If I Can't Have My Rights, I Can Have My Pleasures, and If They Won't Give Me Wages, I Can Take Them:' Gender and Slave Labor in Antebellum New Orleans," in the *Louisiana Purchase Bicentennial Series in Louisiana History*, vol. 11 part A, *The African American Experience in Louisiana*, ed. by Charles Vincent (Lafayette, La.: Center for Louisiana Studies, 1999), 348.

4. *New Orleans Times*, January 5, 1874.

5 *Daily Picayune*, December, 11, 1864

6. Herbert Asbury, *The French Quarter: An Informal History of the New Orleans Underworld* (St. Simons Island: Mockingbird Books, 1964), 184; Henry Castellanos, *New Orleans As It Was*, ed. George Reinecke (1895; reprint, Baton Rouge: Louisiana State University Press, 1978), 159; *Daily Picayune*, October 12, 1879; Federal Writers' Project, folder 118B, Cammie G. Henry Research Center, Watson Memorial Library, Northwestern State University of Louisiana.

7. *Daily Picayune*, October 12, 1879; Castellanos, *New Orleans As It Was*, 159; Asbury, *French Quarter*, 184; Federal Writers' Project, folder 118, Cammie G. Henry Research Center, Watson Memorial Library, Northwestern State University of Louisiana; Jessical Harris, "Foodways to Freedom," *American Legacy Woman* 9, no. 3 (Fall 2003).

8. Castellanos, *New Orleans As It Was*, 159; *New Orleans Times*, January 5, 1874.

9. Alcée Fortier, *A History of Louisiana 1512-1768* (New York: Goupil and Company of Pairs, 1904) 4:87-94.

10. Benjamin French, ed., *Historical Memoirs of Louisiana, From the French Settlement of the Colony to the Departure of Govenor O'Reilly in 1770* (New York: Lamport, Blakemann and Law, 1853), 5:120. This is a translation of the historical memories of Jean-Francois-Benjamin Dumont de Montigny.

11. Antoine Simon Le Page du Pratz, *The History of Louisiana*, ed. Joseph G. Tregle, Jr. (1758; reprint, Baton Rouge: Louisiana State University Press, 1975), 387.

12. James Thomas McGowan, *Creation of a Slave Society, Louisiana Plantations in the Eighteenth Century* (Ph.D. dissertation, University of Rochester, 1976), 197.

13. George Washington Cable, *Dance in Place Congo Square and Creole Slave Songs* (New Orleans: Faruk von Turk, 1974), 21.

14. Gwendolyn Midlo Hall, *Africans in Colonial Louisiana* (Baton Rouge: Louisiana State University Press, 1992), 201.

15. Francis Burns, "The Black Code: A Brief History of the Origin, Statutory Regulation and Judicial Sanction of Slavery in Louisiana," in *The Louisiana Purchase Bicentennial Series in Louisiana History*, vol. 13, *An Uncommon Experience: Law and Judicial Institution in Louisiana 1803-2003*, ed. by Judith K. Schafer and Warren M. Billings (Lafayette, La.: Center for Louisiana Studies, 1997), 308; Charles Garyarre, *History of Louisiana, the Spanish Domination* (1866; reprint, Gretna, La.: Pelican Publishing Company, 1974), 3:313; S. Gleason Stevens, *Log Book of a Trip to New Orleans, Feb. 1–March 13, 1845*, (1970), Microfilm, Howard-Tilton Memorial Library, Tulane University.

16. Marcus Christian, *Negro Iron Workers in Louisiana 1718-1900* (Gretna, La.: Pelican Publishing Company, 1972), 28-29; Thomas Marc Fiehrer, "The African Presence in Colonial Louisiana: An Essay on the Continuity of Caribbean Culture," in *Louisiana's Black Heritage*, ed. Robert Macdonald et. al. (New Orleans: Louisiana State Museum, 1979), 30; Loren Schweninger, ed., *The Autobiography of James Thomas: From Tennessee Slave to St. Louis Entrepreneur* (Columbia: University of Missouri Press, 1984), 112.

17. Joseph Tregle, "Early New Orleans Society: A Reappraisal," *Journal of Southern History* 18, no. 1 (February 1952): 34; *The Bee*, November 8, 1837; *Daily Picayune*, November 5, 1839.

18. *Daily Picayune*, December 11, 1864.

19. George Eaton Simpson, "Peasant Songs and Dances of Northern Haiti," *The Journal of Negro History* 25, no. 2 (April 1940): 203-15; Camille Nickerson, *Afro-Creole Music of Louisiana* (M.A. thesis, Oberlin Conservatory, 1932), 65.

Chapter 9: Conclusion

1. Keith Weldon Medley, "New Orleans Congo Square, African Seeds in American Soil," *New Orleans Tribune*, August, 1986.

Timeline

1. Antoine Simone Le Page du Pratz, *Histoire de la Louisiane*, (Paris: De Bure, l'aine, 1758), 3:226-7; also see Antoine Simon Le Page du Pratz, *The History of Louisiana*, ed. Joseph G. Tregle, Jr. (1758; reprint, Baton Rouge: Louisiana State University Press, 1975), 387.

2. Richard J. Shenkel et. al., *Archaeology of the Jazz Complex and Beauregard (Congo) Square, Louis Armstrong Park, New Orleans, Louisiana: Research Report* (New Orleans: University of New Orleans, 1980), 162; Roulac Toledano and Mary Louise Christovich, *New Orleans Architecture*, vol. 6] *Faubourg Treme and the Bayou Road* (Gretna, La.: Pelican Publishing Company, 1980), 7.

3. Charles Gayarre, *The History of Louisiana* (1866; reprint, Gretna, La.: Pelican Publishing Company, 1974), 2:361-367.

4. Shenkel, *Archaeology of the Jazz Complex*, 162.

5. Minutes of the Cabildo, January 19, 1781, Louisiana Division/City Archives, New Orleans Public Library.

6. C. M. Chambon, *In and Around the Old St. Louis Cathedral of New Orleans* (New Orleans: Phillippe's Printery, 1908), 33.

7. Minutes of the Cabildo, June 2, 1786, Louisiana Division/City Archives, New Orleans Public Library.

8. Gayarre, *History of Louisiana*, 2:313; Francois X. Martin, *The History of Louisiana* (1882; reprint, Gretna, La.: Pelican Publishing Company, 1963), 257.

9. Shenkel, *Archaeology of the Jazz Complex*, 121.

10. John Pope, "Progress Mislaid Many Meant to Rest in Peace," *Times-Picayune*, August 18, 1985.

11. James Pitot, *Observations on the Colony of Louisiana from 1796-1802* (Baton Rouge: Louisiana State University Press, 1979), 29.

12. Francis Baily, *Journal of a Tour in Unsettled Parts of North American in 1796-1797* (Carbondale: Southern Illinois University, 1969), 173.

13. Toledano and Christovich, *Faubourg Treme*, 95.

14. Fortescue Cuming, *Sketches of a Tour to the Western Country* (Pittsburg: Cramer, Speer and Eichbaum, 1810), 333, 336.

15. Henry Arnold Kmen, *Music in New Orleans, The Formative Years, 1791-1841* (Baton Rouge: Louisiana State University Press, 1966) 46; Henry Arnold Kmen, *Singing and Dancing in New Orleans: A Social History of the Birth and Growth of Balls and Opera, 1791-1841* (Ph.D. dissertation, Tulane University, 1961), 76.

16. Berquin-Duvallon, *Travels in Louisiana and the Floridas in the Year 1802, Giving a Correct Picture of Those Countries*, trans. John Davis (New York: I. Riley, 1806) 26-27; Kmen, *Music in New Orleans*, 38.

17. John Watson, "Notitia of Incidents at New Orleans, 1804-5," *The American Pioneer* 2, no. 5 (1843): 232.

18. Toledano and Christovich, *Faubourg Treme*, 63.

19. Christian Schultz, *Travels on an Inland Voyage* (New York: Issac Riley, 1810), 2:197. The "rear of town," as used here, commonly referred to Congo Square.

20. *Code de Police* (New Orleans: Renard Printer, 1808), 48, 272.

21. Paul LaChance, "The 1809 Immigration of Saint-Dominque Refugees," in *The Road to Louisiana: the Saint-Domingue Refugee, 1792-1809*, ed. Carl A. Brasseaux and Glenn R. Conrad (Lafayette, La.: Center for Louisiana Studies, 1992), 247.

22. Conseil de Ville, Louisiana Division/City Archives, New Orleans Public Library.

23. *Louisiana Gazette*, June 23, 1810.

24. Charles, the enslaved of Deslondes, can be found in Gwendolyn Midlo Hall's

Louisiana Slave Data Base, *Afro-Louisiana History and Genealogy, 1699-1860* (Baton Rouge: Louisiana State University Press, 2000).

25. *Montiteur de Louisiana,* January 9, 1811.

26. Ordinance and Resolutions of the Municipal Council, January 16, 1811, Louisiana Division/City Archives, New Orleans Public Library.

27. Albert Thrasher, *On to New Orleans! Louisiana's Heroic 1811 Slave Revolt* (New Orleans, Cypress Press, 1995), 64, 239.

28. Letters of the Mayor, Louisiana Division/City Archives, New Orleans Public Library.

29. Conseil de Ville, Louisiana Division/City Archives, New Orleans Public Library.

30. Letters of the Mayor, Louisiana Division/City Archives, New Orleans Public Library.

31. Ibid.

32. Ibid.

33. Ibid.

34. Ibid.

35. Ibid.

36. Conseil de Ville, Louisiana Division/City Archives, New Orleans Public Library.

37. Ibid.

38. Kmen, *Music in New Orleans*, 85-86; *Historical Sketch Book and Guide to New Orleans & Environs With Map*, (New York: Will Coleman, 1885), 297.

39. Felix Flugel, ed., "Pages from a Journal of a Voyage Down the Mississippi to New Orleans in 1817," *Louisiana Historical Quarterly* 7, no. 3 (1924): 432.

40. Johann Ulrich Buechler, *Land-und Seereisen* (Louisville: Lost Cause Press, 1959), 129-30, 160-61.

41. New Orleans City Ordinances of 1817, Louisiana Division/City Archives, New Orleans Public Library, translated for the author by Frieda Arwe.

42. Estwick Evans, "A Pedestrian Tour of 4000 Miles in Western and Southwestern States and Territories During the Winter & Spring of 1818," in *Early Western Travels, 1748-1846*, ed. by Ruben Gold Thwaites (Cleveland: A. H. Clark, 1904), 3:336.

43. Letters of the Mayor, Louisiana Division/City Archives, New Orleans Public Library.

44. The fact that this observation occurred after the 1817 ordinance and the traveler referred to the location as "the green" suggests that it was Congo Square.

45. Henry Cogswell Knight [Arthur Singleton, pseud.], *Letters from the South and West* (Boston: Richardson and Lord, 1824), 127.

46. Benjamin H. Latrobe, *The Journals of Benjamin Latrobe, 1799-1820 From Philadelphia to New Orleans*, ed. Edward C. Carter, John C. Van Horne, and Lee W. Formwalt (New Burns Haven: Yale University Press, 1980), 204.

47. Letters of the Mayor, September 16, 21, 1820, Louisiana Division/City Archives, New Orleans Public Library; John Adams Paxon, *New Orleans Directory and Register* (New Orleans: Benj. Levy and Co., 1822), 40; Henry Castellanos, *New Orleans As It Was*, ed. George Reinecke (1895; reprint, Baton Rouge: Louisiana State University Press, 1978), 19.

48. The "suburbs of the city" refers to "back-a-town" and Congo Square.

49. Thomas Nuttall, *A Journal of Travels into the Arkansas Territory* (Philadelphia: T. H. Palmer, 1821), 245.

50. *Louisiana Gazette*, August 19, 1820.

51. Issac Holmes, *An Account of the United States of America* (London: H. Fisher, 1823), 332.

52. Paxton, *New Orleans Directory* (1822), 40; John Adams Paxton, *The New Orleans Directory and Register* (New Orleans: Printed Privately, 1823), 139.

53. Frank H. Severance, *The Journeys and Journals of an Early Buffalo Merchant [John Lay]* (Buffalo: Buffalo Historical Society, 1896), v, 4.

54. Welcome Arnold Greene, *The Journals of Welcome Arnold Greene*, ed. Howard Greene and Alice E. Smith (Madison: State Historical Society of Wisconsin, 1956), 122-23.

55. Ordinances of the City of New Orleans, Louisiana Division/City Archives, New Orleans Public Library.

56. Theodore Pavie, *Souvenirs Atlantiques: Voyage aux Etats-Unis et au Canada, par Theodore Pavie*, trans. F. Peterson (Paris: Roret, 1833), 319-20.

57. Shenkel, *Archaeology of the Jazz Complex*, 26.

58. James Stuart, *Three Years in North America* (London: Edinburgh, 1833), 2:210.

59. Georges J. Joyaux, ed., "Forest's Voyage aux Etats-Unis de l'Amérique en 1831," *Louisiana Historical Quarterly*, 39, no. 4 (1956): 457-72.

60. *New Orleans Bee*, September 24, 1831.

61. Municipal Council Ordinances & Resolutions, April 18, 1832, Louisiana Division/City Archives, New Orleans Public Library.

62. *New Orleans Bee*, February 19, 1833.

63. Ibid., June 13, 1833.

64. James Creecy, *Scenes in the South* (Philadelphia: Lippincott and Company, 1860), 20-23.

65. Joseph Holt Ingraham, *The South-West By a Yankee* (New York: Harper and Brothers, 1835), 1:162.

66. Edward Durell [Henry Didimus, pseud.], *New Orleans As I Found It* (New York: Harper & Bros., 1845), 34.

67. Municipal Council Ordinances & Resolutions, March 21, 1835, Louisiana Division/City Archives, New Orleans Public Library.

68. Ibid., August 5, 1835.

69. *New Orleans Bee*, November 30, 1835.

70. Municipal Council Ordinances & Resolutions, February 17, 1836, Louisiana Division/City Archives, New Orleans Public Library.

71. First Municipals Council Ordinances & Resolutions, May 17, 1837, Louisiana Division/City Archives, New Orleans Public Library.

72. Ibid., August 28 1837.

73. *New Orleans Bee*, November 8, 1837.

74. *New Orleans True American*, January 1, 1839.

75. *Daily Picayune*, November 5, 1839.

76. Ibid., September 24, 1840.

77. Ibid., November 19, 1840.

78. Ibid., January 12, 1841.

79. Ibid., July 22, 1841.

80. Ibid., August 19, 1841.

81. First Municipal Council, January 2, 1843, Louisiana Division/City Archives, New Orleans Public Library.

82. *Daily Picayune*, September 23, 1843.

83. Ibid., October 18, 1843.

84. Ibid., December 10, 1843.

85. *Weekly Picayune*, July 15, 1844.

86. Benjamin Moore Norman, *Norman's New Orleans and Environs*, ed. Matthew J. Schott (1845; reprint, Baton Rouge: Louisiana State University Press, 1976), 182.

87. City Council Ordinances & Resolutions, April 28, 1845, Louisiana Division/City Archives, New Orleans Public Library.

88. *Daily Picayune*, June 24, 1845.

89. Ibid., July 15, 1845.

90. Loren Schweninger, ed., *The Autobiography of James Thomas: From Tennessee Slave to St. Louis Entrepreneur* (Columbia: University of Missouri Press, 1984), 109.

91. *Louisiana Courier*, February 23, 1846.

92. *Daily Picayune*, March 22, 1846.

93. A. Oakey Hall, *The Manhattaner in New Orleans* (New Orleans: J. C. Morgan, 1852).

94. *New Orleans Bee*, April 27, 1846.

95. *New Orleans Bee*, June 12, 1846.

96. First Municipal Council Ordinances & Resolutions, March 1, 1847, Louisiana Division/City Archives, New Orleans Public Library.

97. Ibid., December 11, 1848.

98. *Daily Picayune*, December 31, 1848.

99. First Municipal Council Ordinances & Resolutions, January, 15, March 19, April 30, 1849, Louisiana Division/City Archives, New Orleans Public Library.

100. *Daily Picayune*, July 31, 1850; and *New Orleans Louisiana Courier*, July 31, 1850.

101. *Louisiana Courier*, October 15, 1850.

102. First Municipal Council Ordinances & Resolutions, November 11, 1850, Louisiana Division/City Archives, New Orleans Public Library.

103. Toledano and Christovich, *Faubourg Treme*, 65.

104. *Daily Picayune*, February 1, 1851.

105. *Daily True Delta*, July 20, 1851.

106. Ibid., July 25, 1851.

107. Ibid., July 26, 1851.

108. *Louisiana Courier*, February 16, 1853.

109. *Daily True Delta*, February 22, 1853.

110. *Louisiana Courier*, March 5, 1853; City Council Ordinances & Resolutions, March 5, 1853, Louisiana Division/City Archives, New Orleans Public Library.

111. *Daily True Delta*, June 15, 1853; *New Orleans Bee*, June 15, 1853.

112. *Daily Crescent*, July 4, 1853.

113. Marie Fontenay de GrandforGrandfort, *The New World*, trans. by Edward C. Wharton

(Wharton and Company, 1855).

114. *Daily Delta*, November 3, 1854.

115. Schweninger, *Autobiography of James Thomas*, 8.

116. New Orleans City Council Ordinances & Resolutions, December 2, 1856, Louisiana Division/City Archives, New Orleans Public Library.

117. Ibid., December 8, 1856.

118. Henry Jefferson Leovy, *The Laws and General Ordinances of the City of New Orleans: Revised & Digested* (New Orleans: E. C. Wharton, 1857), 258.

119. *New Orleans Tagliche Deutsch Zeitung*, February 16, March 23, 30, 1858.

120. New Orleans City Council Ordinances & Resolutions, April 1858, Book 13, No. 3847, Louisiana Division/City Archives, New Orleans Public Library.

121. *Daily True Delta*, October 9, 1859.

122. Ibid., October 2, 1860.

123. *New Orleans Times*, February 20, 1861.

124. *Daily True Delta*, May 8, 1861.

125. Shenkel, *Archaeology of the Jazz Complex*, 26.

126. *Daily Delta*, July 30, 1861.

127. *Daily Picayune*, August 14, 1861.

128. *New Orleans Era*, June 3, 5, 1863.

129. Keith Medley, *We as Freemen: Plessy v. Ferguson* (Gretna, La.: Pelican Publishing Company, 2003), 75.

130. *New Orleans Times*, February 20, 1864

131. Administrations of the Mayor's of New Orleans: 1803-1936. Compiled and edited by Works Progress Administration, 1940, Louisiana Division/City Archives, New Orleans Public Library.

132. *Daily True Delta*, June 12, 1863; *New Orleans Era*, June 12, 1863.

133. *New Orleans Era*, December 10, 30, 1864; *New Orleans Times*, December 10, 23, 30, 1864; *Daily Picayune*, December 12-14, 18, 21, 27, 30, 1864; *Daily True Delta*, December 14, 31, 1864.

134. *Daily Picayune*, December 11, 1864.

135. Ibid., December 13, 1864.

136. *Black Republican*, April 29, 1865.

137. *Daily Crescent*, October 23, 1865.

138. *New Orleans Tagliche Deutsch Zetung*, December 2, 1865.

139. *New Orleans Daily Crescent*, August 6, 1866.

140. *New Orleans Times*, May 7, 1867.

141. *New Orleans Crescent*, September 11, 1868.

142. *Daily Picayune*, August 24, 1869; *New Orleans Republican*, September 17, 1869.

143. *New Orleans Republican*, September 29, 1869; *Daily Picayune*, October 12, 1869.

144. *New Orleans Republican*, March 11, 1870.

145. *New Orleans Tagliche Deutsch Zeitun*, June 17, 1870.

146. *Daily Picayune*, October 1879.

147. *Item Tribune*, October 14, 1928.

148. *New Orleans Democrat*, June 17, 1881.

149. Ibid., July 8, 1881.

150. *Daily Picayune*, August 5, 1881.

151. *Historical Sketch Book*, 298.

152. Charles Dudley Warner, *Studies in the South and West* (New York: Harper and Brothers, 1889), 64-71.

153. *The Daily States*, June 23, 1887.

154. *Times Democrat*, June 24, 1887.

155. Ibid., March, 15, 1891.

156. *The Times Democrat*, June 19, 1892.

157. *Daily Picayune.*, March 24, 29, 1893.

158. Mayor Martin Berhman's Administration, Park Commissioners Reports, 1906, Louisiana Division/City Archives, New Orleans Public Library.

159. Ibid., October 14, 1928.

160. Ibid., April 15, 1928.

161. Ibid., October 14, 1928.

162. Toledano and Christovich, *Faubourg Treme*, 65.

163. *New Orleans States*, June 29, 1945.

164. Ibid., August 2, 1949.

165. Ibid., August 3, 1949.

166. *New Orleans State Item*, October 31, November 18, 1963.

167. Shenkel, *Archaeology of the Jazz Complex*, 163.

168. *New Orleans Times-Picayune*, April 11, 1980.

169. Funders for the historical marker included: New Orleans Jazz & Heritage Foundation, House of Blues, Essence Communications, Tambourine & Fan Organization, New Orleans Jazz National Historical Park, City of New Orleans, and White Buffalo Day Organization.

Selected Bibliography

"The African Slave Trade." Review of *Captain Canot or Twenty years of An African Slaver*, by Brantz Mayer. *De Bow's Review* 18 (1855): 16-20.

Allain, Helene d'Aquin. *Souvenirs d'Amerique et de France, par une Creole*. Paris: Bourguet-Calas, 1883.

Allen, William Francis. *Slave Songs of the United States*. New York: Simpson and Company, 1867.

Ancelet, Barry Jean. "Zydeco/Zarico: Beans, Blues and Beyond." *Black Music Research Journal* 8, no. 1 (1988): 33-49.

Asbury, Hebert. *The French Quarter: An Informal History of the New Orleans Underworld*. St. Simons Island: Mockingbird Books, 1964.

Baily, Francis. *Journal of a Tour in Unsettled Parts of North America in 1796-1797*. Carbondale: Southern Illinois University Press, 1969.

Bean, Annemarie, James V. Hatch, and Brooks McNamara. *Inside the Minstrel Mask – Readings in Nineteenth-Century Blackface Minstrelsy*. London: Wesleyan University Press, 1996.

Bell, Caryn Cossé. *Revolution, Romanticism, and the Afro-Creole Protest Tradition in Louisiana 1718-1868*. Baton Rouge: Louisiana State University Press, 1997.

Berjot, Eugene. *Un Voyage a' la Nouvelle-Orleans*. Par le Dr. E. Berjot. [N. p., 18--].

[Berquin-Duvallon.] *Travels in Louisiana and the Floridas, in the Year 1802, Giving a Correct Picture of Those Countries*. Translated by John Davis. New York: I. Riley, 1806.

Birden, Earl F. "Kemble's 'Speciality' and the Pictorial Countertext." In *A Case Study in Critical Controversy: Adventures of Huckleberry Finn*, ed. by Gerald Graff and James Thelan. New York: Bedford Books, 1995.

Bland, Elizabeth, ed. *Life and Letters of Lafcadio Hearn Including the Japanese Letters*. Vol. 1. New York: Houghton Mifflin Company, 1923.

Blesh, Rudi and Harriet Janis. *They All Played Ragtime*. New York: Oak Publications, 1966.

Blockson, Charles L. *African Americans in Pennsylvania, a History and Guide*. Baltimore: Black Classic Press, 1994.

Brown, William Wells. *My Southern Home: or the South and Its People*. New York: Negro Universities Press, 1880.

Buechler, Johann Ulrich, *Land-und Seereisen*. Louisville: Lost Cause Press, 1959.

Burns, Francis P. "The Black Code: A Brief History of the Origin, Statutory Regulation and Judicial Sanction of Slavery in Louisiana." In *The Louisiana Purchase Bicentennial Series in Louisiana History*, vol. 13, *An Uncommon Experience Law and Judicial Institutions in Louisiana 1803-2003*, edited by Judith Schafer and Warren M. Billings, 305-311. Lafayette: Center for Louisiana Studies, 1997.

Cable, George Washington. *The Dance in Place Congo and Creole Slave Songs.* New Orleans: Synoeceosial Farukvon Turk, 1976.

Cable, Mary. *Lost New Orleans.* Boston: Houghton Mifflin, 1980.

Castellanos, Henry. *New Orleans As It Was.* Baton Rouge: Louisiana State University Press, 1978.

Chambon, C. M. *In and Around the Old St. Louis Cathedral of New Orleans.* New Orleans: Phillippe's Printery, 1908.

Chase, Gilbert. *America's Music from the Pilgrims to the Present.* Chicago: University of Illinois, 1987.

Christian, Marcus. *A Black History of Louisiana.* Louisiana and Special Collections, Earl K. Long Library, University of New Orleans Library, unpublished, 1980.

————. *Negro Iron Workers in Louisiana 1718-1900.* Gretna, La.: Pelican Press, 1972.

Christy, Edwin Pearce, *Christy's Plantation Melodies, No. 4.* Philadelphia: Fisher and Brothers, 1854.

Coleridge-Taylor, Samuel. *Twenty Four Negro Melodies, Op.59.* Boston: O. Ditson, ca. 1905.

Conrad, Glenn R. "Emigration Forcee: A French Attempt to Populate Louisiana 1716-1720." In *The Louisiana Purchase Bicentennial Series in Louisiana History,* vol. 1, *The French Experience in Louisiana,* edited by Glenn R. Conrad, 125-135. Lafayette: Center for Louisiana Studies, 1995.

Courlander, Harold. *Negro Folk Music, United States of America.* New York: Columbia University Press, 1963.

————. *Haiti Singing.* New York: Cooper Square Publications, 1973.

————. "Musical Instruments of Cuba." *The Musical Quarterly* 28, no. 2 (1942): 227-40.

————. "Musical Instruments of Haiti." *The Musical Quarterly* 27, no. 3 (1941): 371-383.

Creecy, James. *Scenes in the South.* Philadelphia: Lippincott and Company, 1860.

Cuming, Fortescue. *Sketches of a Tour to the Western Country.* Pittsburg: Cramer, Speer and Eichbaum, 1810.

Daniel, Yvonne. *Dancing Wisdom: Embodied Knowledge in Haitian Vodou, Cuban Yoruba, and Bahian Candomble.* Chicago: University of Chicago Press, 2005.

Dart, Henry P., "The Slave Depot of the Company of the Indies at New Orleans." *Louisiana Historical Quarterly,* 9 (April 1926): 286-287.

Davis, Edwin Adams. *Louisiana: A Narrative History.* Baton Rouge: Claitor's Publishing Division, 1971.

Donaldson, Gary A. "Window on Slave Culture: Dance at Congo Square in New Orleans, 1800-1862." *Journal of Negro History* 69 (Spring 1984): 63-72.

Dunbar, Alice Nelson. "People of Color in Louisiana: Part II." *The Journal of Negro History* 1, no. 4 (1916): 361-376.

Durell, Edward [Henry Didimus]. *New Orleans As I Found It.* New York: Harper and Bros., 1845.

Early, Eleanor. *New Orleans Holiday*. New York: Rinehart and Company, Inc., 1947.

Elie, Louis E. *Histoire d'Haiti*. Port-au-Prince, Haiti: Droits de Traduction, de Reproduction, 1944.

Emerson, Ken. *Doo – dah!, Stephen Foster and the Rise of American Culture*. New York: Simon and Schuster, 1997.

Emery, Lynne Fauley. *Black Dance in the United States from 1619 to 1970*. Palo Alto, Cal.: National Press Books, 1972.

Epstein, Dena J. *Sinful Tunes and Spirituals*. Chicago: University of Illinois Press, 1977.

Estes, David C. "Traditional Dances and Processions of Blacks in New Orleans as Witnessed By Antebellum Travelers." *Louisiana Folklore Miscellany* 6, no. 3 (1990): 1-14.

Evans, Estwick. "A Pedestrian Tour of 4000 Miles in Western and Southwestern States and Territories during the Winter and Spring of 1818." In *Early Western Travels, 1748-1846*, vol. 8, edited by Reuben Gold Thwaites. Cleveland: A. H. Clark, 1904.

Farrison, William Edward. *Wells Brown, Author and Reformer*. Chicago: University of Chicago Press, 1969.

Fiehrer, Thomas M. "The African Presence in Colonial Louisiana: An Essay on the Continuity of Caribbean Culture." In *Louisiana's Black Heritage*, edited by Robert MacDonald et. al, 3-31. New Orleans: Louisiana State Museum, 1979.

Flint, Timothy. *Recollections of the Last Ten Years in the Valley of the Mississippi*. Carbondale: Southern Illinois University Press, 1968.

Floyd, Samuel. "Black Music in the Circum-Caribbean." *American Music* 17, no. 1 (Spring 1999): 1-38.

Flugel, Felix, ed. "Pages From a Journal of a Voyage Down the Mississippi to New Orleans in 1817." *The Louisiana Historical Quarterly* 7 (1924): 414-440.

Fortier, Alcee. *History of Louisiana 1512-1768*. Vol. 2. New York: Goupil and Company of Paris, 1904.

Fossier, Albert E. *New Orleans, the Glamour Period, 1800-1840*. New Orleans: Pelican, 1957.

Freiberg, Edna B. *Bayou St. John in Colonial Louisiana 1699-1803*. New Orleans: Harvey Press, 1980.

French, Benjamin, ed. *Historical Memoirs of Louisiana, From the French Settlement of the Colony to the Departure of Governor O'Reilly in 1770*. Vol. 5. New York: Lamport, Blakemann and Law, 1853.

Gayarre, Charles. *History of Louisiana, the Spanish Domination*. Vol. 3. Gretna: Pelican Publishing Company, 1974.

Gilbert, Chase. *America's Music from the Pilgrims to the Present*. Chicago: University of Illinois Press, 1987.

Giraud, Marcel. *A History of French Louisiana*. Vol. 1. Translated by Joseph C. Lambert. Baton Rouge: Louisiana State University Press, 1974.

Gould, Virginia. "'If I Can't Have My Rights, I Can Have My Pleasures, and If They Won't Give

Me Wages, I Can Take Them': Gender and Slave Labor in Antebellum New Orleans."
In *The Louisiana Purchase Bicentennial Series in Louisiana History*, vol 11, *The African American Experience in Louisiana*, Part A, edited by Charles Vincent, 340-357. Lafayette: Center for Louisiana Studies, 1999.

Grattan, H. P. "The Origin of the Christy's Minstrels." *The Theatre – A Month Review of the Drama, Music, and the Fine Arts* 5 (1882): 129-133.

Green, Frances H. *Shahmah in Pursuit of Freedom or The Branded Hand.* New York: Thatcher and Hutchinson, 1858.

Greene, Welcome Arnold. *Journals.* Edited by Howard Greene and Alice E. Smith. Madison: State Historical Society of Wisconsin, 1956.

Gura, Philip F. and James Bollman. *America's Instrument, the Banjo in the Nineteenth Century.* Chapel Hill: The University of North Carolina Press, 1999.

Hall, Abraham Oakey. *The Manhattaner in New Orleans.* New Orleans: J. C. Morgan, 1851.

Hall, Gwendolyn Midlo. *Africans in Colonial Louisiana.* Baton Rouge: Louisiana State University Press, 1992.

———. "Myths About Creole Culture in Louisiana." *Louisiana Cultural Vistas* 12 (Summer 2001): 79-85.

———. *Slavery and African Ethnicities in the Americas.* Chapel Hill: University of North Carolina Press, 2005.

Haas, Edward F., ed. *Louisiana's Legal Heritage.* Pensacola: The Perdido Bay Press, 1983.

Hanger, Kimberly A. *A Medley of Cultures, Louisiana History at the Cabildo.* New Orleans Louisiana Museum Foundation, 1996.

Hardy, James D., Jr. "The Transportation of Convicts to Colonial Louisiana." In *The Louisiana Puchase Bicentennial Series in Louisiana History*, vol. 1, *The French Experience in Louisiana*, edited by Glenn R. Conrad, 115-124. Lafayette: Center for Louisiana Studies, 1995.

Hare, Maude Cuney. *Six Creole Folk Songs.* New York: Carl Fischer, 1921.

Harris, Jessica. *Beyond Gumbo: Creole Fusion Food from the Atlantic Rim.* New York: Simon and Schuster, 2003.

———. *Iron Pots and Wooden Spoons.* New York: Simon and Schuster, 1999.

Hearn, Lafcadio. "The Scenes in Cable's Romances." *Century Magazine* (November 1883): 40-47.

———. *Two Years in the French West Indies.* New York: Harper, 1923.

Holloway, Joseph E. "The Origins of African-American Culture." In *Africanisms in American Culture*, edited by Joseph Holloway, 1-17. Bloomington: Indiana University Press, 1990.

Holmes, Isaac. *An Account of the United States of America, Derived from Actual Observations During a Residence of Four Years in that Republic: Including Original Communications.* London: H. Fisher, 1823.

Hurston, Zora Neale. *Mules and Men.* New York: Harper Perennial, 1935.

Ingersoll, Thomas N. *Mammon and Manon in Early New Orleans.* Knoxville: University of Tennessee Press, 1999.

Ingraham, Joseph Holt. *The South-West By a Yankee.* Vol. 1. New York: Harper and Brothers, 1835.

Johnson, Jerah. *Congo Square in New Orleans.* New Orleans: Louisiana Landmarks Society, 1995. Originally published as "New Orleans' Congo Square: An Urban Setting for Early Afro-American Culture Formation." *Louisiana History* 32 (Spring 1991): 117-157.

Johnson, Walter. *Soul by Soul: Life Inside the Antebellum Slave Mart.* Cambridge: Harvard University Press, 1999.

Joyaux, Georges J. "Forest's Voyage aux Etats-Unis de l'Amerique en 1831." *Louisiana Historical Quarterly* 39 (January 1956): 457-472.

Kendall, John Smith. *History of New Orleans.* Vol. 2. New York: Lewis Publishing Company, 1922.

———. "Notes On the Criminal History." *The Louisiana Historical Quarterly* 34 (July 1951): 147-173.

King, Grace. *New Orleans, the Place and the People.* New York: Macmillan Company, 1899.

Kmen, Henry A. *Music in New Orleans - The Formative Years 1791-1841.* Baton Rouge: Louisiana State University Press, 1966.

———. "The Roots of Jazz and the Dance in Place Congo: A Re-Appraisal." *Inter-American Musical Research Yearbook* 8 (1972): 5-17.

———. "Singing and Dancing in New Orleans: A Social History of the Birth and Growth of Balls and Opera 1791-1841." Ph.D. diss., Tulane University, 1961.

Knight, Henry Cogswell [Arthur Singleton]. *Letters from the South and West.* Boston: Richardson and Lord, 1824.

Krehbiel, Henry E. *Afro-American Folksongs.* New York: G. Schirmer, Inc., 1914.

Kubik, Gehard. "Drum Patterns in the 'Batuque' of Benedito Caxias," *Latin American Music Review/ Revista de Música Latinoamericana* 11, no. 2 (Autumn – Winter,1990): 115-181.

Labat, Jean Baptiste. *Nouveau Voyage Aux Isles de l'Amerique.* Vol 2. Paris: La Haye, P. Husson, 1724.

LaChance, Paul. "The 1809 Immigration of Saint-Dominique Refugees." In *The Road Louisiana: The Saint-Domingue Refugees, 1792-1809,* edited by Carl A. Brasseaux and Glenn R. Conrad, 245-284. Lafayette: The Center for Louisiana Studies, 1992.

Le Page Du Pratz, Le Page, Antoine Simone. *Histoire de la Louisiane.* Vol. 3. Paris: De Bure, l'aine, 1758.

———. *The History of Louisiana.* Edited by Joseph G. Tregle, Jr. Baton Rouge: Louisiana State University Press, 1975.

Latrobe, Henry Benjamin. *The Journals of Benjamin Latrobe 1799- 1820 From Philadelphia to New Orleans.* Vol. 3. Edited by Edward C. Carter II, John C. Van Horne, and Lee W. Formwalt. New Haven: Yale University Press, 1980.

Le Blanc de Villeneufve, Paul Louis. *The Festival of the Young Corn or The Heroism of Poucha-Houmma.* Lafayette: University of Southwestern Louisiana, 1964.

Leovy, Henry Jefferson. *The Laws and General Ordinances of the City of New Orleans*. New Orleans: E. C. Wharton, 1857.

Logsdon, Joseph and Caryn Cossé Bell. "The Americanization of Black New Orleans, 1850-1900." In *Creole New Orleans: Race and Americanization*, edited by Arnold R. Hirsch and Joseph Logsdon, 201-261. Baton Rouge: Louisiana State University Press, 1992.

Long, Carolyn Morrow. *Spiritual Merchants*. Knoxville: University of Tennessee Press, 2001.

Long, Ellen Call. *Florida Breezes or Florida, New and Old*. Jacksonville: Ashmead Brothers, 1883.

Mariana, Myriam Evelyse. *African Influences in Brazilian Dance* in *African Dance: An Artistic, Historical and Philosophical Inquiry*. Edited by Kariamu Welsh Asante. Trenton, N.J.: African World Press, Inc., 1996.

Martin, Francois X. *The History of Louisiana*. New Orleans: Pelican Publishing Company, 1882.

Mbiti, John. *African Religions and Philosophy*. Portsmouth, N.H.: Heinemann Educational Publishers, 1969.

McGowan, James Thomas. "Creation of a Slave Society, Louisiana Plantations in the Eighteenth Century." Ph.D. diss., University of Rochester, 1976.

Medley, Keith Weldon. "New Orleans Congo Square, African Seeds in American Soil," *New Orleans Tribune*, August 1986.

Monroe, Nina. *Bayou Ballads, Twelve Folk Songs from Louisiana*. New York: G. Schirmer, Inc., 1921.

Moreau De Saint-Mery, Mederic-Louis-Elie. *A Civilization That Perished: The Last Years of White Colonial Rule in Haiti*. Translated, abridged and edited by Ivor D. Spencer. Lanham, Md.: University Press of America, 1985.

———. *Dance*. Translated by Lily and Baird Hastings. Philadelphia: A Dance Horizon Publication, 1976.

———. *Description Topographique, Physique, Civile, Politique et Historique de la Partie Francaise de l'Isle Saint-Dominque*. Philadelphia: Chez l'auteur, 1797.

Mulira, Jessie Gaston. "The Case of Voodoo." In *Africanisms in American Culture*, edited by Joseph Holloway, 34-67. Bloomington: Indiana University Press, 1990.

Nasatir, Abraham and Ernest R. Liljegren, "Materials Relating to the Mississippi Valley, From the Minuets of 1795, The Spanish Supreme Councils of State, 1787-1797." *The Louisiana Historical Quarterly* 21 (January–October 1938): 5-75.

Nettel, Reginald. "Historical Introduction to 'La Calinda." *Music and Letters* 27 (1946): 59-62.

Nickerson, Camille Lucie. *Africo-Creole Music in Louisiana*. Master's thesis, Oberlin Conservatory of Music, 1932.

'Nketia, J. H. Kwabena. *The Music of Africa*. New York: W. W. Norton and Company, 1974.

———. "Drums, Dance, and Song." *Atlantic Monthly 203* (April 1959): 69-72.

Norman, Yetman. *Life Under the "Peculiar Institution"- Selections from the Slave Narrative Collection*. New

York: Robert Krieger Publishing Company, 1976.

Norman's New Orleans and Environs [1845]. Baton Rouge: Louisiana State University Press, 1976.

Nuttal, Thomas. *A Journal of Travels into the Arkansas Territory.* Philadelphia: T. H. Palmer, 1821.

Olmstead, Frederick, L. *The Cotton Kingdom.* New York: Modern Library, 1984.

Pavie, Theodore. *Souvenirs Atlantiques. Voyage aux Etats-Unis et au Canada, par Theodore Pavie.* Translated by Mrs. F. Peterson. Paris: Roret, 1833.

Peterson, Clara Gottschalk. *Creole Songs From New Orleans in the Negro Dialect.* New Orleans: L. Grunewald, ca.1909.

Phelps, Albert. *Louisiana: A Record of Expansion.* New York: Houghton Mifflin, 1905.

Pitot, James. *Observations on the Colony of Louisiana from 1796 – 1802.* Baton Rouge: Louisiana State University Press, 1979.

Reinders, Robert. *End of an Era: New Orleans, 1850 – 1860.* New Orleans: Pelican Publishing Company, 1964.

Richards, Dona Marimba. *Let the Circle Be Unbroken: Implications of African Spirituality in the Diaspora.* Trenton, N.J.: The Red Sea Press, 1980.

Roberts, John Storm. *Black Music of Two Worlds.* New York: William Morrow and Company, Inc., 1974.

Robin, Charles C. *Voyage to Louisiana.* New Orleans: Pelican Publishing Company, 1966.

Rothschild, Salomon de, Baron. *A Casual View of America: The Home Letters of Salomon de Rothschild, 1859-1861.* Translated and edited by Sigmund Diamond. London: Cresset Press, 1962.

Saxon, Lyle. *Old Louisiana.* New Orleans: Robert L. Crager and Company, 1950.

Schultz, Christian. *Travels on an Island Voyage.* Vol. 2. New York: Issac Riley, 1810.

Schweninger, Loren ed. *The Autobiography of James Thomas: From Tennessee Slave to St. Louis Entrepreneur.* Columbia: University of Missouri Press, 1984.

Searight, Sarah. *New Orleans.* New York: Stein and Day Publishers, 1973.

Severance, Frank. *The Journeys and Journals of an Early Buffalo Merchant [John Lay].* Buffalo, N.Y.: Buffalo Historical Society, 1896.

Shenkel, Richard J., Robert Sauder, and Edward R. Chatelain. *Archaeology of the Jazz Complex and Beauregard (Congo Square), Louis Armstrong Park, New Orleans, Louisiana: Research Report.* New Orleans: University of New Orleans, 1980.

Siegel, Martin. *New Orleans: A Chronological and Documentary History 1539-1970.* Dobbs Ferry: Oceana Publishers Inc., 1975.

Simpson, George Eaton. "Peasant Songs and Dances of Northern Haiti." *The Journal of Negro History* 25, no.2 (April 1940): 203-215.

Sitterson, J. Carlyle. "The Savior of Louisiana." In *The Louisiana Purchase Bicentennial Series in*

Louisiana History, vol. 16, *Agriculture and Economic Development in Louisiana*, edited by Thomas A. Becnel, 210-220. Lafayette: Center for Louisiana Studies, 1995.

Sloat, Susanna, ed. *Caribbean Dance from Abakua to Zouk: How Movement Shapes Identity.* Gainsville: University Press of Florida, 2002.

Southern, Eileen. *The Music of Black Americans.* New York: Norton and Company, 1971.

Stevens, S. Gleason. *Log Book of a Trip to New Orleans, Feb. 1 – March 13, 1845.* Microfilm, Howard-Tilton Memorial Library, Tulane University, 1970.

Stuart, James. *Three Years in North America.* London: Edinburgh, 1833.

Sublette, Ned. *Cuba and Its Music: From the First Drums to the Mambo.* Chicago: Chicago Review Press, 2004.

———. *The World That Made New Orleans – From Spanish Silver to Congo Square.* Chicago: Lawrence Hill Books, 2008.

Tallant, Robert. *New Orleans City Guide.* Boston: Houghton Mifflin Company, 1952.

Taylor, Joe Gray. *Negro Slavery in Louisiana.* Baton Rouge: The Louisiana Historical Association, 1963.

Thompson, Robert Farris. *Flash of the Spirit.* New York: Vintage Books, 1984.

———. *Tango.* New York: Pantheon Books, 2005.

———. "When the Saints Go Marching In: Kongo Louisiana, Kongo New Orleans." In *Resonance from the Past: African Sculpture from the New Orleans Museum of Art*, edited by Frank Herreman. New York: Museum of African Art, 2005.

Thompson, Thomas. "National Newspaper and Legislative Reactions to Louisiana's Deslondes Slave Revolt of 1811." *Louisiana History* 33, no.1 (1992): 5-29.

Thorpe, Edward. *Black Dance.* New York: The Overlook Press, 1990.

Toledano, Roulhac and Mary Louise Christovich. *New Orleans Architecture.* Vol. 6, *Faubourg Treme and the Bayou Road.* Gretna: Pelican Publishing Company, 1980.

Thrasher, Albert. *On To New Orleans! Louisiana's Heroic 1811 Slave Revolt.* New Orleans: Cypress Press, 1995.

Tregle, Joseph. "Early New Orleans Society: A Reappraisal." *The Journal of Southern History* 18 (1952): 21-36.

Tregle, Joseph, Jr. *Louisiana in the Age of Jackson.* Baton Rouge: Louisiana State University Press, 1999.

Usner, Daniel H. Jr. "American Indians in Colonial New Orleans." In *Powhatan's Mantle: Indians in the Colonial Southeast*, edited Peter H. Wood, Gregory A. Waselkov and M. Thomas Hatley. Lincoln: University of Nebraska Press, 1989.

———. "From African Captivity to American Slavery: An Introduction of Black Laborers to Colonial Louisiana." *Louisiana History* 20 (1979): 25-47.

———. *Indian, Settlers, and Slaves in a Frontier Exchange Economy.* Chapel Hill: North Carolina University Press, 1992.

Washburn, Beatrice. "First and Last Nights: I." *The New Orleanian,* December 1930, 16.

Washburn, Christopher. "The Clave of Jazz: A Caribbean Contribution to the Rhythmic Foundation of an African-American Music." *Black Music Research Journal* 17, no.1 (Spring 1997): 59-80.

Watson, John. "Notitia of Incidents at New Orleans 1804-5." *The American Pioneer* 2, no. 5 (1843): 227-237.

Wegener, Werner A. *Negro Slavery in New Orleans.* Microfilm, Baton Rouge: Louisiana State University Photo Duplication Service, 1935.

Whitman, Walt. *Three New Orleans Sketches.* New York: Farrar, Straus, and Company, 1948.

Villiers, Marc de. "History of the Foundation of New Orleans (1717-1722)." *Louisiana Historical Quarterly* 3, no. 2 (April 1920): 161-251.

Young, Jason R. *Rituals of Resistance.* Baton Rouge: Louisiana State University Press, 2007.

Zacharie, James S. *New Orleans Guide With Descriptions of the Routes to New Orleans, Sights of the City Arranged Alphabetically, and Other Information Useful to Travellers; Also, Outlines of the History of Louisiana.* New Orleans: The New Orleans News Company, 1855.

IMAGE CREDITS

Front cover, *Danis 1* by Elizabeth Calett; cover art © Elizabeth Catlett/Licensed by VAGA, New York, NY; viii, courtesy the New Orleans Museum of Art, bequest of Victor K. Kiama 77.135; 4, from *Century Magazine*, 1886; 11, both maps are reprinted from *The Architecture of Colonial Louisiana* (Lafayette: Center for La. Studies, 1987); 14, from *The Architecture of Colonial Louisiana*; 16, *Plan of New Orleans the Capital of Louisiana . . . in the Year 1720* by Thomas Jefferys (London, 1759); 17, *Map of New Orleans and Vicinity* by Vicente Sebastian Pintado (Havana, 1819; copy New Orleans, 1873), courtesy the Library of Congress; 21, courtesy The Historic New Orleans Collection, 1985.127.12; 27, *Plan of the City and Suburb of New Orleans . . . in 1815* by Jacques Tanesse, courtesy the Library of Congress; 28, *Norman's Plan of New Orleans & Environs, 1845* by Henry Moellhausen, courtesy the Library of Congress; 31, from *Digeste Des Ordonnances En Force Dans La Municipalite No. Un, Le 13 Mai 1846* by Christoval Morel and T. W. Collens (New Orleans: Auguste Brusle); 34, Slavery Manuscripts, 1153, courtesy the Louisiana Collection, Tulane University, New Orleans; 41, *Los Companillas*, courtesy Xavier University Archives, New Orleans; 41, *Grande Polka Des Chasseurs*, from the Louisiana State Museum, courtesy Xavier University Archives, New Orleans; 60, courtesy The Historic New Orleans Collection, 1977.79.19; 64, from the original manuscript journals of Benjamin Latrobe, courtesy the Maryland Historical Society, Baltimore; 66, all courtesy the Amistad Research Center, New Orleans, (bottom two drums, photographed by J. R. Thomason); 67, both courtesy the Louisiana State Museum, (photographed by J. R. Thomason); 68 and 69, both catas, the elongated gourd, and the mule's jawbone courtesy the Summers Multi-Ethnic Institute of Arts, (photographed by J. R. Thomason); 68-69, banza-style string instrument, marimba, and kalimba at left from the author's collection, (photographed by J. R. Thomason); 69, kalimba in far right corner courtesy the Southern University Archives, New Orleans; 70, from *Century Magazine*, 1886; 82, from *Creole Songs from New Orleans* by Clara Gottschalk Peterson (New Orleans, La.: L. Grunewald Co., 1909); 84, from *Piano Music of Louis Moreau Gotschalk* (New York: Dover Publications, Inc., 1973); 85, from *Twenty-Four Negro Melodies, op. 59* by Samuel Coleridge-Taylor and Booker T. Washington (Philadelphia: O. Ditson Co., 1905); 88, *Calinda: Danse des Négres en Amérique* by François Aimé Louis Dumoulin, from the Musée historique de Vevey; 114, photographs by J. R. Thomason; 118, photograph by Christopher Porché West; 122 top, courtesy the Library of Congress; 122 bottom, courtesy the Southeastern Architectural Archive, Special Collections Division, Tulane University, New Orleans; 123 top, courtesy The Historic New Orleans Collection, 1974.25.2459; 123 bottom, courtesy the Louisiana State Museum; 124 top, courtesy The Historic New Orleans Collection, 1979.325.5821; 124 bottom, courtesy Louisiana State Museum; 125, courtesy The Historic New Orleans Collection, 1979.325.5822; 126 and 127, courtesy the New Orleans Public Library; 128 top, courtesy the Louisiana State Museum; 128 bottom right, from the Jazz and Heritage Festival Archives, courtesy artist Bruce Brice; 128 bottom left, courtesy William Fagaly; 129 top, photograph by Jules Cahn, courtesy The Historic New Orleans Collection; 129 bottom, photograph by Michael Smith, courtesy The Historic New Orleans Collection; 130 all, courtesy Jazz at Lincoln Center; 131-133, photographs by the artists and J. R. Thomason; 134, from *Robinson's Atlas of the City of New Orleans, Louisiana* (New York: E. Robinson, 1883); rear cover, courtesy the New Orleans Museum of Art, bequest of Victor K. Kiama 77.135.

INDEX

1811 Slave Revolt, 15, 25-26, 54, 139

Acolapissa (Indians), 9
Addy, Yacub, 121, 130
"Adeline" (song), 81
Adenle, Adewale, 131
Adó, 47
Adventures of Huckleberry Finn, 3
Africa, ix, x, 1-2, 6-7, 13, 15, 24-5, 37, 40,
    42, 45, 47, 50, 53, 55, 65-66, 70-
    75, 81, 89, 101, 104-05, 109, 115,
    136, 144-45
African-American Folksongs, 73
African cultural practices: body percus-
    sion, 71, 106; call and response,
    75, 86, 90; dance styles, 95, 117;
    gathering in circles, 75, 89; gris
    gris, 48, 55; habanera rhythm and
    derivatives, 86, 107, 95, 117; influ-
    ence of, 43, 117; integration of
    drum, song and dance, 52, 75, 86,
    89, 92, 98, 117; improvisation, 79,
    86, 87, 104, 105; marketing prac-
    tices, 109, 113, 117; in Mississippi,
    91; musical instruments, 63-74,
    95; participation of all gatherers,
    89; ring shout, 104; singing styles,
    75, 86-87; in South Carolina and
    Georgia, 104; syncopated and
    poly rhythms, 89, 90, 107, 95, 117;
    wanga, 53
African Diaspora, 37, 53, 71
African Liberation Day Rally, 120
African nations (ethnic groups): Adó
    (Edo), 47; Bambara, 7, 47, 121,
    136; Caraba, 47; Chamba, 47; Fon,
    47, 52-53, 121; Foulah, 7, 136;
    Fulbe, 47; Ibo, 47; Kanga (Canga),
    47; Kissy, 47; Kongo (Congo,
    see also Kongo nation), 6-7, 38,
47-48, 52-53, 55, 70-72, 75-76,
    90-95, 96, 99, 103, 105, 121;
    Mandinga (Maninga), 7, 47; Mina
    (Minah), 47; Moko, 47; Nard, 47;
    Wolof (Yolof), 7, 47, 136; Yoruba
    (Nago), 47, 53
African retentions & survivals: see Afri-
    can cultural practices
African Slave Trade, 35
African Treasury, ix
Africans in Colonial Louisiana, 112
"Ah, Suzette" (song), 77, 83
"Aine, de' Trios" (song), 81
Algiers, La., 13, 135
Allain, Hélène d'Aquin, 3, 5, 76
All Congregations Together, 120
Allen, William, 104
"Allons Danser, Colinda" (song), 102
Amenkum, Ausettua Amor, xiii, 117
American Revolution, 24
Amsterdam Avenue (New York), x
Angola (Kongo-Angola region), 6, 7, 71,
    92, 95, 103, 121
Annals of Philadelphia, 24
Annunciation Street, 45
"Anons au Bal Colinda" (song), 102
Arada, 73
archaeological excavations, 9, 18, 162
Armstrong, Louis, xi, 119-21, 133, 162-63
Armstrong, Lucille, 162
Armstrong Park, 119-21, 162-63
Asbury, Herbert, 91, 102-04
Ascension Parish, La., 28
attire of enslaved Africans: blanket coats,
    58; chemise, 59; of dancers, 97,
    106, 148; of gatherers in Congo
    Square, 59, 61; grandiers, 58; pan-
    taloons, 58; regulation clothing,
    58; *tignons*, 59, 109
Augustin, Alexandre, 73, 96

"Aurore Pradère" (song), 81, 104
"Aurore Pradère (Bradaire)" (song), 79
"A Voudoo Tree: Haunted Sycamore of Congo Square" (article), 56
"Azelie" (song), 81

Baião (Brazilian beat), 39
Baily, Francis, 137
Bambara, 7, 47, 121, 136
Bamboula: art music compositions, 51, 81, 83-85; dance, 7, 55, 71, 81, 83, 99, 102-04, 136, 156; dancers, 102-04; drum, 121; origin of term, 102; relation of dance to Tango and Congo dances, 7, 103; rhythm, 37-38, 42; use of term, 7, 102; in the West Indies, 102-03
Bamboula 2000, 116
The Bamboula – African Dance (music), 83, 85-86
Banda-Linda, 73
Bando de Buen Gobierno, 59
Bandouliers de Mississippi, 12
banjo, 33, 44, 70, 74, 78, 96, 149-51, 153, 158
"Banjo, Op. 15" (music), 79
banza (musical instrument), 68, 70, 73, 96
Barber of Seville, 156
Barès, Basile Jean, 40-41
Barker, Danny, 97
Barnes, Harrison, 35
Barracks Street, 33
Basin Street, 139
Bata (rhythm), 42
Battle of New Orleans, 142
Batuque (dance), 72, 95
Bayogoulas (Indians), 9
Bayou Barataria, 48
Bayou Choupic, 9
Bayou Road, 9, 18, 96, 139, 154
Bayou St. John, 9, 13, 18-19, 52, 57, 135, 137
Beauregard, P. G. T., 161; Beauregard Park, 33, 161; Beauregard Square, 20, 35, 119, 124-25, 161

"Beautiful Layotte" (song), 79; see also "Belle Layotte"
Bechet, Sidney, 116, 131, 163
Bee, New Orleans (newspaper), 109, 113
Behrman, Martin, 33
"Belle Layotte" (song), 79, 81, 100, 104
Bernard, Shane, 102
Berquin-Duvallon, 137
Bienville, Sieur de (Jean Baptiste Le Moyne), 9-10, 12-13, 18, 135, 153
The Big Sea, ix
Bight of Benin, 47
Bight of Biafra, 47
Biloxi, Miss., 135
Black Code, 15, 28, 112, 135, 139; see also *Code Noir*
Black Dance, 93
Blanchard, Terrence, 116
Blesh, Rudi, 104
Bolden, Charles "Buddy," 36, 132
Bomba: dance, 72, 76, 103; meaning, 76; music, 39, 73, 76; in song lyrics, 75-76
Bonano, "Sharkey," 161
Boniquet, Jose, 137
Borders, Florence, 95-96
Boston, Mass., 79
boula: drum, 73; mule's skull, 96
Bourbon Street, 153
Bras Coupé, 104, 116
Brazil, 52, 72, 95
Broadway (New York), 44, 46, 106
Brown, William Wells, 5
Buechler, Johann, 59, 61, 143
Buffalo, N.Y., 35, 44
bula (drum): see boula
bullfights, 19
Burgundy Street, 10, 32, 154
Butler, Benjamin, 32, 157

Cabildo, 36, 121, 155, 170, 172, 181
Cable, George Washington, 3-5, 48-49, 65, 71, 76-77, 83, 86-87, 91, 94, 103-04, 112, 116
Café Du Monde (New Orleans), 9

Cailloux, Andre, 157
Cajon (drum), 72
Cajun culture: African influence on cui-
    sine, 13; African influence on song
    and dance, 102
Calas (food), 110
Calinda (Calenda, Kalenda, Kalinda):
    descriptions of, 99-101; early
    accounts of, 23, 99; origin of, 98;
    influences of, 101-102; in other
    countries, 99-101
call and response: see African cultural
    practices
The Camp, 51-52
Los Campanillas (music), 40
Camp Street, 45
Canada, 44, 86
Canal Street, 45, 146
Candomblé (beliefs), 52
Canga, Thélémaque, 75
cannon, 19, 147
Canot, Captain, 35
Caraba, 47
Caribbean, 2, 37, 39, 42, 47, 72-74, 83,
    115, 120
Caribbean Carnival Friends and Culture
    Festival, 120
Carabine (dance), 106
Carolina Sea Coast, 40
"Caroline" (song), 81, 104
Carondelet, Baron Hector, de: ban on
    enslaved Africans from the West
    Indies, 53; regulation clothes, 58;
    wages for the enslaved, 112, 136
Carondelet Canal, 19, 122, 136-37, 143
Carriacou, 101
carriage shows, 19
Carriere, Noel, 137
cassuto (musical instrument), 73
Castellanos, Henry, 35, 76
cata (musical instrument), 68, 73, 96
Catlett, Elizabeth, xiii, 131, 133, 163
Catlett, Franciso Mora, 73, 117
Cayetano's Circus, 19, 45, 142
Celebration of the African American

Child, 120
"Celeste" (song), 80
Celestin, Oscar "Papa," 128, 161
Center for Black Music Research, 39
Century Magazine, 3, 91
Chamba, 47
Chambon, C. M., 136
"Chanson Creole" (song), 99
Charity Hospital, 139
Charles (slave of Deslondes), 54
Charleston, S.C., 106
Chase, Gilbert, 3
Chaute par les Voudou sur la place Congo, 57
Chica (dance), 93-94, 98-99, 102-103
Chicago, Ill., x, 39, 95, 117
Chinese, 3, 19, 73
Chitimachas (Indians), 9
Chretien, Abel, 131
Christian, Marcus, 32, 77
Christy, Edwin Pearch (E. P.): appropria-
    tion of African culture, 43-45,
    106, 116; circus performances,
    43-46; at Congo Square, 43, 45-46;
    influence on minstrelsy, 44-46, 78,
    106, 117
Christy's Minstrels, 44-45, 78
churches: catholic, 56; St. James A.M.E.,
    32; worship in, 54
cinquillo (rhythm), 38-39, 42
Circus Fans Association, 45
Circus Park, 20, 45
Circus Place, 20, 29, 154; see also Place
    du Cirque
Circus Square, 20, 45, 142, 145, 149, 153
Circus Street, 153
Civil War, 5-6, 19, 21, 31-32, 55, 58, 71,
    76, 94, 97, 110, 115, 157, 161
Claiborne Avenue, 96-97
clave (rhythm), 39
Clemens, Samuel L., 86; see also Twain,
    Mark
Clotelle, 5
cockfights, 19
Code Noir, 1, 15, 18, 25, 52, 110, 135
Coleridge-Taylor, Samuel, 83, 86

"'Colinda': Mysterious Origins of a Cajun
    Folksong," 102
Coliseum Place, 45
College of Orleans, 36
Columbia College (Chicago), 39
Columbia University (New York), x
Company of the Indies, 10, 13, 18, 135
Company of the West, 10, 12
Company Plantation, 13, 18; see also
    King's Plantation
concessions, 12
congo: meanings of term, 6-7; uses of
    term, 6
Congo (dance), 83, 91-94; ethnic origin
    of, 94; influence of, 95-98; in other
    countries, 94-95, 103; in other
    states, 91; popularity of, 36, 83,
    94, 145-46; relation to Chica and
    Fandango dances, 93; relation to
    Tango and Bamboula dance, 7,
    103; songs of, 81, 83; variations of,
    94-95
Congo Circus, 142
"Congo Creole" (dance), 94
"The Congo Dance," 5, 94, 159
Congo dances, 97, 143, 146-47
"Congo Franc" (dance), 94
"Congo Layet" (dance), 95
"Congo Mazonne" (dance), 94
"Congo Pailette" (dance), 94
Congo people: see Kongo
Congo Square: archaeological investiga-
    tions, 162; became Place d' Armes,
    19; changes to, 18, 35, 119, 121,
    136, 145, 149, 151, 153, 155, 161,
    163; different names for, 20, 43;
    enclosed with fence, 145; festivals
    held in, 20, 116, 120-21; food
    items sold in, 96, 110, 113; historic
    marker, 163; influence on local
    culture, 2, 43, 94-96, 107, 116-
    117; influence on national culture,
    45, 106, 116-117; interruption of
    gatherings, 26-28; marketing at, 2,
    36, 109, 113; name changed by or-
dinance, 35, 119, 161; in Philadel-
    phia, Pa., 24; placed on National
    Registry, 163; post Civil War, 5,
    55-58, 97; as tourist attraction, 51,
    94; uses of, 18-19
Congo Square Foundation, xiii, 163
Congo Square International Festival, 120
Congo Square Rhythms Festival, 116,
    121, 129, 163
Congo Square Symposium, 120
Conjurors, 53
Conrad, Glenn, 12
Conti Street, 155
Coonjai (dance), 81; see also Counjaille
Coquet, Bernando, 137
Cotton Exposition (1884-85), 56, 160
Counjaille (dance), 81, 102, 104
Courlander, Harold, 73, 94, 104
Creecy, James, 26, 35-36, 49-51, 70, 86,
    89, 147
creole: beer, 96, 110, 113; cuisine, 13;
    dances, 97, 113; 18th century
    usage, 78; language, 75-76, 94,
    112, (see also Louisiana Creole);
    people, 79, 91, 110, 112; songs,
    77-87, 94, 100, 102, 112
Creole Dance, 97-98, 103, 113
Creole Slave Songs, 5, 77, 83, 112
Crozat, Antoine, 10
Cuba, 2, 15, 24-26, 37-38, 47-48, 52-53,
    71-74, 94-95, 101, 105, 115, 138,
    143
Cuming, Fortescue, 137
Cungi (dance), 98
Curaçao, 101
Customhouse Street, 154
Cyrillo, Bishop (Cirilo Sieni), 7, 55, 103,
    136

D*aily Crescent*, New Orleans (newspa-
    per), 159
Daily Picayune, New Orleans (newspaper),
    5, 30, 32-33, 35, 42, 48, 61, 89, 94,
    151, 159
Daily True Delta, New Orleans (newspa-

per), 32, 157
dances (African-based): children, 105,
     107; demographic composition of,
     89-90; formation of, 90; interrup-
     tion of in Congo Square, 26-28,
     140; locations in the city, 7, 13,
     18, 25-26, 33, 52, 54, 89, 91, 94,
     97; Mardi Gras Indians, 46, 96,
     107; musicians and instruments
     for, 63-71, 90; post Civil War, 97,
     98, 113; receiving money for, 107;
     use of kerchiefs, 90, 92-93, 97-98,
     100, 106-07;
dances (titles): Bamboula, 7, 55, 71,
     81, 83, 99, 102-104, 136, 156;
     Bartuque, 72, 95; Calinda (Kal-
     inda, Kalenda, Calenda), 23, 77,
     81, 83, 97-99, 101-102; Carabine,
     106; Chica, 94; Congo, 83, 91-98;
     Counjaille (Counja, Counjale,
     Counjai, Coonjine), 81, 104; Fan-
     dango, 93; Jim Along Josey, 150;
     Juba, 44, 71, 105-106, 146; Jump-
     ing Jim Crow, 105; Pilé Chactas,
     105; Rubin Rede, 105; The Shout,
     104; Tumba Francesa, 72
"The Dance in Place Congo,", 3, 5, 79
The Dance in Place Congo & Creole Slave
     Songs, 5
Daniel, Yvonne, 95
"Dansé La Counjale" (song), 105
Danse des Nègres, 38, 81, 83
Da pa Laba, 55
d'Aquin Allain, Hélène, 3, 76
D'Artaguette, 13
Dauphine Street, 18, 135, 153
Davis, Edwin Adams, 65
Decatur Street, 9, 97
De Haner's Circus, 159
"Delaide Mo la Reine" (song), 80
Delgado, Lydia, 76
Delord Street, 157
Democrat, New Orleans (newspaper), 23
Democratic Republic of the Congo, 24
Dent, Tom, 97

De Paris, Wilbur, xi
Deslondes, Charles: see Charles (slave of
     Deslondes)
"Dé Zab" (song), 77
"Dialogue d'Amour" (song), 81, 100
Didimus, Henry, 149
Dirman, Rose, 161
Djouba (dance), 105; see also Juba
Djuka (dance), 72
Domino, Antoine "Fats," 116
Donaldson, Gary, 49
Dryades Street, 159
Le Duc du Maine (ship), 13
Duke of Orleans, 10
Dumaine Street, 10
Dummons, Kimberly, 132
Dumont de Montigny, Jean-Francois-
     Benjamin, 111
Dunbar, Alice Nelson, 38, 83, 94, 103

Early, Eleanor, 50
East Feliciana Parish, La., 28
"Eh! Eh! Bomba!" (song), 75-76
Elie, Louis, xiii, 75
Ellington, Duke, 117
Emancipation Proclamation, 19
Emerson, Ken, 44
Emery, Lynne, 94
England, 44, 136
English, Joseph, 155
enslaved Africans: attire of, see attire;
     curfew for, 19, 147; domestic slave
     trade, 48; early presence in colony,
     12-13; ethnic origins, 47-48, 52;
     executed in Congo Square, 20;
     gatherings and dancing, 18, 23;
     hired-out, 5, 49, 110-13; paid for
     work on Sundays, 28, 36, 112-13;
     punishment of, 20-21, 32; skills of,
     13-15, 17; smuggling of, 48
Epstein, Dena, 24
Esplanade Avenue, 45, 146
Ethiopia, 30, 40, 43-44, 46, 78, 152
Ethiopian minstrels, 40

Evans, Estwick, 143
Evanston, Illinois, x

Fandango (dance), 93, 149
Faubourg Marigny, 25-27, 54, 141
Faubourg Ste. Marie, 25-27, 48, 54, 141-
    42
Federal Writers' Project, 5, 20, 33, 55, 65,
    74, 80, 96, 101, 103, 105; see also
    Works Progress Administration;
    Interviewees: Augustine, Alexan-
    dre, 73, 96; Morris, Joseph, 55;
    Felix, Oscar, 56-57, 97; Homer,
    Bill, 65; Rivaros, Raymond, 56;
    Miss White, 33; Wilson, Wash, 65
Felix, Oscar, 56-57, 97
Ferdinand, Fort: see Fort St. Ferdinand
Fernandez (of Havana), 25
"Festival of the Young Corn" (play), 9
Fiehrer, Thomas Marc, 13, 113
firework exhibitions, 19
First Municipal Council, 30-31, 147, 149,
    151, 154-55
First Municipality, 32, 149, 152
Flint, Timothy, 20, 42, 94, 96, 146
Floyd, Samuel, 39, 42
Flugel, J. G. (a traveler), 25, 48, 142
Fon, 47, 52-53, 121
Forest, P., 51, 147
Fortier, Alceé, 92-93, 102, 106
Fort St. Ferdinand (Fernando), 17, 19, 25,
    54, 136-38, 141
Fort St. Louis, 26, 142
Fort Wayne Daily Gazette, 86
Forty-Seventh Massachusetts Regiment,
    158
Foster, Stephen, 44
Foulahs, 7, 136
France, 3, 10, 18, 25, 53, 137-38
free people of color, 6, 19, 25, 28, 31-33,
    36, 49-50, 53-54, 110, 113, 135,
    137-38, 140, 146, 151, 154, 156; at
    Congo Square, 31, 49, 149; free-
    dom restricted, 28, 31-32; Haitian

immigrants, 25, 49, 138; Tremé
    Neighborhood, 19
French Market, 50
French Quarter, 9-10, 91, 135
Fulbe, 47

"Gardé Piti Mulet Là (Musieu Banjo),"
    79
Geggus, David, 53
Georgetown, Md., 147
Georgia Sea Coast, 40
Ghana, ix, xi, 72
Gilbert, Henry, 79
Giouba (dance), 105; see also Juba
Girod, Nicolas, 25, 140-42
Girouard, Julia, 102
Globe Ball Room, 19, 30-31, 155
Globe Hall, 30, 35
Gold Coast, 47
"Gold Dust Twins," 3
Gome (drum), 72
Gottschalk, Louis, 38, 51, 79-81, 83, 86,
    116
Gould, Virginia, 109
Gov. Nicholls Street, 18
Grand Army of the Republic, 97
Grand Bayou de St. Jean, 9; see also
    Bayou St. John
Grande Polka Des Chasseurs (music), 41
Gravier Street, 97
Gray, Bessie Richardson, 95
Gray, Luther, xiii, 116, 121, 163
Greene, Welcome Arnold, 146
Grenada, 101
gris gris, 3; see also wanga
Guadeloupe, 102
Guerrier, Peniel, 94
Guinea, 25, 143
Gulf Coast, 10
Gulf of Mexico, 9
Gullah, 42

Habanera (rhythm), 38, 40, 81, 86, 103,
    117

habitations, 12

Haiti, 2, 15, 24-25, 37-38, 48, 52-53, 70-
    76, 78, 81, 83, 93-94, 100-03, 105,
    113, 115

Haitian Revolution: ban on slave impor-
    tation, 53; and Cuba, 37-40; and
    immigrants, 25-26, 53, 81; impact
    on New Orleans, 48, 53

Hall, A. Oakey, 30, 153

Hall, Gwendolyn Midlo, xiii, 10, 13, 35,
    42, 47, 53, 78, 80, 112

Hambone (dance), 106; see also Juba

Hare, Maude Cuney, 31, 65, 79, 98

Harlem, New York, x, 6

Harlem Renaissance, 6

Harris, Jessica, 110

Harrison, Donald, 116

Havana, Cuba, 13, 25, 38, 142-43, 206

Hearn, Lafcadio, 5, 71-72, 76, 81, 87,
    91-94, 102

Hennessy, David, 160

Hermeneutic circle, 6, 45

"Heron Mande" (song), 100

Herskovits, Melville, x, 2

"Hey Jim Along" (song), 78

"Hey Pockey Way" (song), 38

Holmes, Isaac, 91

Holy Ghost, 56

Los Hombres Calientes, 116

Homer, Bill, 65

horse shows, 19

Houma (Indians), 9

House of Representatives (U.S.), 53

Hughes, Langston, ix, 117

Humboldt Square, 159

Huntsville, Ala., 5

Hurston, Zora Neale, 56

Iberville, Sieur de (Pierre Le Moyne),
    10, 135

Ibo, 47

Indian Portage, at New Orleans 9-10

indigo, 15

Ingraham, Joseph Holt, 148

Institute of African Studies, xi

International Middle Passage Remember-
    ance Day, 120

Item Tribune, New Orleans (newspaper),
    50, 59

Jackson, Andrew, 142

Jackson, Mahalia, 131; Theater of Per-
    forming Arts, 120-21, 163

Jackson Square, 109

Jamaica, 47, 70, 73, 101

Jazzin' in the Park, 120

Jesuits, 15

J&M Record Shop, 116

Johnson, Jerah, xiii, 23

Jones-Adenle, Sheleen, 132, 133

Juba (dance): influence of 106; origin of
    105; in other countries, 105; used
    by minstrels, 44, 106; variations
    of, 106

Julia Street, 45

"Jumping Jim Crow" (dance), 105

Juneteenth, 120

Kalimba (musical instrument), 65, 206

Kanga (canga), 47

Katrina, Hurricane, 119-20, 130, 163

Kemble, Edward, 3-4

"Kemble's Coons," 3

Kendall, John Smith: on the location of
    Congo Square, 9; on the meaning
    of term "congo," 7

Kimbundu, 53

King, Grace, 36

Kings of Dixieland, 161

King's Plantation, 13-14, 23, 26, 36, 100;
    see also Company Plantation

Kissy, 47

Kline, Steve, 132

Klinger, Tom, 79

Kmen, Henry, 28

Knight, Henry Cogswell, 1, 143

Kongo, 52; Catholicism among, 52; danc-
    ing style, 91; drumming style, 90;
    influence of, 7; prevalence of, 48,

94; royalty of, 48
Krehbiel, Henry, 73, 76, 83, 87, 91, 104
Kubik, Gerhard, 39
Kumbuka African Drum and Dance Collective, 117
Kumbundu, 73
Kwanzaa, 120

La Bamboula—Dance des Nègres (music), 38, 51, 81
Labat, Jean Baptiste, 99-100
"La Crocodile, Deux Canards" (song), 83
Lafayette Square, 26
"La Fête du Petit Blé ou l'Héroisme de Poucha-Houmma" (play), 9
Lake Pontchartrain, 9-11, 19, 57, 97, 120, 152
La Mora: see Perez Prades, Danys, 95
La Salle, Sieur de (Rene-Robert Cavelier), 10
LaSalle, Alex, 76, 103
Latrobe, Benjamin, 1, 34-35, 50, 63-64, 70-72, 76, 86, 89-91, 93-94, 96-97, 143
L'Aurore (ship), 13
Laveau, Marie, 5, 55-56, 159
Law, John, 10, 12
Lay, John, 35, 146
Leeward Islands, 98
Legacy Blues Festival, 120
Le Page du Pratz, 13, 18, 23, 36, 98, 100, 111, 135
Leveau, Marie: see Laveau, Marie
Levee Street, 146, 149
Lever Brother, 3
Liberia, 110
Lincoln, Abraham, 19, 121, 158
Lincoln Jazz Center Orchestra, 121
Little Richard (Penniman), 116
Livingstone, Rodney, 73
"Lizette" (song), 80
Long, Carolyn Morrow, 3
Long, Ellen Call, 109
Louisiana: early African presence, 12-13; early settlements, 9-18; enslaved

Native Americans, 10; King's Plantation (Company Plantation), 13-14, 18, 23, 26, 36, 100; recruitment of colonists, 10-12; ships transporting enslaved Africans, 13, 47-48
Louisiana Black Heritage Festival, 120
Louisiana History, 54
Louisiana Purchase, 48, 77
Louis XIV, 10

Macarty, Augustin de, 26
Mandigoes, 7, 136
Mandinga, 47
Manhattan, New York, ix
Manhattaner in New Orleans, 153
Marcus Garvey Birthday Celebration, 120
Mardi Gras, 19, 38, 46, 86, 107, 117, 153; Indians, 38, 46, 86, 107, 117; parades, 19
Marie, Teena, 117
Marigny; see Faubourg Marigny
marimbas (musical instrument), 65
Mariotini, Cayetano, 142
markets: city markets (including French Market), 109; at Congo Square, 2; petty marketing, 109
Maroons, 49
Marsalis, Jason, 116
Marsalis, Wynton, 116, 121, 130
Martin Luther King Day, 120
Martinique, 47, 71, 94, 99, 101
Matassa, Cosimo, 116
Mayfield, Irvin, 116
mbira (musical instrument), 65, 72
Mbiti, John, 52, 54, 58
McGowan, James, 111
Medley, Keith, 117
Menagerie of Messrs. Purdy & Welch, 43
Messrs. Purdy, Welch & Delavan (Circus Caravan), 44
Metropolitan Opera Company, 79
Mexico, 101
Middle Passage, 115, 120
military drills, 19

Mina, 47
minstrels: features of shows, 44, 106; re-
lation to circuses, 44-45; standard
band of, 44, 74; see also Christy's
Minstrels
Miró, Esteban Rodriguez, 7, 59, 103, 136
Missié d' Artaguette, 80
Mississippi, 9-10, 12-13, 15, 21, 91, 104,
111, 135; Bandits, 12; River, 9,
111, 135; Valley, 12
Missouri River, 104
Mobile, Ala. 10
Moko, 47
Montana, Allison "Big Chief Tootie," 133
Montiteur De Louisiana, New Orleans
(newspaper), 139
Morand, 18-19
Moreau de Saint-Méry, Médéric-Louis-
Elie, 3, 5, 19, 49, 51, 70, 76, 79,
93, 98, 100, 102-03
Morning Star Benevolent Association,
157
Moro, Pablo, 19, 73
Morris F. X. Jeff Municipal Auditorium:
see Municipal Auditorium
Morris, Joseph, 55-56
Morton, "Jelly Roll," 39, 117
"Mo Té Ain Negresse" (song), 101
Mozambique, 47
Mukuna, Zawadi wa, xiii, 72, 75
mulattoes, 50
Mungier, George François, 123
Municipal Auditorium, 35, 120, 124, 127,
161, 162
musical instruments: African prototypes,
1, 63-74; body percussion, 71, 106;
of European origin, 71; impro-
vised sound makers, 71; Latrobe's
sketches of, 64
"Musieu Bainjo" (music), 79-80
My First Book of Africa, ix
*My Southern Journey or The South and Its
People*, 5

Nagin, C. Ray, 121

Nard, 47
Natchez, Miss.13
Natchitoches, La., 92, 105, 147
National Dance Commission (Cuba), 95
National Register of Historic Places, 163
Native Americans, 9-10, 12, 19, 23, 51,
135; assisted colonists, 10; corn
festivals and gatherings, 9, 23;
dancing with Africans, 51-52;
enslavement of, 10, 12; Indian
Portage, 9
Native Guards, 97
Neville, Cyril, 116
Neville Brothers, 116
New Orleans and South African Connec-
tion Culture and Music Festival,
120
New Orleans as It Was, 35
New Orleans City Council, 54, 119,
159-61
New Orleans Creole Fiesta Association,
161
New Orleans & Environs, 29, 152
New Orleans Gas Company, 50
New Orleans Jazz and Heritage Founda-
tion, xiii, xiv, 116, 121, 129
New Orleans Jazz & Heritage Festival,
20, 116, 120, 128-29, 162
New Orleans Police, 54
New Orleans Register & Directory, 146
New Orleans Word Festival, 120
New World, 1, 7, 24, 37, 47, 52, 54-55,
58, 70-71, 75, 95, 109, 113
New York, ix-x, 24, 44, 79, 87, 91, 106,
117
Nicaud, Rose, 109
Nickerson, Camille, 87, 89, 97, 102, 113
Nile River, 106
`Nketia, J. H. Kwabena, ix-xii, 7, 39,
73-74
Noble, Jordan B., 142
Norman, Benjamin Moore, 152
Norman's New Orleans and Environs, 78, 107
Notes of a Pianist, 81
Nubia, 106

Nuttall, Thomas, 109, 145

Odadaa, 121
Ohio River, 104
okra, 15
Old Folks at Home (song), 44
"Old Virginia Never Tire" (song), 78
Olmsted, Frederick, 34, 169
On to New Orleans!, 54
Orleans Ballroom, 32
Orleans Parish Prison, 122, 160
Orleans Theater Company, 149
Ouachita Parish, La., 65
Ouachita River, 147
"Ouendé, Ouendé, Macaya" (song), 77
Ouma, 9

Palo (belief), 52
Panama, 95
panpipes, 65, 73
Paris, France, xi, 10, 12
Partner (dance), 105
Pat Juber: see Juba
Pavie, Theodore (traveler), 70, 72, 92-93, 105, 146
Paxton, Norman, 146
peas, 15, 55
People's Hurricane Relief Fund, 120
Pepin (King of the Congo), 25, 143
Percussion Inc., 116
Perez, Manuel, 36
Perez Prades, Danys "La Mora," 95
Perier, Etienne, 18
Peru, 101
Peters-Muhammad, Jamilah, 163
Peterson, Clara Gottschalk, 80
Pétro (drum), 71
Petwo (rhythm), 39
Philadelphia, Penn., 24, 43
picallions, 106
Picayune, New Orleans (newspaper), 3, 5, 30, 32-33, 35-37, 42, 48, 50, 61, 89, 94, 113, 151, 159; see also *Times Picayune*
Pilé Chactas (dance), 92

pillory, 20
Pinkster, 24
Pitot, James, 136
Place d'Armes, 19-20, 26, 30, 147, 155-56, 158-59
Place des Nègres, 20
Place du Cirque, 20; see also Circus Place
Place Publique, 20, 26-27
Place Washington, 26-27; see also Washington Square
planters, 15, 47, 53
playground equipment (Congo Square), 19, 161
Plaza de Armes; see also Place d'Armes
polyrhythms: see African cultural practices
Pontchartrain and New Orleans Railroad Company, 49-50
Pork Chops and Kidney Stew (entertainers), 161
Port au Prince, Haiti, 25, 143
Portobelo, 95
Port Royal, 104
Puerto Rico, 72-73, 76, 95, 101-03

"Quand mo-té Jeune" (song), 100
"Quand mo te jeune (Bal fini)" (song), 83
"Quan Patate-Latchuite" (song), 38, 81, 86, 94, 103
Quan Patate-Latchuite (music), 82
quills (musical instrument), 65, 70
Quinipissa (Indians), 9

Race Street, 45
Rampart Street, 20, 30, 33, 45, 51, 116, 146, 147, 153, 156, 158-59
Reconstruction, 40
Red Brick and Tile Company, 50
Redd, Douglas, 121
Rejoicin' in the Park, 120
"Remon" (song), 81, 104
rhythmic cells: Cinquillo, 38, 42; Clave, 39; Habanera and derivatives, 38, 42, 81, 86, 103, 117; Tango, 38;

Tresillo, 38-42
Ring Shouts, 40
Rivaros, Raymond, 56
Roach, Max, xi
Rockefeller Foundation, ix
Roots of Music Cultural Sculpture Garden, 121, 131-33, 163
roots persons, 53
Rousseau, Jean Jacques, 99
Rubin Rede (dance), 105
Rumba (dance), 38-39, 68, 72
Rumba Guaguancó (dance), 38-39, 95

St. Ann Street, 9, 10, 55, 112, 155
St. Charles Avenue, 45, 30, 33, 35, 155
St. Charles Parish, La., 54, 139
St. Croix, 102
St. Domingo, (Haiti), 15, 25, 83, 143
St. Domingue, 3, 12-13, 15, 19, 24-25, 38
   47, 53, 70, 73, 78, 81, 93, 102-03;
   see also Haiti
St. John's Day, 98; eve of, 159-60
St. James African Methodist Episcopal
   Church, 32
St. James Parish, La., 92
St. Julien, Aline, 95, 96
St. Louis Cathedral (New Orleans), 26,
   109
St. Lucia, 102
Ste. Marie: see Faubourg Ste. Marie
St. Peter Street, 9, 30, 35, 155
St. Philip Street, 96
St. Thomas, 101-02
Santeria (beliefs), 42, 52
Santiago, Chile, 95
sanza (musical Instrument), 65
Satchmo Festival, 120
Schultz, Christian, 55, 63, 89, 138
sculptured eagle (Congo Square), 20, 119
Sculpture Garden; see Roots of Music
   Cultural Sculpture Garden
Senagalese, 70
Senegambia, 47, 70
Seth B. Howe's Circus, 158

Shahmah, 106
Shake (dance), 95
Shimmy (dance), 95
Shout (dance), 104
Shreveport, La., 65
Sierra Leone, 47, 110
Singleton, Arthur, 143
Skinkus, Michael, 39
Slave Revolt of 1811, 25-26, 54, 139
slaves: see enslaved Africans
Soards City Directory, 35
songs (in Congo Square): in African languages, 75-76, 91, 94, 86; characteristics of, 86; in combinations of
   languages, 75-77, 86; in Louisiana
   Creole, 75, 78-87, 90, 94
songs, Creole: art musical compositions
   based on, 79-85; influence on
   white elite, 80; national performances of, 86-87, 116; various
   terms for, 78
songs, Creole (titles): "Ah, Suzette,"
   83; "Aurore Pradère" (also
   "Bradaire"), 79, 81, 104; "Belle
   Layotte," 79, 81, 100, 104;
   "Caroline" (also "Aine, déTrios,"
   "Adeline," "Azelle"), 81; "Celeste,"
   80; "Chante par les Voudou sur
   la Place Congo," 57; "Dansé La
   Counjale," 105; "Delaide, Mo la
   Reine," 80; "De Zab," 77; "Dialogue d' Amour," 81, 100; "Duex,
   Canards," 83; "La Crocodile,"
   83; "Lizette," 80; "Mo Té ain
   Negresse," 101; "Missié d' Artaguette," 80; "Musieu Bainjo," 79,
   80; "Quan Patate Latchuite," 38,
   81, 83, 94, 103; "Quand mo-té Jeune," 83, 100; "Ouendé, Ouendé,
   Macaya," 77; "Remon," 81, 104;
   "Tant Sirop Est Doux," 81
songs, European (titles): "Get Along
   Home You Yallow Girls," 78;
   "Hey Jim Along," 78; "Old Virginia Never Tire," 78

songs: West Indian (titles): "Ah Suzette,"
    83; "La Crocodile," 83; "Duex,
    Canards," 83; "Eh! Eh! Bomba,"
    75-76; "Quan Patate Latchuite,"
    38, 81, 83, 94, 103; "Tant Sirop
    Est Doux," 81
Song of the Voudous on Congo Square, 57
South Carolina, 42, 48, 53, 104
South Prieur Street, 56
*Souvenirs D'Amérique Et De France, Par une
    Créole,* 3
Spain, 25, 53, 93, 136-38
Spanish Independence Day Festival, 120
Squire: see Bras Coupé
S.S. Malone (ship), ix
Stevens, S. Gleason, 112
Stuart, James, 147
Sublette, Ned, xiii, 38, 76
sugar, 15, 145
Summers, Bill, xiii, 39, 116
"Suzette" (song), 80
swimming pool (Congo Square), 19, 161

Tafia (rum),110
Tanesse, Jacques, 26-27
tango, 7, 38, 103, 136; meaning), 103
Tango (dance): origin of, 7; relation to
    Bamboula and Congo dances, 7,
    103
"Tant Sirop Est Doux" (song), 81
Taylor, Joe Gray, 51
Tchoupitoulas Street, 45
Terspichore Street, 156
Texas, 65
Theatre d'Orleans (New Orleans), 156
Theatre of Performing Arts: see Mahalia
    Jackson Theater of Performing
    Arts
Thomas, James, 42, 50-51, 63, 105, 152,
    156
Thompson, Robert Farris, 55, 70, 72,
    102, 105
Thompson, Thomas, 54
Thorpe, Edward, 93-94

Thrasher, Albert, 54
tignons, 59, 109, 136
Times, New Orleans (newspaper), 110
Times Democrat, New Orleans (newspa-
    per), 42, 160
Times Picayune, New Orleans (newspaper),
    3, 94; see also *Picayune*
Tobago, 101
Treat It Gentle, 116
Treaty of Fontainbleau, 136
Tregle, Joseph, Jr., 28
Tremé (neighborhood), 19, 26, 119, 127,
    137, 139, 146, 162
Tremé, Claude, 19, 137, 139
Treme Street, 96
tresillo (rhythm), 38-39, 42
Trinidad, 101-02
Tucker, Earl "Snake Hips," 96
Tumba Francesa, 72
Tunicas (Indians), 9
Turner, Nat, 28
Twain, Mark, 3, 86
Twenty Four Negro Melodies Op. 59, 83
Two Years in the French West Indies, 71, 81

Umoja, 120
Uncle Tom's Cabin, 3
Union (Army), 19, 32, 40, 97, 157-58
United States, ix, 45, 53-54, 86, 94, 104,
    138
University of Ghana, ix, xi
University of New Orleans, 162
University Place, 97
Usner, Daniel, 9

Virginia, 48, 78, 107, 109, 150
Virgin Islands, 71, 102
Voodoo: see Voudou
"Voodoo and Orgies Held Sway Here," 6
Voodoo Festival, 120
Voudou (Vodu, Voudaux): ceremonies,
    3, 103; commercialization of, 5; in
    Congo Square, 3-5; customs vs.
    organized religion, 5; emergence

in Louisiana, 52-53; followers
of, 75; gris gris, 48, 55; Haitian
impact, 49, 53; Laveau, Marie, 5,
55-56, 160; origin of, 52; relation
to Candomble, Palo, Santeria, 52;
root workers, 53; Thélèmaque
Canga, 75; wanga, 53; W.P.A.
interviews, 55-58

Wanga, 53; see also gris gris
Warner, Charles Dudley, 42
Washington, Booker T., 83, 206
Washington Square, 24, 159; see also
        Place Washington
watermelons, 15
Watson, John, 138
Way Down upon the Swanee River (song), 44
Wegener, Werner, 50
West Africa, 42, 73
West Indies, 2, 5, 12, 24-25, 37, 49, 53,
        70-73, 81, 83, 94, 98-99, 101-03,
        113, 115, 135, 145
West, Mae, 96
"When I was Young (The End of the
        Ball)" (song), 83
White Buffalo Day Celebration, 120
White, Michael, xiii, 107
Wilson, Wash, 65, 71
Windard Coast, 47
Wolof, 47
W. P. A.(Works Progress Administration),
        42, 65, 73, 97, 101, 113; see also
        Federal Writer's Project

Xylophones: see marimbas

Yankee Doodle (song), 149
Yolofs, 7, 47, 136; see also Wolof
Yuca (dance), 95

ABOUT THE AUTHOR

FREDDI WILLIAMS EVANS is an alumna of Tougaloo College, Tougaloo, Mississippi where, as a music major, she began studying traditional African music on a study-travel to the University of Ghana at Accra. Evans is the award-winning author of three historically-based children's books: *A Bus of Our Own* (2001), *The Battle of New Orleans: the Drummer's Story* (2005), and *Hush Harbor: Praying in Secret* (2008). Her writings for general audiences have appeared in local newspapers, as well as several compilations and anthologies including *The Storytelling Classroom: Applications Across the Curriculum* (2006) and *Kente Cloth: Southwest Voices of the African Diaspora* (1998).

Evans has presented widely on Congo Square at schools, museums, and festivals and her essay "New Orleans' Congo Square: A Cultural Landmark" will appear in *Ancestors of Congo Square: African Art in the New Orleans Museum of Art* (2011). Her research on Congo Square has taken her to numerous archives, local and national, and back to West Africa. Evans resides in New Orleans and works as an arts educator and administrator as well as an independent scholar.